*Doing
Literary
Business*

Gender & American Culture

Coeditors

Linda K. Kerber

Nell Irvin Painter

Editorial Advisory Board

Nancy Cott	Mary Kelley
Cathy Davidson	Annette Kolodny
Thadious Davis	Wendy Martin
Jane DeHart	Janice Radway
Sara Evans	Barbara Sicherman

Doing Literary Business

American Women Writers in the Nineteenth Century

Susan Coultrap-McQuin

*The University
of North
Carolina
Press
Chapel Hill
and London*

© 1990 Susan Coultrap-McQuin
All rights reserved

Library of Congress Cataloging-in-Publication Data
Coultrap-McQuin, Susan Margaret.
   Doing literary business : American women writers in the
nineteenth century / by Susan Coultrap-McQuin.
      p.   cm.—(Gender & American culture)
   Includes bibliographical references.
   ISBN 0-8078-1914-X (alk. paper).—ISBN 0-8078-4284-2 (pbk.
: alk. paper)
   1. Women and literature—United States—History—19th
century.   2. American literature—Women authors—History
and criticism.   3. American literature—19th century—History
and criticism.   4. Authors and publishers—United States—
History—19th century.   5. Literature publishing—United
States—History—19th century.   6. Authorship—History—
19th century.   I. Title.   II. Series.
PS147.C68   1990
810.9'9287'09034—dc20   90-12006
                                                          CIP

The paper in this book meets the guidelines for permanence
and durability of the Committee on Production Guidelines for
Book Longevity of the Council on Library Resources.

Manufactured in the United States of America
94 93 92 91 90   5 4 3 2 1

*To my parents
with gratitude
for all you have
given me*

Contents

Preface xi

Acknowledgments xv

1 Why Try a Writing Career?: The Ambiguous Cultural Context for Women Writers of the Mid-Nineteenth Century 1

2 Gentlemen and Ladies: Ideals and Economics in the Literary Marketplace 27

3 The Place of Gender in Business: The Career of E.D.E.N. Southworth 49

4 The Impact of Domestic Feminism: Harriet Beecher Stowe's Mature Career 79

5 The Battle for a Fair Marketplace: Mary Abigail Dodge versus James T. Fields 105

6 "Very Serious Literary Labor": The Career of Helen Hunt Jackson 137

viii   *Contents*

7 The Demise of Feminine Strength: The Career of
Elizabeth Stuart Phelps (Ward)   167

8 A Final Word: Literary Professionalism
and Women   193

Abbreviations   201

Notes   203

Bibliography   229

Index   243

Illustrations

Eminent Women   1

Negotiating with a Publisher   27

E.D.E.N. Southworth   49

Harriet Beecher Stowe   79

Mary Abigail Dodge   105

Helen Hunt Jackson   137

Elizabeth Stuart Phelps (Ward)   167

Writer's Desk   193

Preface

This study focuses on the literary careers of five women writers of the nineteenth century: E.D.E.N. Southworth, Harriet Beecher Stowe, Mary Abigail Dodge who used the pseudonym "Gail Hamilton," Helen Hunt Jackson who used the pseudonyms "H. H." and "Saxe Holm," and Elizabeth Stuart Phelps (Ward). Although I had first planned to write a composite history of women's literary professionalism in the nineteenth century based on studies of the careers of twenty writers, I eventually decided that a composite approach obscured important differences between the women by emphasizing somewhat misleading similarities. Therefore, I turned my attention to the five writers named above. I chose these particular writers because I had developed an enormous respect for them as individuals facing particular problems in their careers and because, though individuals, they also show what I believe are some typical experiences and responses of women in the literary marketplace.

My choice of individuals will, perhaps, be faulted for one reason or another: I have left out some important writers; I have not looked at those women who failed; I have not adequately represented women's cultural diversity. I would claim, however, that my five writers provide a good cross section from the very popular to the moderately successful, from the well-to-do to the occasionally impoverished; their social class and race are typical of writers of their time, although their approaches to and experiences in the world were quite varied. They also represent women's participation in a variety of literary fields—fiction, poetry, and nonfiction; they used literary approaches from the sensational to the serious. In addition, the overlapping years of these writers' careers provide a useful time line for women's participation in the literary marketplace from the 1840s to the early 1900s. Although I do not claim they represent every woman's experiences in that marketplace, I do believe these five women can teach us much about women writers and about literary professionalism in the nineteenth century.

This study centers on the women's professional activities—the ways in which they pursued their careers—rather than on their private lives. Though I trace the biography of each writer, I emphasize those aspects of her life that seem to have shaped her career; I particularly explore the ways in which a woman's definitions of womanhood and authorship influenced her career. I have not been primarily concerned with the quality of or the themes in the women's literary works, although I have discussed writings when they illuminate professional lives. Throughout the book, but particularly in the first two and final chapters, I have tried to situate these women's literary activities within the histories of women, the literary marketplace, and literary professionalism in the nineteenth century.

As my investigation shows, nineteenth-century America was not wholly restrictive to the aspirations of women who chose to be writers; rather, in its ambiguous cultural messages and social circumstances, the nineteenth century enabled more (usually white, middle-class) women than ever to choose literary careers. Furthermore, because literary business, especially at mid-century, was conducted within author-publisher relationships that idealized such values as personal regard, benevolent paternalism, loyalty, noncommercialism, and advocacy of Victorian morality, the atmosphere of the literary marketplace was not particularly alienating to women who could successfully integrate their female values and behaviors into the pursuit of their literary careers. In fact, as Mary Abigail Dodge pointed out, the inequalities in author-publisher relations meant that all writers, male and female, were expected to relate to publishers in "female" ways. Thus, the mid-century marketplace may actually have been more congenial to women than any later one, since by the end of the century there was a good deal of emphasis on developing a more impersonal, modern, and "masculine" approach to literary business.

Women's use of female values and behaviors in pursuit of their careers did not mean that they were less serious or less professional than male writers; women took their skills seriously, were highly creative, understood their audience, were aware of developments in literary and critical circles, and learned to handle the business of their careers. Many of their behaviors that sometimes have been identified as evidence of women's anxiety of authorship—anonymity or pseudonymity, claims of writing for the good of humanity, denial of professional status, postures of moral superiority or of self-effacement—actually were common among men as well as women and, when expressed by women, are indications of their understanding of the expectations of the nineteenth-century marketplace. They were literary professionals in the most positive sense of those terms.

Although all women writers were confronted by similar cultural messages about woman's sphere, they did not all respond to those messages in the same way; each writer's temperament, ideals, and life circumstances shaped her response to the cultural prescriptions of her time. Thus, E.D.E.N. Southworth, who accepted fairly conventional views of woman's sphere, achieved her phenomenal success in an author-publisher relationship that mirrored her private values. In quite a different way, Harriet Beecher Stowe experienced a great deal of power and autonomy in her career, justified by her belief in what I will call "domestic feminism." A third individual, Mary Abigail Dodge (Gail Hamilton), desired to be an "androgynous" woman; when she discovered the gendered nature of author-publisher relations, she refused to trust or to be bound to any publisher again. By contrast, Helen Hunt Jackson (H. H. and Saxe Holm), whose individuality was not dampened by her belief in separate spheres, developed a professional life-style involving serious literary study, superb business skills, and mentorship of other writers. Finally, Elizabeth Stuart Phelps (Ward), who always maintained her mid-century "feminine" values, struggled valiantly at the end of the century in a marketplace increasingly indifferent to those values.

Of course, as a group women did have some different experiences as writers than men did, both because they lived in a patriarchal culture that undervalued them and their work and because their domestic responsibilities interfered with their professional ones in ways that men's usually did not. But women writers do not deserve to be seen only in terms of that discrimination; nor should we ignore what they shared in common with their literary brothers. Literary women in the nineteenth century succeeded in their careers, despite the disadvantages they faced, and as a result of certain circumstances we have never before recognized. Their life stories are complex and inspiring. It is my hope that each reader who picks up this book will find these lives as fascinating as I have.

Acknowledgments

I incurred many debts while working on this book. Without the help of librarians across the country, I could not have located the thousands of pages of author-publisher correspondence that are the foundation of my work. I am particularly grateful to the universities and libraries that granted me permission to quote from manuscript sources in their collections and to use pictures from their archives. They include the American Antiquarian Society, Boston Public Library, Bowdoin College, Brigham Young University, Colorado College, Columbia University, Cornell University, Duke University, Essex Institute, Haverford College, Historical Society of Pennsylvania, Harvard University, Huntington Library, Jones Library, Louisiana State University, Macmillan Publishing Company, Massachusetts Historical Society, Minnesota Historical Society, New York Public Library, Pennsylvania State University, Princeton University, Rutherford B. Hayes Presidential Center, Radcliffe College, Smith College, Stanford University Libraries, Stowe-Day Foundation, Trinity College, Vassar College, University of Virginia, and Yale University. In addition, I deeply appreciate the cooperation and efficiency of Susan Kesti and Mary Palzer, librarians at the University of Minnesota-Duluth (UMD) who expedited my many minitex and interlibrary loan requests.

I am also sincerely grateful for the grants I received from the University of Minnesota Graduate School, the College of Letters and Sciences-UMD, and the College of Liberal Arts-UMD that helped me to defray expenses during the research and writing process. In addition, I wish to thank Randi Freesol and Karla Ward especially, as well as Jean Nygaard and Barb Williams, who each had a hand in typing the manuscript. My research assistants over the years—Randi Freesol, Belinda Loosen, Holly Nordquist, and Debra Ogston—never lost patience or care with the endless bibliographies and library searches. And Stevie Champion, my copyeditor at the University of North Carolina Press, made many helpful suggestions. Thank you all.

I owe a special debt of gratitude to those colleagues, including Carol Farley Kessler, Nina Baym, Janice Radway, Jane Tompkins, Carol Bock, Elizabeth Bartlett, and Mara Kirk Hart, who helped by commenting on drafts of the manuscript at various stages. My thanks to Bilin Tsai and Don Poe, who loaned me an attic in which to work at a crucial time. In addition, I extend special thanks to Sandra Eisdorfer, my editor, whose encouragement and patience brought this book along.

Finally, my heartfelt thanks go to the Coultraps and the McQuins who never complained about my working on my book, and especially to my own family—David, Katherine, and Christopher—who have deferred many pleasures and assumed many responsibilities so I would have time to finish this project.

*Doing
Literary
Business*

1

Eminent Women
Courtesy of the Arthur and Elizabeth Schlesinger Library, Radcliffe College, Cambridge, Massachusetts

Why Try a Writing Career?

The Ambiguous Cultural Context for Women Writers of the Mid-Nineteenth Century

On December 17, 1877, H. O. Houghton and Company, publishers of the prestigious *Atlantic Monthly*, hosted a dinner party to celebrate the twentieth anniversary of their literary magazine and the seventieth birthday of one of its major contributors, the poet John Greenleaf Whittier. Among the sixty guests were such famous writers as Henry Wadsworth Longfellow, Ralph Waldo Emerson, Oliver Wendell Holmes, and Samuel Clemens (Mark Twain). Held in the East Room of the fashionable Hotel Brunswick in Boston, the event included a seven-course dinner, served with various wines and followed by lively speeches marking the historic occasion.[1] But one group of *Atlantic* contributors was missing. Women had not been invited to the celebration, even though they were a considerable percentage of the contributors to the *Atlantic* in the 1870s, had been a significant part of the American literary community since before the 1850s, and were good friends with many of the *Atlantic* writers who attended the party, especially with its guest of honor, John Greenleaf Whittier.

Although absent from this important dinner in literary history, women authors were very popular and prominent in the nineteenth century, particularly during and after the 1850s. Statistics clearly reveal their increasing visibility as the nineteenth century passed. Before 1830 about one-third of those who published fiction in the United States were women. During the antebellum years, almost 40 percent of the novels reviewed in journals and newspapers were by women, which suggests that an equally high percentage were being published. Best-seller lists reveal that by the 1850s women were authors of almost half of the popular literary works. Among them was Susan Warner's *Wide, Wide World* (1851), the first of many books of "women's fiction" with sales that went far beyond 100,000 copies. Another, Harriet Beecher Stowe's *Uncle Tom's Cabin* (1852), surpassed the 300,000 mark within the first year of publication. By 1872 women wrote nearly three-quarters of all of the novels published. In the same year, patrons of the Boston Public Library called for books by E.D.E.N. Southworth, Mary Jane Holmes, and Caroline Lee Hentz more frequently than any other works, and Mary Jane Holmes received a thousand fan letters a week. Women were hardly invisible as writers.[2]

Among the most successful writers between the 1840s and the 1880s were the five women whose careers are examined in depth in later chapters: E.D.E.N. Southworth, Harriet Beecher Stowe, Mary Abigail Dodge (Gail Hamilton), Helen Hunt Jackson (H. H. and Saxe Holm), and Elizabeth Stuart Phelps (Ward). But there were many other women writers from those years whose careers and writings should not be forgotten. Rose Terry Cooke, for instance, so impressed her peers that she was given the lead story in the premier issue of the *Atlantic* in 1857. Harriet Prescott Spofford, short story writer and poet, intrigued the nation with her story "In a Cellar," published in the *Atlantic* in 1859, and continued to be prominent in literary circles for the rest of the century. Rebecca Harding Davis has been credited with introducing realism to the *Atlantic* with her "Life in the Iron Mills" in 1861. Outside the pages of the *Atlantic*, women were equally successful. Louisa May Alcott, who had published some early work in the *Atlantic*, earned her popular following with the publication by Roberts Brothers of *Little Women* in 1868. The poetry of Louise Chandler Moulton was considered among the finest in the second half of the century. Sara Payson Parton (Fanny Fern) and Sara Jane Lippincott (Grace Greenwood) had thousands of readers for their essays on social and domestic topics, as did Maria Cummins for her novels. The list of well-known women writers could go on.

The prominence of women writers and their absence from the *Atlantic* dinner reveal a major paradox confronting literary historians of the nineteenth century: How can we explain women's persistence and success as writers in the face of attitudes and behaviors that could render them invisible? What ideas and social circumstances sustained their literary work in spite of the frequent devaluation of it? To answer those questions, we need to examine some cultural beliefs and social circumstances in nineteenth-century America that both created the possibility of *woman writer* and devalued her efforts. By doing so, we will begin to discover some reasons why women pursued literary careers.

At the outset, it is important to recognize that women writers caught in the paradox of their situation were often quite outspoken on their own behalf. Not long after the *Atlantic* dinner, the following "bagatelle" appeared in a western newspaper:

Mr. Houghton's Mistake

We are glad to learn that the lady contributors to the Atlantic, who did not attend the Whittier dinner were not disappointed. Indeed, they had intended all along not to be present, and they so indicated to Mr. Houghton in letters written the very day before the dinner. "I hear it intimated," writes Mrs. Stowe, "that I am to be selected to sit at the right hand of Mr. Whittier. Now, my dear Mr. Houghton, while I am deeply grateful for the compliment, I cannot accept. I believe in the largest freedom for everybody, and I am sure the gentlemen who participate in the festivities would not be pleased to have their programme embarrassed by the presence of ladies. He, he! I suppose you know what I mean. One of these days, perhaps the ladies of the Atlantic will have a dinner, and I think they are selfish enough to desire to be alone."

Mr. Houghton read the letter and said, passing his hand through his hair, "I think I have forgotten something. I detect sarcasm in this."

"I am glad, Mr. Houghton," wrote Harriet Prescott Spofford, "that you have decided not to call the ladies from their sylvan solitude. I am deeply engaged in studying the peculiarities of some rushes that grow upon the banks of the beautiful river that rolls by my door, crystallized at present, by the way—I mean the river—in the mellowest moonlight that ever sifted its gold upon a beautiful world; so I couldn't attend anyhow. Thank you for sending no invitation. It would have embarrassed me greatly.

"Have you heard that Mrs. Stowe is about to give a dinner? Are you aware that there is to be a new ladies' magazine? But I cannot write more. Thank you again, and good-bye."

"I am quite confident," said Mr. Houghton, looking worried, "that there is an inadvertence somewhere. It's very singular I did'nt [sic] think of these ladies before." He turned wearily and opened a letter from Gail Hamilton [Mary Abigail Dodge].

"Well, my boy," wrote this lady, "so you're going to give a dinner, are you? To Mr. Whittier, the dearest and best for whom my soul longeth? And without us? I didn't think it of you, Mr. Houghton. I was about to say I didn't think anything of you, but I won't. You can thank your true goodness for that. O, say nothing of that last check. Seriously, however, I don't blame you. If there's anything unpleasant in this world, it is a woman in a wide house—I mean in a banquet hall. I will not stop to argue the wine question; I have no liquid by me to create the necessary inspiration. I suppose it would do no good either—you men are determined to have your own way always, and ours as often as possible. I write to say that I won't come, and to insist that Mr. Whittier and the rest shall not break their hearts over it. Sufficient is it on these occasions to break bread, and, perhaps, also heads. I have just seen a circular in behalf of a new ladies' magazine. Have you seen it? Excuse me now. I have an engagement to spank the Administration at this very moment. Do you know, by the way, that Mrs. Spofford is about to give a grand dinner to the lady contributors of the Atlantic?"

"Alas! for my stupidity!" remarked Mr. Houghton, his face growing pale, and his knees knocking together. "This great moral earthquake will be after me next."

"Oh, Mr. Houghton," wrote H. H. [Helen Hunt Jackson], enthusiastically, "I am so pleased to hear of the honor to grand old Mr. Whittier. My pleasure is only exceeded by my joy that I am not to be there. I should be highly honored by being permitted to be in such company, of course, but I am timid, and I fear that literary men do 'cut up' dreadfully—you will pardon the expression—on these occasions. Do you know, Mr. Houghton, that Gail Hamilton talks of starting a magazine? and they do say that there is to be a grand literary reunion at her house, or rather at the house of Mr. Blaine. I shall not be able to send you anything for some time to come."

"Merciful Heavens!" exclaimed Mr. Houghton, "this must be a conspiracy. They are all of them pleased, and yet they all seem to be contemplating the worst kind of retaliation. I do not understand this!"

He turned with a sigh to a letter from Philadelphia. "You will accept my regrets," said Rebecca Harding Davis. "I cannot possibly be present. I have not received my invitation, but of course it has been delayed in the mail. However, none of that brilliant gathering will feel my absence. I am not so presuming as to suppose that such a slight vacancy in so immense a place will be noticeable. And I do know, Mr. Houghton, that gentlemen delight to be by themselves at times. I hear Helen Hunt and Louisa M. Alcott have put their heads together in behalf of a ladies' magazine and I understand that Rose Terry is to give a dinner to several well-known writers of the gentler sex. Such a magazine might be profitable, and I know the dinner would be delightful."

"Now this is dreadful," said Mr. Houghton, striking the desk with his clenched hand. "I have actually been applying the paper-cutter to my own nose. It is the stupidest thing I ever did in my life. Why, oh! why could I not have seen this result before?" He thought very fast a moment, and then his face brightened and he laughed right out. "I have it!" he exclaimed. "Two months hence there shall be a dinner to the lady contributors of the Atlantic Monthly. It shall be given in honor of Gail Hamilton's seventieth birthday."[3]

Henry O. Houghton's mistake in not inviting "lady contributors" reflected the paradoxical nature of nineteenth-century beliefs about women writers. On the one hand, Houghton often published and paid well for literary works by women that accorded with his Victorian sense of morality, didacticism, and literary excellence; on the other hand, he never considered women's literature to be as important as men's. A rather typical gentleman of his time, he believed in male superiority and the more honorable place of women in the home. No doubt he felt he could relax more with men and wine than with women and water (which he served at a breakfast for Oliver Wendell Holmes in 1880 when he did invite women).[4] In many respects, Henry Houghton exemplified the ambiguous response of nineteenth-century American society to the woman writer.

"Mr. Houghton's Mistake" illustrates the variety of responses women showed to those attitudes. Whether the article was actually written by one or more of the women parodied in it (the humor and style suggest Mary Abigail Dodge), or by another humorist, it demonstrates women's ability to define themselves beyond their culture's most limiting values and expectations. It is absolutely true, of course, that women's lives and careers were controlled by their society's patriarchal perspectives; even after building successful careers, women had to respond to social circumstances, stereotypes, and assumptions about women and women writers that were largely created and perpetuated by men. Nevertheless, women were not uniformly molded by those social expectations; they developed a variety of responses, such as those illustrated in the letters to Houghton—responses that ranged from Spofford's poetic conformity to Dodge's abrasive defiance. Even when faced by cultural prescriptions and social institutions that undervalued women's capabilities and achievements in comparison to men's, women demonstrated remarkable individuality and determination in their pursuit of a literary career. "Mr. Houghton's Mistake" is a good reminder that patriarchal perspectives did not completely define women's options nor their views of themselves in the world. If patriarchal views had been wholly accepted, the article would never have been written.

The article also makes the important point that, by virtue of their connections with one another and their popularity with their audiences, women were not without power in the literary arena. "Mr. Houghton's Mistake" demonstrates, even if through fiction, that there was a network among the women writers that sustained and encouraged each others' efforts. Furthermore, these writers had an audience familiar enough with their works to understand the humorist's allusions to spanking the Administration and meeting in Mr. Blaine's house. (See Chapter 5 on Mary Abigail Dodge.) Collectively at least, and in many cases individually, women writers were important to the economics of the literary marketplace; if they decided to start a new magazine, it would have to be taken seriously. In fact, their threats (or those of the humorist) seem to have had some impact on Houghton himself, although they did not prevent the same sort of discrimination against women writers from happening again and again. Although Houghton never gave a dinner for Mary Abigail

Dodge, he was careful to include women in his next big celebration, the Holmes breakfast in 1880, and he honored Harriet Beecher Stowe similarly in 1882.[5]

In short, the position of women writers in the mid-nineteenth century—say, from the 1840s to the 1880s—was paradoxical: they had a place in the literary world, yet that world often rendered them invisible. The explanation of the paradox lies, first, in the ambiguous nature of cultural messages to and about women. While the ideology of woman's sphere in the nineteenth century could restrict women's participation in society, other messages about ideal Americans and about authorship sometimes did accommodate women. The changing social circumstances of women, particularly middle-class ones, also provided opportunities for fuller public participation, despite messages that woman's place was in the home. Both cultural prescriptions and social circumstances provided the context within which women writers pursued their careers.

The subjects of this study grew up in antebellum America, a time of great possibilities created by industrial and urban growth, westward expansion, and improved communications. They were aware of voluntary associations, utopian experiments, and reform crusades, including those for abolition and women's rights, that were changing the ways people ordered their private and public lives. And, they probably heard much debate about individualism, equality, and self-government, for there was not unanimity on what those ideals meant or to whom they applied.[6] In addition, they, like their brothers, were encouraged to adopt ethical views that historians have come to label "Victorian."

To simplify greatly, we can say that American Victorianism encouraged moral, didactic, and patriarchal approaches to life. Victorians promoted strict sexual codes, social responsibility, and genteel, patriarchal social standards. They stressed hard work, deferred gratification, sobriety, and conscientiousness—qualities that were essential to an industrializing society. They also encouraged competition but warned that too much of it would destroy the rational social order.[7] Victorians urged conformity to genteel social standards as the humane, democratic route to status and success. Sentimentalism and emotional expression, according to them, were inappropriate in the business world but acceptable in literature, the church, and the home—all three areas seen primarily as the province of women.

The ideal American who attempted to conform to these views was said to have "character." A person of character felt a sense of obligation to promote the general welfare of society as well as to improve the self—educationally, culturally, and morally. In their words, Victorians wanted "well-informed minds, pure hearts, and refined manners."[8] With that end in mind, they worked to master their weaknesses through self-discipline and restraint. Character building, a lifelong process, was supposed to begin in the (ideal middle-class) home under the direction of a devoted mother.[9]

Though espoused by the majority of Americans (the dissenters coming particularly but not entirely from outside the white middle class), Victorian ideals were most thoroughly articulated by northern, middle-class, Protestant males and carried the stamp of their class, race, and gender.[10] These men assumed that everyone should adopt their values, and, in fact, their ideas ultimately permeated much of nineteenth-century society. As public education became more common, male and female students across the country learned lessons reflecting Victorian beliefs. In addition, the rapidly expanding publishing industry, as demonstrated in the next chapter, became a mouthpiece for the expression of Victorian values. Orators and community programs took Victorian values to rural hamlets, spreading the worldview still further.

While the values of American Victorianism were derived primarily from the values of white males and were meant to apply primarily to men in society, they were also heard by and had an influence on women. We can see this in the women writers studied in this book. E.D.E.N. Southworth, for example, argued strongly in defense of the moral rectitude of her writings, as did most other Victorians. Mary Abigail Dodge urged women to develop their character more than their looks. Harriet Beecher Stowe felt it appropriate to speak out against Lord Byron's sexual immorality. Other women writers expressed Victorian views when they encouraged genteel manners, hard work, and the social importance of familial ties. To some extent anyway, Victorian perspectives were shared by women and men.

But Victorians also expected men and women to be essentially different and to have separate "spheres" of activity; women, for example, were thought to be more sentimental and emotional and less interested in competitiveness and the public arena than men were. Although the ideology of separate spheres could be restrictive to women, it also gave them an area of authority (the home) and an expertise (domesticity and morality) that some of them eventually used to justify an expanded role in society. Within their separate sphere women developed bonds with other women that nourished a rich female culture and spawned the collective activity of nineteenth-century women in voluntary associations and reform crusades. Nevertheless, the rhetoric of separate spheres usually emphasized women's dependence and subordination.[11]

Like other nineteenth-century values, the belief in separate spheres was both a cause of and a response to what was actually happening to women and men in their lives. As America industrialized, adult activities were more frequently segregated by sex than they had been in earlier times.[12] The separation between home and business meant that the control of economic resources shifted from the home to employed males in the marketplace, leaving women and children in the middle-class or affluent home, who did not have income-producing jobs, in a more subordinate and dependent position. The ideology of separate spheres seems to have arisen to justify these middle- and upper-class circumstances, though the concept was used as an ideal against which to judge people in all classes. Such a prescription was not simply imposed by men to justify the patriarchal social order, although men certainly did argue for separate spheres to that end. Women themselves, seeking to cope with the social changes, often embraced the ideology of separate spheres and argued that their position was one of significance, not subordination. Others in varying degrees chafed against its restrictions and demanded equal rights.

But what exactly was a nineteenth-century woman supposed to be? Actually, there was no single view of womanhood, but a continuum of views ranging from conservative to more liberal perspectives.[13] The conservative view was widespread in the media of antebellum America, which included books on etiquette, sermons, literary gift books, and annuals; those who supported this view insisted that "true women" were naturally domestic, submissive, and morally pure. The more liberal perspective, which was definitely a minority view in antebellum America, although one that increased in popularity as the century passed, was expressed by proponents of women's education, legal rights, suffrage, and career opportunities; this group maintained that "true women" were morally superior to men and valued family relations, but could and should be as self-reliant and competent as men. According to the conservative view, women were emotional and had few rational capabilities; according to the more liberal view, women were capable of affection *and* intelligence. The conservatives believed that women were assigned by God and nature to their separate sphere of activity and should rejoice in that. The liberals felt that the restrictions on woman's sphere, imposed only by social circumstances, should be eliminated, while the values of the sphere—nurturance, love, and morality—should be spread throughout society.

The conservative view has been called the "Cult of True Womanhood" because of what appears from a twentieth-century perspective to be an obsessive, almost ritualistic repetition of very narrow views of women.[14] The liberal view might be called the "Vision of New Womanhood" because it often provided the justification for women's participation in many new areas of society, including the literary marketplace, in the nineteenth century. In between the two poles were various arguments, including those for honoring Domesticity—the role of the mother in the home. What all the views shared in common was a belief in women's morality, spirituality, and nurturance; they can be distinguished by their disagreements over (1) whether those values restricted women to the home or justified their participation throughout society; and (2) whether they made women superior to, subordinate to, or separate but equal to men.

True Womanhood, the conservative view, influenced most writings about nineteenth-century women, especially, but not exclusively, before the Civil War. For example, Mary Jane Holmes's minister described the private life of this best-selling writer in its terms, saying she "possesses in a high degree, those Christian graces and virtues which alone give lustre to mental accomplishments. . . . She prefers the quiet of home life. . . . Her piety is deep, serene and unostentatious." With a similar vision of purity, piety, and domesticity in mind, Harriet Prescott Spofford praised the poet Louise Chandler Moulton as "a being of absolute uprightness, incapable of untruth, faithful to her ideals, ingenuous, confiding, unsuspicious, without guile, caring nothing for place or power, for social rank and position, or for wealth; of childlike nature throughout life, a triumphant woman, but always a child." Indeed, the image of True Womanhood was so appealing that even advocates of expanding woman's role in society, like Sara Jane Lippincott (Grace Greenwood), sometimes felt compelled to use it, saying, for instance, "true feminine genius is ever timid, doubtful, and clingingly dependent; a perpetual childhood. A true woman shrinks instinctively from greatness."[15]

Despite the fervor of these claims, none of the above descriptions accurately reflect or describe the authors themselves. Holmes was a smart, determined, and ambitious writer; Moulton, a woman capable of using literary friendships to her own advantage in building her career; and Lippincott, a proponent of woman suffrage. Yet so luminous was the ideal of the True Woman that other characteristics of women often fell into deep shadow and were not seen or remarked upon at all. Thus, behaviors demonstrating ambition or assertion or the use of literary influence were often denied or ignored, and, if seen, were criticized resoundingly. In other words, while there is ample evidence that women themselves did not wholly conform to prescriptions of True Womanhood, nevertheless, those prescriptions exerted a strong influence on what was seen, understood, and said about women's lives. True Womanhood was the ideal against which most women's activities, including their literary ones, were judged.

Being woman was the primary fact and being womanly the major glory, according to proponents of True Womanhood. A woman of her time, Ellen Olney Kirk, called it "the essential need of being womanly" against which other characteristics and motives faded. From this perspective being a True Woman was a vocation in itself, more distinguished than any other. According to its most conservative proponents, therefore, being a True Woman was incompatible with being a woman writer. As one such commentator said, "If women were wise they would understand that they have a mission quite as grand as that of literary authorship. It is the mission of keeping alive for men certain ideas, and ideals too, which would soon pass out of the world." The True Woman's special responsibility was to be guardian of the cultural, religious, and moral values of Victorian society in America. She was to maintain the noncommercial values of love, hope, and charity in a secular age fascinated with business, competition, and endless expansion. With her innocence and charm, woman was to create a home life that was a refuge for men and children from the cruelty and unpredictability of the world.[16]

Literary critics of the period, like most other social commentators, not only accepted but also preached the conservative vision of True Womanhood. While they commended male characters in novels for displaying individuality, they praised female characters who were True Women: pious, pure, domestic, and pleasing to others.[17] For example, a critic in the *Christian Examiner* (September 1852) said of the main character in *The Sunny Side* that she was "the good man's crown" because she was "the cheerer of her husband in despondency, the kind and wise guide of her children in the right way, with modesty prompting the wish to shrink from publicity, but high principle curbing the indulgence of that wish, she appears the true pastor's wife, ready when occasion calls to be the friend and counsellor of those around her, but finding her peculiar sphere of duty in her own home." Like twentieth-century advice columnists, nineteenth-century literary reviewers, both male and female, encouraged female readers to pattern their lives after those heroines who best conformed to the role of True Woman. Reviewers praised most highly those novels that kept women in their sphere, rather than legitimizing their discontent with it. They also created idealized descriptions of literary women, like those quoted above, as models for other women to follow. Finally, they usually argued that "women ought to write not as individuals, but as exemplars of their sex." The conservative message of True Womanhood was widespread.

Despite its popularity, True Womanhood as an ideal was criticized in its own time by liberals espousing a Vision of New Womanhood. The most radical of the critics, like the suffragist Elizabeth Cady Stanton, argued that women were, most importantly, human beings like men with aspirations for achievement and only incidentally wives and mothers with their special responsibilities. Moderate critics like Catharine Beecher saw womanhood as primary but would not concede that this made women weaker or less important than men.[18] Actually, most liberals agreed with conservatives that women were prepared to nurture and care for others because they were morally superior, but liberals also argued that women could and should move beyond the home into volunteer and career opportunities to make society a better place in which to live. Many thought men should imitate women's piety, purity, and gentleness; conversely, women in their sphere or beyond it should be as intelligent, self-reliant, and courageous as men. This Vision of New Womanhood sometimes called for blending masculine and feminine characteristics as the nineteenth century defined them, but it usually did not go so far as to say that women and men could be the same. As Mary Abigail Dodge (Gail Hamilton) wrote, "They make a great mistake, who think a strong, brave, self-poised woman is unwomanly. The stronger she is, the truer she is to her womanly instincts."[19]

Women themselves varied in their attitudes toward their society's prescriptions for womanhood, but, whatever their view, the values they were socialized to accept did not make them wholly distinct from their male counterparts. With men they were expected to share Victorian beliefs in, for example, moral purity, self-improvement, hard work, genteel behavior, and, in some cases, self-reliance. When articulating any of the shared values, women might be heard as *women* or as *Victorians* like the men. This is an important point because it begins to explain why women were ambivalently accepted in the literary world and also how they might step beyond the prescriptions of separate spheres. The rhetoric of separate spheres coupled with that of Victorianism helped to create an ambiguous intellectual context for women's participation in society beyond the home: one in which at least middle-class white women were both insiders (Victorians) and outsiders (women), or, as the 1877 *Atlantic* dinner illustrated, both prominent writers and uninvited guests. While this intellectual context made responses to women contradictory, it simultaneously created the possibility that some women would believe they had something to say to the world in regard to either those shared values or their separate sphere.

While, on the one hand, the overlapping, sometimes contradictory messages to Victorian women made it possible for at least some of them to think they could legitimately speak to their whole society, even when being told to remain in their separate sphere, on the other hand, equally ambiguous messages about authorship made it possible for them to persist as writers, even when they were discouraged and discriminated against. Ideas about womanhood and about writing in the nineteenth century were not wholly dichotomous, though many proponents of separate spheres tried to make them seem so. Although people usually assumed authors were male—seen by implication in the necessity of saying "lady" contributor or "authoress" when talking about women—authors' characteristics were not wholly "masculine," as the nineteenth century understood the term. Similarities between the role and characteristics of women and of writers also may have facilitated women's adoption of and persistence in literary careers.

In the first place, the ideal of the leisured writer that pervaded authorship in America until mid-century was compatible with social expectations for middle-class women. In the early nineteenth century, people assumed, often rightly, that a writer was a gentleman of leisure who wrote for his own enjoyment and that of his literary equals. If he did not have wealth enough to support this activity, the ideal writer was supposed to depend on others, a patron or his family, for support. He wrote when the spirit moved him, not because he needed money or because he wanted popularity. When he published his work, it was anonymously as a sign of his modesty and noncommercial aims.[20] According to Charles Brockden Brown, one of the first Americans who tried and failed to earn a living by writing, a respectable author was "the man who devotes to composition the leisure secured to him by hereditary affluence, or by a lucrative profession or office." Writing was an embellishment, a luxury, a pursuit for the leisured or for those with a lucrative career and time to spare. Negative portrayals in the press of commercial writers as grasping lowbrows reaffirmed the desire of many writers to be seen as amateurs, even if they were not. Thus, many echoed Catharine Maria Sedgwick who said, "Literary occupation is rather a pastime than a profession with me." This ethic of "genteel amateurism," as Lawrence Buell calls it, persisted as an ideal, if not a reality, throughout the antebellum period.[21] Here, then, was the first aspect of authorship compatible with the expectations of (middle-class) womanhood. There was no better term than "genteel amateur" to describe the woman whose talents were supposed to be used for the entertainment of others; in this sense at least, her literary career did not challenge the expectations of her sphere.

Even as writing became more acceptable as a way of earning a living, the ideal of the leisured writer persisted. Those who earned their living by writing in antebellum America clung to the ethic of genteel amateurism, most notably by insisting that they did not have commercial aims.[22] In addition, the concept of writer took on a particularly Victorian cast: while literature might be written for the pleasure of the audience, the ideal writer would incorporate moral and social lessons as well; one corollary of that assumption was that only the morally upright person could write good works. Like ideal women, "respectable" writers were expected to be above commercial concerns and to be not only models but also teachers of good morals. In these ways, too, being a writer and being a woman were not antithetical.

Moreover, in industrializing America writing was viewed as a somewhat deviant activity because it involved writers in a sphere of social life that was not as productive as business. While writers tended to view themselves as superior to those with commercial concerns, their detractors said writers did not understand finances. As one publisher said at the end of the century, "Most writers have few financial dealings, and they often innocently propose impracticable things. But this is not a peculiar trait of writers. Most preachers and many women show it."[23] This perceived impracticality made writers as deviant as women and preachers in commercial society. It is significant, therefore, that the responses from authors themselves to their deviant position were not unlike the responses of women to their separate sphere. Some were apologetic and self-deprecating, while others argued the comparability or superiority of their work to business.

Although on the whole these similarities in status and attributed characteristics between women and writers were not noticed in the nineteenth century, sometimes commentators of the period did make the comparison. At mid-century several noted the "feminine" nature of writers. Rufus Griswold remarked in passing in 1849 that "the most essential genius in men is marked by qualities which we may call feminine." Another literary reviewer, writing on "Female Novelists," pointed out that "there is a race of masculine writers, with feminine delicacy of mind," including Richard Dana, Nathaniel Hawthorne, and Washington Irving.[24]

Nevertheless, other assumptions about writers, their literary works, and their professional practices were clearly related to the idea of author as male. The greatest writers were assumed to have a wide knowledge of the world, to be educated and to be familiar with many people and places. Such knowledge was, of course, more accessible to and assumed more appropriate for men. Furthermore, the greatest writing was described as "vigorous" and, although not identified exclusively with men's writing, was considered "masculine," both in literature and in social life.[25] Some assumed that, when it came to selling one's literary work, women would have a harder time. One commentator observed that, from her point of view, "A man going from office to office to sell a poem or a leader must be a sorry sight. A woman compelled to peddle by voice and eye such a ware must be a sadder sight still."[26]

Given the pervasiveness of the ideology of separate spheres, it is not surprising that attitudes toward women writers often mirrored attitudes toward women. Thus, in praising Sara Jane Lippincott (Grace Greenwood), a reviewer wrote, "There is a delightful absurdity about her wit, into which only a genuine woman could fall." Likewise, an article on Louise Chandler Moulton, written at the beginning of the twentieth century but reflecting patriarchal Victorian attitudes, begins with a comparison of Moulton to Elizabeth Barrett Browning, claiming the work of each "could have been written only by a woman." Moulton won praise from this reviewer for "never letting her imagination, however willing, stray beyond the boundary of her own experience. . . . She never wished to cope with events great or small outside her own sphere. . . . She was always a poet and always a woman." Earlier in the century another poet, Lydia H. Sigourney, had been commended for her poems that "commonly express, with great purity and evident sincerity, the tender affections which are so natural to the female heart, and the lofty aspirations after a higher and better state of being."[27]

Often, in fact, literary critics seemed incapable of distinguishing between an author and her text. Although men's character also was presumed to be reflected in their texts, the connections expected in women's works were strongly influenced by the cultural prescriptions for women. Again, the review of Moulton's poetry illustrates this: "Her poetry is the mirror, clear, limpid, unspotted by any blemishes of style, which contains the beautiful reflection of her personality and experience."[28] Sometimes a woman's art was seen as a test of her femininity; other times, her life, the final test of her art. Using this second argument, Sara Jane Lippincott reassured readers that even shocking writings by Sara Payson Parton (Fanny Fern) were acceptable because "whatever masks of manly independence, pride, or mocking mischief Fanny Fern may put on, she is, at the core of her nature, 'pure womanly.'"[29] Apparently, Fanny Fern's personal traits could redeem her prose.

In addition to contending with critics who confounded their womanhood and their literary work, women also had to confront negative images of the woman writer. Women writers were stereotyped as "bluestockings" and as "strong-minded" women whose intelligence made them "tough, aggressive, pedantic, vain, and ugly."[30] Even when they were not considered unfeminine, female authors were regarded by many as having certain disadvantages as women. One journalist, commenting on Adoradim Judson's marriage to the popular writer Emily Chubbuck, claimed that the only reason Judson accepted "the drawback" of a woman with "a reputation which was growing into fame" was that he got a woman "of uncommon loveliness of mind and character." But criticism could go further than that. After she published the controversial *Ruth Hall*, critics said they could tell that Fanny Fern was "not sufficiently endowed with female delicacy," and "nothing more than a high-stepping, skirt-flouncing, self-puffing divorcee of 'a certain age.'"

As scholar Nina Baym has pointed out, most antebellum reviewers accepted women as writers as long as their works made clear their primary identification as True Women. Thus, the reviewers expected womanhood to be reflected in women's literary style as diffuseness, gracefulness, or delicacy; in their subject matter as the domestic, the social, or the private; and in their tone as purity, morality, idealism, and didacticism.[31] According to the writer Ann S. Stephens, who was fond of turning feminine stereotypes to women's advantage, these feminine characteristics qualified women as greater literary geniuses than men: "Deep and sensitive feelings alone give that delicacy and pathos which will ever distinguish the creations of a truly feminine author from those of men. The very word genius comprehends all that makes the loveliness of woman. It signifies but the power to feel, deeply combined with an intellect capable of embodying feeling into language, and of conveying images of truth and beauty from the heart of the writer to the heart of the reader."

In spite of Stephens's advocacy, works by women were usually not recognized as greater than or equal to men's, even when the authors did conform to the expectations of the True Woman writer. It was a catch-22. Women, who were expected to write of domestic scenes, were criticized for doing so. One critic complained that "the majority of lady writers do not rise above the atmosphere of the tea-table, which is the element of the common novel, and have a constant downward tendency towards the kitchen." Though diffuseness was expected of women, Harriet Prescott Spofford was criticized for using "far too many words, synonymous words and meaningless words. Like the majority of female writers—Mrs. Browning, George Sand, Gail Hamilton, Mrs. Stowe—she possesses in excess the fatal gift of fluency." According to Rufus Griswold, it was difficult to judge women's works at all because it was so easy to find oneself "mistaking for the efflorescent energy of creative intelligence, that which is only the exuberance of personal 'feelings unemployed.' We may confound the vivid dreamings of an unsatisfied heart, with the aspirations of a mind impatient of the fetters of time, and matter, and mortality."[32]

By such reasoning the True Woman writer, though honored, was always inferior to male authors. If she reached the heights of artistic excellence, it was often assumed to be at the sacrifice of her womanhood. As the author of "Literary Women" warned in 1864, "To understand by long experience the meannesses of the world, to comprehend the various ways in which men undergo moral declension and decay, and yet be able to take a broad and comprehensive view of life after all the destruction of one's ideals and utopias, is part of the necessary qualification for a great writer. The women who attain to it must attain to it by undergoing a defeminizing process; after which they gain much strength and breadth of view at the sacrifice of that nameless beauty of innocence which is by nature the glory of the woman."[33] Agreeing with this perspective, a reviewer in the *New Englander* criticized Harriet Beecher Stowe for her representation of the villain Aaron Burr in *The Minister's Wooing*, doubting it was possible for a "pure and true woman" to conceive of a villain so wicked as he was.

Despite the negative criticism, women's writing continued unabated. Indeed, it began to seem to some commentators that there must be a natural affinity between women and fiction; one wrote that fiction was "woman's appropriate sphere, as much as the flower-garden, the drawing room, and the nursery." Another noted, if condescendingly, that "the average merit of the sexes as novel-writers is decidedly in favor of woman." Similarly, an article in the *Democratic Review* in 1855 declared that female "genius" had its place; while it was most honorable when "confined to its proper sphere," it was necessary for "the completeness of any national literature." Women's tenderness and sensibility, their finer, more delicate minds aided through fiction "the full development of human nature." In 1853 the Reverend Jesse T. Peck prophesied that woman "in the world of literature . . . yet has room for indefinite expansion."[34]

As the century passed, the idea of a "New Woman" writer gradually took hold. This ideal of female authorship benefited from the increasing national acceptance of the Vision of New Womanhood that was broader than True Womanhood. An example of this appeared in an 1883 article in the *Literary World*; it declared, "the woman of letters must have some masculinity in her composition; her finer metal must be streaked with iron-ore; she must carry the sledge-hammer in her hand as well as wear the flower at her throat. She must be a Miriam, a Deborah, prophetess as well as poet; a woman who fathoms philosophies as well as fashions." From this perspective Sara Jane Lippincott (Grace Greenwood) was admired for ranging "beyond the usual limits of woman's sphere" with a language "more virile and pungent" than most women's. And Rufus Griswold, who also had claimed to have a hard time evaluating women's poetic abilities, advocated an understanding of the true female poet whose "feminine" characteristics contained other Victorian (male) strengths: "We should deem her the truest poet, whose emotions are most refined by reason, whose force of passion is most expanded and controlled into lofty and impersonal forms of imagination."[35]

Almost no one in the nineteenth century (or the twentieth, for that matter) was entirely able to separate the evaluation of literary work from the sex of the author. The frustration this created in women writers was intense and expressed for all of them by the heroine in Fanny Fern's *Ruth Hall* who exclaimed, "I wish *I* had a paper. Wouldn't I call things by their right names? Would I know any sex in books? Would I praise a book because a woman wrote it? Would I abuse it for the same reason?"[36] Of course, this cry did not stop reviewers of *Ruth Hall* from making comments related to the author's sex, most of them negative, as indicated above.

The interesting thing is that the cultural messages promoting separate spheres in the literary world did not stop all women from pursuing literary careers. Though they could be overlooked and undervalued, they still pushed on. Again, an ambiguous intellectual context may explain the paradox. In the nineteenth century, the attributes of woman and of writer were not conceived in wholly dichotomous ways; rather, they had some remarkable affinities. By concentrating on certain aspects of authorship, such as genteel amateurism or its moral goals and noncommercial aims, women could feel they did not compromise their womanhood by being writers, even if their critics said they did. At the same time, those affinities probably led critics who wished authorship would remain predominantly, if not completely, in the hands of males to make exaggerated pronouncements about woman's separate sphere. Thus, as women became visible successes in the literary marketplace, there was a struggle over literary territory, played out in the words of literary critics—male and female—and male writers who wanted to keep women writers in their own sphere. But the ambiguous nature of the boundaries would not hold women out. Though uninvited to the *Atlantic* dinner, women writers would have their place.

How they felt about their place as women writers has been debated by scholars. While some women certainly must have experienced self-doubt and conflict in the pursuit of a literary career, others, like the subjects of this study, were relatively comfortable in their role as women writers. The latter seem not to have internalized, though they were aware of, the negative views of women writers. Similarly, Judith Fetterley has argued, based on her readings of works by prominent nineteenth-century writers like Sara Payson Parton, Harriet Beecher Stowe, and Mary Abigail Dodge, that they "seemed to manifest a considerable degree of comfort with the act of writing and with the presentation of themselves as writers and relatively little sense of disjunctiveness between 'woman' and 'pen.'"[37] Fetterley found that many women showed skill and self-confidence in their literary works that focused on the woman writer.

Many women's novels of the period also suggest that writers felt confident about women's ability to overcome obstacles in their lives. Nina Baym illustrates this point in her study of *Woman's Fiction . . . 1820–1870* (1978):

> The many novels all tell, with variations, a single tale. In essence, it is the story of a young girl who is deprived of the supports she had rightly or wrongly depended on to sustain her throughout life and is faced with the necessity of winning her own way in the world. . . . At the outset she takes

> herself very lightly—has no ego, or a damaged one, and looks to the world to coddle and protect her. . . . By the novel's end she has developed a strong conviction of her own worth as a result of which she does ask much from herself. She can meet her own demands and, inevitably, the change in herself has changed the world's attitude toward her. . . . The end of change, finally, is a new woman and, by extension, the reformation of the world immediately around her.[38]

Though the stories may have been a type of wish fulfillment (there was not a dramatic reformation of the world around women writers), they do seem to reflect the self-confidence and seriousness about women's lives that women writers themselves often showed.

There are other indications of women's acceptance of themselves as writers. In addition to speaking out in their own defense, as in "Mr. Houghton's Mistake," they were able to joke about the criticism that came to them as women. Rose Terry Cooke, for example, in a humorous piece for the *Atlantic Monthly*, poked fun at one of the stereotypes of women writers: "I am case-hardened to the instantaneous scattering and dodging of young men that ensue, the moment I enter a little party, because 'gentlemen are so afraid of literary women.' I don't think gentlemen are; I know two or three who never conceal a revolver in the breast of their coat when they talk to me."[39] Popular women writers also took pride in their literary skills and said that, though they wrote to earn money, they also had serious artistic aspirations.[40]

Given this variety of evidence, it is apparent that, by the middle of the nineteenth century, many women writers could be comfortable with their own literary aspirations, though undoubtedly there were others whose attitudes toward themselves reflected their society's ambivalent or negative views.[41] It may have been possible for some women to overcome the social ambivalence toward women writers, in part, because of the overlapping nature of expectations about Victorianism, womanhood, and authorship. On the whole, the authors examined in this study did not seem to accept the idea that a literary career was inappropriate for women; they were not particularly anxious about being a woman who was pursuing literary work.

This is not to say that being a writer was easy for women in the nineteenth century or that they were not bothered by the criticism of peers. Obviously, some cultural views and social circumstances created situations that disadvantaged women as writers in comparison to men. By the predominant cultural view, women were not only different, they were less. Furthermore, in their social situations they had to balance women's responsibilities—childrearing, housekeeping, visiting, and so forth—with their literary careers. They suffered, as contemporary women do, from having two careers, home and paid work. Nevertheless, it was possible for some women writers to persist, in fact, triumph against cultural devaluation, supported in part by the particular ambiguity of the values and concepts described here.

While cultural views made it possible for women to think of themselves as writers, societal and personal circumstances also made authorship a popular career choice. It is important to recognize, however, that it was not a career choice for all types of women. Lawrence Buell has described the typical successful antebellum woman writer from New England as follows: She was born to New England–born parents, more affluent and better educated than average. She was white, had been born in New England (Massachusetts, in fact) and lived there most of her life, and was most often affiliated with either the Congregational or Unitarian church. In addition, she was more likely to write fiction than her male counterparts and more likely to devote herself to writing than to any other pursuit as a way to earn a living.[42] In the case of the five women writers analyzed in upcoming chapters, all except E.D.E.N. Southworth had New England–born parents who were better educated than most and at least for part of their lives were more affluent than average. Four of the writers were born in New England and three were of Congregational background; all ultimately chose writing as a way of earning a living over (the most popular alternative) teaching.

In other words, for women, writing as a career choice was generally limited at mid-century to white, Protestant, middle-class women (there were exceptions, of course)—women of the same race, class, and economic background as those men who were the predominant spokespersons of Victorianism. These women benefited not only from their society's ambiguous messages to women, but also from expanding educational opportunities for women, the presence of other achieving women as role models, the declining rate of childbirth, and the support of those around them. As individuals, they were intelligent, verbally creative, and often felt "different" from others when they were growing up. However, the pursuit of a career was not easy. Economic necessity often drove their careers. Housework and other responsibilities of woman's role frequently got in the way. Ultimately, it took perseverance and creativity on each woman's part to succeed.

Without a doubt, the large number of women who became writers in the nineteenth century benefited from the expansion of education for women. By 1850, at least 50 percent of white women could read and write, and in New England literacy was almost universal. By the 1860s, 75 percent of all females between the ages of five and nineteen who lived in New England were in school. Still, women's education was not comparable to men's, either in its level of sophistication or in its expectations of outcome. Each of the five women highlighted in this study had at least some high school or academy education, but none attended college as did many of their male peers. Though often encouraged in their studies by family members or teachers, they were always expected in the end to become wives and mothers. While their educations gave them some of the literary skills they needed to be writers, they were not the same skills their male peers had.[43]

Although they did not have comparable educations to those of their male counterparts, women who became writers were often known for their intelligence as children, at least in retrospective accounts of their lives. The biographies of some, like Mary Abigail Dodge, indicate that they began reading or learning when they were very young. Those who started their educations at older ages, like E.D.E.N. Southworth, were eager and quick learners. Most of the writers themselves reported an early fascination with storytelling or writing—sometimes, as in Southworth's case, in hearing stories; sometimes, as in Elizabeth Stuart Phelps's case, in telling stories. As intelligent girls, they must have been caught up in their country's passion for novel reading, encountering in those books messages advocating not only female education but also the virtues of writing well.[44]

As they were growing up, the women who eventually adopted writing careers were all taught, and to some degree rebelled against, the expectations of True Womanhood. In each of the writers examined here and in many others, there was some sense of alienation or of being different from other girls during their childhood. Some of the young girls spent considerable time outdoors and were called "tomboys." Others, like Elizabeth Stuart Phelps, later characterized themselves in that way.[45] Some, like Mary Abigail Dodge, felt different because temperamentally or physically they could not conform to popular expectations of young women. Others, like Helen Hunt Jackson, were troublemakers as children. When grown, however, women writers in general were satisfied with being women and supporting women's values, though their views ranged from conservative to liberal.

Furthermore, when these writers were young, some women around them gave them a vision of woman's place in the world that was wider than a True Woman's sphere. In antebellum America, female moral reformers were working for temperance, moral purity, and, later, women's rights, stirring up controversy, even while they argued that their participation in society was an expression of their domesticity and other women's values. Other middle-class women were beginning to take jobs as teachers and nurses. Moreover, the future writers also knew about the many women writers who had come before them; they had, it must be noted, a knowledge of a female literary tradition in America and England. The writers in this study were familiar with the works of such authors as Fanny Burney, Maria Edgeworth, Anne Radcliffe, Susanna Rowson, Catharine Sedgwick, Lydia Maria Child, and Lydia Sigourney. Finally, they probably all read (in fact, Harriet Beecher Stowe contributed to) the enormously popular *Godey's Lady's Book*, whose editor, Sarah Josepha Hale, while advocating True Womanhood and domesticity, also argued for women becoming authors of moral literature.[46]

Although they were not raised with the idea they would sometime have a career, like other women of their time they had seen enough economic disruptions in middle-class families to be aware that some women of their class in society had to earn a living. They would have known that the precariousness of the American economy in antebellum America quickly elevated some Americans to good fortune and as quickly ruined others in the panics of the time. Indeed, some, like Southworth, personally experienced just such a plunge into poverty as a child. Historians have pointed out that downward social mobility often prompted women in the nineteenth century to choose professional careers.[47] For many, the death of a spouse, the inadequacy of family income, or other economic needs motivated the adoption of a literary career.

Economically, a literary career was a good choice for women, though it did not bring all of them great riches. Women, even more than men who had other vocational opportunities, were lured to writing, knowing that by mid-century some people were earning substantial incomes from their literary careers.[48] Both single women and married women whose husbands' incomes were inadequate found that, if they wrote even moderately well, they could earn a better living by writing for newspapers and magazines than by sewing or teaching, other popular alternatives for genteel women. Furthermore, while women like Rose Terry Cooke, Elizabeth Stuart Phelps (Ward), and Rebecca Harding Davis actually began their careers to express their creative impulses, they, too, came to rely on the income from their writing to support themselves and their families later in life. In fact, their earnings from published writings often kept women and their families in the middle class, a status they might not otherwise have been able to maintain.

Nevertheless, as wage earners, women writers were doing something that was uncommon for women, especially middle-class single or married ones. By 1860, only about 15 percent (up from 10 percent in the 1840s) of all women were wage earners outside the home, and those were predominantly young, poor, black, immigrants, or widows. As writers, women earned money but not outside the home. Their work made them more like the uncounted numbers of married women in the nineteenth century who were wage earners in their homes, selling surplus products, taking in boarders, or making garments. Undoubtedly it was important that writing could be done in the home, because the middle-class response to women workers was that they were either neglecting their families or risking their virtue.[49] Class, race, and gender biases against women working were mitigated somewhat by their doing the work at home.

Work at home was also important because, like their contemporaries, most women writers were or had been married and most were parents, though the proportion of women writers before the Civil War who were single (and childless) was higher than the national average.[50] As a group of mostly married women, writers benefited from the decline in national birthrates, from 7.04 in 1800 to 5.92 in 1850 to 3.56 in 1900, with the most precipitous drop among the middle class in towns and cities. The five writers studied in this book illustrate a similar decline: Harriet Beecher Stowe, born earliest in the century, had seven children; Helen Hunt Jackson and E.D.E.N. Southworth had two—and Jackson's died before she started her career; and Mary Abigail Dodge and Elizabeth Stuart Phelps (Ward) had none. Though, on the whole, the drop in childbirths meant fewer children to care for and fewer years of care giving, the responsibilities connected with parenting created conflicting choices for most women writers. In making choices, some, like Rebecca Harding Davis, ranked family over career, and others, like Stowe and Southworth, alternated priorities between family and career. Only a few, like Dodge and Phelps, could emphasize their career because they had remained single and/or childless.

No matter what their marital or parental status, it was very difficult, almost impossible, for them to avoid the many social obligations of nineteenth-century women—from housework to entertaining to caring for family members. In this regard, single women were as tightly bound as married ones to the duties of their sphere.[51] Above all, there were, for most women, unending household responsibilities in the nineteenth century. Urban middle- or upper-class women benefited most quickly from advances in household technology, while women on the frontier or in rural areas lived in much more work-intensive situations. But even those with access to technology were likely not to have gas until the mid-century or electricity until the end. Without those conveniences, they had to cook over wood or coals, market daily for fresh food, clean the house without powered vacuum cleaners, and do laundry by hand. When there were domestic servants, women often worked along side of them, rather than having total relief from all the housework. Thus, for women, careers were sometimes facilitated by household conveniences or servants, but those careers still had to be sustained through personal will and the support of family or friends.[52]

Fortunately, many women writers had someone who encouraged them.[53] Some husbands like Calvin Stowe, or family members like Augusta Dodge, Mary Abigail Dodge's sister, assisted the woman's career either psychologically or by helping out with household tasks. Other women found support in the strong network of women writers illustrated in "Mr. Houghton's Mistake." Nevertheless, no woman's domestic or familial responsibilities were totally relieved because she was a writer or supporting her family with a literary career, even when she did not experience rejection from her family as Sara Payson Parton (Fanny Fern) did. What is finally most impressive is the depth of women's commitment to their careers—careers that were sustained even when they conflicted with the other responsibilities in women's lives.

Cultural ambiguities and social circumstances both played a role in creating the paradoxical place of the woman writer in nineteenth-century America. As we have seen, these women lived in a culture that tried to confine them to their separate sphere; unending messages described and prescribed women's domesticity, spirituality, and purity. Arguments about woman's separate sphere extended to discussions about all aspects of life and work, including authorship. But like all subordinate classes, women had knowledge of the dominant class' views, including its Victorian ideals and its concept of authorship, which were not wholly distinct from the ideals and concepts of woman's sphere. The overlapping nature of the ideals and concepts made it possible for women to be accepted as writers and yet as often devalued and ignored. Moreover, the social circumstances of middle-class women—their background, education, role models, economic position, and marital and childbearing status—while by no means as favorable as men's to the pursuit of a career, nevertheless opened the way for some women to become authors.

What any individual woman did for herself in this society depended on her personal temperament, on what ideals she accepted, and on how she interpreted her life circumstances. If she seized the opportunities of the ambiguous cultural context and social order, she might consider becoming a writer. Later on, her temperament, ideals, and social circumstances would also influence her attitudes toward herself and her literary career. Like the attitudes of those represented in "Mr. Houghton's Mistake," women's attitudes toward their lives and literary careers varied from Mary Abigail Dodge's defensiveness to Helen Hunt Jackson's enthusiasm to Rebecca Harding Davis's gentle, self-effacing stance. Although they each confronted a similar cultural situation, their responses were not uniform. Having chosen literary careers, they pursued them in various ways.

But how did women who chose to be writers succeed in a career that asked them to be more than writers, that is, to be business people as well? Did they have a hard time negotiating their compensation, placing their work, and dealing with male publishers and editors? Was the literary marketplace alienating to women? The answers to those questions are considered in the next chapter.

2

Negotiating with a Publisher
From Mrs. M. L. Rayne, What Can a Woman Do: Or, Her Position in the Business and Literary World *(Albany, N.Y.: Eagle Publishing, 1893)*

Gentlemen and Ladies

Ideals and Economics in the Literary Marketplace

Over twenty years before the 1877 *Atlantic* dinner, another celebration brought together publishers, authors, and booksellers in an event that can be seen as representative of the ideals of the nineteenth-century literary marketplace. Sponsored by the New York Association of Book Publishers, the Complimentary Fruit and Floral Festival was held in the spacious Crystal Palace in New York City at the end of September 1855.[1] Organized to devise ways of merchandising books more effectively, the association had decided that one means of doing so would be to improve personal relationships in the industry by sponsoring this event. Six hundred guests, one-tenth of whom were women, gathered under a gas-illuminated banner proclaiming "Honor to Genius." It was a lavish afternoon and evening, with guests feasting on many courses of meats and fruits prepared in ornamental designs representing such scenes as "Graces Supporting a Basket of Flowers"; the highlight was a pastry depicting "The Temple of America." During the evening innumerable toasts and speeches expressed feelings of goodwill among publishers, authors, and booksellers.

In many ways the event captured the ethos of the mid-century literary marketplace. Even though publishing was an economic and often acrimonious enterprise, the major publishers worked hard to create an image of themselves and their profession that was genial and lofty. They thought of themselves as "Gentlemen Publishers" and professed beliefs in personal relationships, noncommercial aims, and moral guardianship. At the Fruit and Floral Festival, therefore, they mingled with authors, trying to build the personal trust they considered so crucial to a successful publishing venture. They hoped the festival would show that they were as interested in promoting culture as in winning profits. And, they presented themselves as models of moral rectitude by foregoing cigars and liquor in deference to the ladies. Their emphasis on personal relationships, noncommercial aims, and moral guardianship, combined with the economic prospects of the industry, made it possible for women to work comfortably in a business that some claimed was far outside their sphere.

The evolution of the Gentleman Publisher ideal is interesting because, even though publishers liked to trace their heritage to the Renaissance patrons of the arts, actually they were the offspring of eighteenth-century tradesmen. Publishing had begun in the eighteenth century as a sideline of printers and booksellers, so at that time publishers called themselves "booksellers," though they secured manuscripts, contracted for printing, paid for production, and marketed the finished product with their imprint on the title page.[2] Printer-publisher-booksellers learned their trade by apprenticeship and became skilled craftsmen like mechanics and artisans. In eighteenth-century society, printer-publisher-booksellers earned prestige by hard work, good business sense, and skill, not because they patronized the arts.

At the turn of the century, the most important American publisher was Matthew Carey, whom the historian John Tebbel calls a "prototype of the early nineteenth-century publisher." As a transitional figure he showed characteristics of both an eighteenth-century craftsman and a nineteenth-century Gentleman Publisher. Apprenticed as a printer, he became an entrepreneur whose career was noteworthy for its many achievements: he published the first really successful magazine in the United States and an impressive list of books, attractively bound. He was the innovator of an exchange system for the distribution of books, in-house specialization of duties, new advertising and circulation methods, and a magazine supplement for his books.

But Carey also embodied ideals that later in the nineteenth century would be associated with the Gentleman Publisher. In other words, for Carey, publishing was more than a business. He had a strong personal interest in books and study and was himself an occasional writer. Furthermore, he brought to his work strong moral values; Carey was, according to Tebbel and many others, "hardworking, careful, frugal, pious, not given to the flamboyant. More than others, perhaps, Carey was rigidly moralistic."[3] Carey also showed some commitment to public service, devoting the last years of his life to philanthropic work. His superb craftsmanship and business ingenuity, combined with his literary tastes, moral values, and public service—typical of the Gentleman Publisher's values—made him the most well-known and well-respected publisher and bookseller of his time.

Just as Carey was first in reputation among his publishing contemporaries, he was also the first of many nineteenth-century publishers to profit from women's best-sellers. When Susanna Rowson came to this country in 1793, she arranged with Matthew Carey to publish *Charlotte Temple* in America. Not only was the book Carey's first big success, but also it was one of the most successful books of the nineteenth century. Eighteen years after its publication, Carey wrote to Rowson, saying, "The sales of *Charlotte Temple* exceed those of any of the most celebrated novels that ever appeared in England. I think the number disposed of must far exceed 50,000 copies, and the sale still continues."[4] Although their association may have been somewhat arbitrary, no doubt Carey's personal values as well as his publishing skills made him an attractive publisher for Rowson. In the future other Gentlemen Publishers would attract many women writers to their fold, both because of their ideals and because of their economic success.

Although individuals like Matthew Carey certainly expressed some of its values, Gentleman Publisher as the prescribed model for all respectable publishers did not reach the height of its influence until mid-century. Emphasis on that ideal seems to have grown in response to the highly competitive market conditions in the first half of the century. "What had been a relatively quiet occupation of printing and semischolarly concern with the printed word became, after 1830," Tebbel reports, "a hardnosed competitive scramble."[5] The opportunities were enormous. Between 1820 and 1850 the publishing industry expanded tenfold in response to increasing national levels of literacy, people's growing interest in reading as cheap entertainment, and an expanding railroad system making national distribution of books possible. In this environment, many publishers abandoned ethics in pursuit of ever greater profits. Changes in printing technology, more radical than any since the fifteenth century—including the advent of the steam-powered cylinder press, the use of stereotyped plates, and cheaper methods of making paper and bindings—made possible the publication of low-priced cloth and cheap paper editions of books. Piracy of British works was common. Competition raged and failure was frequent.

In response to those conditions, leaders in publishing took the first steps toward regulating the industry by establishing the principle of trade courtesy, one of the future tests of adherence to the values of the Gentleman Publisher. First worked out between the Harper brothers and Matthew Carey, trade courtesy was the practice of respecting the prior rights of another firm to an author's works. Under the courtesy principle, publishers arranged for advance sheets from European, usually British, publishers and then claimed the right to be the sole American publisher. When an intention to publish was announced, other firms would agree not to publish a rival edition or to bargain for that writer's future work. Courtesy was also applied to works by American writers; in this case, there was a gentleman's agreement not to try to tempt an author to leave someone else's fold. The principle worked by moral rather than legal suasion to control rampant competition over authors' works; it was particularly beneficial for large companies, which could thereby close out competition from smaller competitors. But even though trade courtesy was at its base an economic ploy, it helped create an atmosphere of cooperation and self-restraint between the more respectable publishers at least. It made the industry appear more genteel. And as an ideal it seems to have had an impact. Historians generally agree that trade courtesy was more often honored than ignored by respectable publishers from the 1840s through the 1860s.[6]

Other efforts at self-regulation intensified as publishing came to be recognized as a distinct profession. Trade fairs, trade catalogs, and publishers' flyers were among the methods used to bring order to the industry through shared information. Another means was the Book Publishers' Association, which was established in 1855. In addition to sponsoring the Fruit and Floral Festival when the association was called the New York Association of Book Publishers, it soon brought out the first trade journal, the *American Publishers' Circular and Literary Gazette*. The *Circular* not only reported publishing news but also was a forum for debate over industry standards. By the 1850s such debate was appropriate, because publishers were now considered to be professionals in their own right with expertise in manufacturing, promotion, and publicity.[7] Regulation of the market and moves toward a more professional concept of publishing encouraged publishers to promote the image of Gentleman Publisher—self-regulating and honorable.

An increasing emphasis on the Gentleman Publisher image also seems to have been linked to growth in the financial stability of author-publisher relations. Early in the nineteenth century, monetary settlements between publishers and authors had been complicated by the unspecialized relationships among printers, publishers, jobbers, and retailers, which often made publishing an unprofitable business. Furthermore, currency and credit, as William Charvat reports, were "so unstable" before 1850 "that the mere process of paying and getting paid was difficult."[8] But by the 1850s, currency was more stable and publishers concentrated on publishing as a primary commitment rather than as a sideline. Retail book prices had risen to the level where publishers could make a profit and writers were less likely to have to share the cost of publication. Periodical publishing—literary monthlies or quarterlies, weekly story papers, and newspapers—had significantly expanded in the marketplace, and publishers could raise payments for writers while still making good profits themselves. Because of the increased financial stability in the marketplace at mid-century, other characteristics in addition to payments—that is, the advantage of working with a Gentleman Publisher—could be emphasized as part of author-publisher business dealings.

While these steps toward stabilization of the publishing industry were being taken, women's participation in the literary marketplace steadily increased. Early successes like *Charlotte Temple* had apparently set the precedent for accepting writing by women. Later publishers also acquired works by women in order to meet the demands of the rapidly expanding marketplace. Thus, thousands of readers became familiar with the works of Catharine Maria Sedgwick, Lydia Maria Child, Lydia H. Sigourney, and others. By the 1850s and 1860s, in fact, women were more prominent as best-selling writers than ever. Thus, the popular Cary sisters, Susan Warner, and Sara Payson Parton (Fanny Fern) were included among the guests at the Fruit and Floral Festival in 1855, while Harriet Beecher Stowe, the most successful of all, sent apologies for her absence. So well known had women writers become that no one had to ask which authors were being referred to in the toast made at the festival to "Our Lady Guests": "*The New England Tale* [Catharine Sedgwick] is re-echoed from the *New Home* [Caroline Kirkland] of the Far West; and from a *Cabin* [Harriet Beecher Stowe] on the banks of the Ohio, a touch of Nature vibrates among *The Lofty and the Lowly* [Maria McIntosh], through *The Wide, Wide World* [Susan B. Warner]."[9] The visibility of the woman writer, the expansion of the marketplace, and the development of the Gentleman Publisher image seem to have gone hand in hand. The question is: how did the ethics of the Gentlemen Publishers affect women's participation in the marketplace?

The image of Gentleman Publisher, which flourished in the mid-nineteenth century, was as widespread a standard for publishers as True Womanhood was for women of the time. Though, of course, all publishers did not live up to the image's expectations, most practitioners who took their careers seriously and who wanted to be respected as professionals by their colleagues, by writers, and by society at large tried to comply with its norms. Advocates believed that "this ideal lifted [publishers'] business up to the dignity of the great professions." The image was so compelling that biographers always characterized the most respected publishers as "Gentlemen," even if their behavior had sometimes suggested otherwise. Although after the 1880s this ideal began to be displaced by a new one, that of "Businessman Publisher," as late as 1900 a commentator in the *Dial* eulogized the Gentlemen Publishers by claiming, "There is probably no commercial occupation which can show names more old and venerable than those which stand as monuments in the book-producing world. The repute of publishing as the trade most nearly resembling a learned profession is fully sustained. . . . The older men, gone from the generation now passing, were men of sound character and cultivated minds, and their example has been followed, until, with rare exceptions, the American publisher stands well for American character and culture."[10]

For publishers themselves, perpetuation of the ideal must have had several psychological benefits. First of all, the image fit the nouveau riche publishers' aspirations for status in society; with it, publishers could claim to be the heirs of the Renaissance patrons of the arts, even if their eighteenth-century predecessors were less elite. The image also was appropriate for businesses, which were still predominantly small, family-controlled operations run by fathers and taken over by sons; the ideal called for the same paternalism and benevolence expected of a man in the family in the nineteenth century. Finally, while acceptance of the ideal before the 1850s had been a means of dealing with the stress of unruly competition, in the second half of the century it helped publishers rationalize the industry's slowed growth and their own smaller fortunes than American manufacturers overall.[11]

The most well-respected publishers in the nineteenth century tried to adhere to the aims of the Gentleman Publisher. Among them were George P. Putnam, Charles Scribner, Daniel Appleton, William Ticknor, James T. Fields, Joshua Lippincott, James Osgood, and to some degree the Harper brothers. In most cases, the sons of these men espoused the values of their fathers when they took over the business. Magazine editors like Henry Mills Alden, William Dean Howells, James Russell Lowell, and Thomas Bailey Aldrich, to name a few, subscribed to the editor's version of the role. Of all of these, the Harpers seem to have adhered least to the ideal, although they did accept some of its aims and were often described in its terms. However, the Harpers' defiance of certain industry standards actually made them the predecessor of the commercial ideal that would take over publishing at the end of the century.[12]

As the preceding list of publishers suggests, the model of Gentleman Publisher presupposed that the publisher was male. Although women had often been involved in printing and publishing during colonial days, by the nineteenth century few of them were publishers in their own right of books or magazines until the last two decades of the century.[13] Sarah Josepha Hale, Caroline Gilman, Ann Stephens, Amelia Bloomer, and others certainly made their marks as editors and publishers, but there were too few women involved in the trade for anyone to think the ideal of Gentleman Publisher was inappropriate for the industry as a whole.

Men, like those mentioned above, who aspired to being known as Gentlemen Publishers, set the terms for much of women's involvement in the literary marketplace. Those publishers and editors shared three aims: they sought to develop trusting, paternalistic, personal relationships with their authors; they claimed to have goals beyond commercial ones to advance culture and/or to provide a public service; and they assumed the role of moral guardian for their society. Although some would argue that those lofty aims were meant to mask competitive, capitalist motives, the evidence suggests that, while profit was never ignored by those who were trying to make a good living at publishing, the Gentleman Publisher's values often influenced respectable publishers' economic decisions.[14] Of course, being human, nineteenth-century publishers sometimes did not act according to their espoused goals; nevertheless, the spirit of their ideals pervaded their publishing houses.

Central to the image of Gentleman Publisher was the emphasis on personal relationships, which almost came naturally to an industry of this size. Because publishing at mid-century was still a relatively small industry of approximately 400 publishers, printers, and booksellers, concentrated in three cities—New York, Boston, and Philadelphia—friendships between publishers were common. On the occasion of his approaching marriage, for example, George Haven Putnam's fellow publishers presented him with a loving cup inscribed, "With love of Scribner, With love of Harper, With love of Holt, For Love of Putnam."[15] Such sociability also occurred within individual businesses, most of which were relatively small. Roberts Brothers, a highly respected Boston firm of the 1870s and 1880s, for example, had only 7 employees. In contrast, with almost 350 employees, 19 power presses, and 7 five-story buildings, Harpers was the largest publisher in the United States by the end of the 1840s. Though Harpers grew still larger in the following decades, James Harper acted as though it still was small by greeting every employee by name. The size of the typical firm, however, was somewhere between the two, closer to Roberts Brothers than Harpers. (Even most twentieth-century publishing establishments—a company may own several establishments—have fewer than 20 employees.) The small number and size of firms was conducive to the valuing of personal relationships.[16]

The operation of editorial and publishing offices under the auspices of Gentlemen Publishers was generally congenial. Publishing offices, as historian Christopher Wilson has said, "self-consciously detached themselves from the grime and pace of printing, mimicking instead the easy tempo of republican men of leisure." Some publishing houses even had quiet places for authors to work on manuscripts. Offices were not standardized, but reflected the personalities of the publishers. At Ticknor and Fields' Old Corner Bookstore in Boston, the publishers' office upstairs was casual, yet inviting: "a wild disorder of piled-up manuscripts, bric-a-brac, and objects of art [amid which was given] business advice, editorial criticism, and professional interviews." Wilson reports that one observer wrote of the Harpers' office in 1885, "'There never seems to be any hurry or bustle[;]' . . . it was a place of 'old-fashioned simplicity' and seeming frictionless regularity." Similarly, the home offices of the *Atlantic* and *Century* maintained a moderate office tempo. Indeed, the "Editor's Easy Chair," a column in *Harper's Monthly*, expressed the ambience of literary business.[17]

Within this informal atmosphere, business was organized in nonspecialized ways. At mid-century it was common for the publisher himself to read and decide on manuscripts' fates without the help of assistants. Similarly, editorial roles on house magazines were often nonspecialized and nonhierarchical. As editor of the *Atlantic*, William Dean Howells involved himself not only in the acceptance of manuscripts but also in proofreading and revisions. Of course, most other businesses of the time were also not very hierarchical or impersonal, but such qualities were even more prominent in publishing. As late as the 1890s, when a greater business orientation was apparent in most newspaper and magazine publishing, the older, more elite magazines like *Atlantic Monthly* and *Century* as well as literary publishing houses resisted the trends toward hierarchy, monopolies, and bureaucratization.[18]

The Gentleman Publisher's emphasis on personal relations grew out of family involvement in the operation of the business. In fact, the major houses, owned by such men as Daniel Appleton, Moses Dodd, William Ticknor, J. B. Lippincott, and George P. Putnam, were family operations from the beginning and were passed from fathers to sons as full participants in the business. Even female family members had occasional roles as advisers, particularly in regard to women's manuscripts. For example, John P. Jewett's wife advised him to publish *Uncle Tom's Cabin*, G. P. Putnam's mother convinced him to publish Susan Warner's *Wide, Wide, World*, and James Fields's wife was responsible for encouraging the publication of Elizabeth Stuart Phelps's *Gates Ajar*.[19] This pattern of family involvement led some publishers to describe their business in private, familial terms. George Haven Putnam, for example, admired publishing offices that had "the character of a family circle." As historian Christopher Wilson has pointed out, editorial offices of the quality magazines also sought the feeling of "a happy and united family." Among magazine editors, Wilson continues, "[Richard Watson] Gilder likened his [editorial] role to picking a bouquet in a garden; Bliss Perry said [choosing manuscripts] was akin to a gentleman of leisure selecting a dinner for his family."[20]

In many ways a familial spirit pervaded offices of those trying to live up to the image of Gentleman Publisher, particularly in the 1850s when personal relationships between authors and publishers were at their height. A letter from the editor George Princhard to Maria Cummins in 1857 reflects the impact of such an ethos on business operations:

> I have had a sort of personal—almost family interest and pride in your success, which has made me quite anxious about this new book. You will not, therefore, consider me as intrusive, if I say—that in its composition, in its moral tone, in its plot (as far as I have read) in its delineations of character, and general execution—it is quite worthy of the author of the Lamplighter.... This good opinion of [the character] Mabel is not mine only. All about the office, who have read the proofs, seem to have the same. My wife—to whom I am required to carry home the proof sheets every day—is enthusiastic in her admiration & praise of the work.[21]

This was the family spirit full blown: editor, proofreaders, and wife all cheering the author on.

Even when publishing was not described in familial terms, personal relationships were emphasized. Attesting to the spirit of friendship that was the aim of many Gentlemen Publishers, James Russell Lowell, in dedicating *The Cathedral* to his publisher James Fields, said, "My relations with you have enabled me to discover how pleasantly the Friend may replace the Bookseller." Stressing yet a third kind of personal relationship appropriate for the Gentleman Publisher, Henry Holt, eulogist of the mid-century values, claimed that relations between authors and publishers were "like those of patient and doctor, parishioner and pastor, client and lawyer."[22]

Because Gentlemen Publishers believed in the importance of personal relationships in publishing, they advocated author-publisher relations that were long term, like marriages, close friendships, or intimate professional associations. Thus, they viewed loyalty and trust as central to the author-publisher alliance. Horace Scudder, who wanted to portray Henry Houghton as a Gentleman Publisher, said Houghton applied "a pretty strong term 'loyalty' to those who held by him in spite of temptations to go after other publishers; but he recognized quite as strongly the reciprocal relations involved and once an author was 'on the list' he would strain a point before he would suffer a new book from the same hand to go elsewhere, even though it might fall below the standard previously set."[23] Many publishers like Houghton felt it was best to keep all of an author's books in the same house. Trade courtesy was a means of honoring those relations; publishers like Daniel Appleton withdrew their intention to publish an author when another house pointed out its prior claim. In the same spirit, editors like Henry Mills Alden and Bliss Perry firmly rejected "Wild West feats of editorial chase, capture, and exhibition," wanting instead long-term bonds of loyalty between authors and editors.[24]

Those who adhered to the goals of the Gentleman Publisher expected commitment from authors and were willing to work for it, some more pleasantly than others. George R. Graham wrote to Henry Wadsworth Longfellow in 1844 expressing exasperation that some authors would not agree to an exclusive commitment to him, even when he paid them well. He vowed to cut those who would not be as loyal to him as he felt he was to them. Other publishers and editors adopted a more genial attitude. Expecting to work with their writers for a long time, these publishers tried to approach their writers with affection and respect. Ik Marvel testified to that cordiality in James Fields, saying, "Whether he criticized or praised or made suggestions, he had the charming art of making one believe thoroughly in his friendliness."[25]

In an effort to ensure commitment, many publishers took on paternalistic roles in their relationships to their writers. In fact, in many ways they took care of their writers. Publishers at mid-century commonly paid authors' bills as directed, advanced money, and sometimes gave advice on investments. At Nathaniel Hawthorne's request, William Ticknor at various times accompanied him on trips, picked out his suits, ordered cigars, paid bills, got postage stamps, and looked for a "good dog." Although it seems odd today, Susan Warner was not doing anything unusual when she asked her publisher G. P. Putnam to sell her picture of George Washington for her. Robert Bonner, Thomas Niles, and James Fields—editors and publishers of the women in this study—each provided such gentlemanly services. There was, of course, a good potential for abuse in this situation and some writers were actually exploited, but authors like Hawthorne probably could not have survived without the paternalism of publishers like Ticknor and Fields.[26]

The paternalism of the Gentleman Publisher was one of several ways in which, regardless of the author's sex, publishers were in a "male" role to the author's "female" one. We have also seen that the image of Gentleman Publisher presupposed the maleness of the publisher, while that of writer had certain affinities with the female role in the nineteenth century. But there were other gender overtones to the relationship as well. The concept, Gentleman Publisher, alluded to another popular male Victorian ideal, that of "Christian Gentleman," the complement of a True Woman. Furthermore, publishers were responsible for instrumental activities and authors for inspirational, expressive ones, as men were supposed to be responsible for business and women for spiritual and emotional affairs. Like men and women, publishers and authors had separate spheres of activity; under this model, Gentlemen Publishers usually gave their writers responsibility for their own sphere, providing some guidance when necessary. Like husbands and wives of the time, many publishers and authors felt themselves bound together by reciprocal obligations and rights. Therefore, after one of her books was attacked in the *New York Evening Post*, Julia Ward Howe, as woman and *as author*, asked James Fields, "Will no chivalrous hand strike a blow for me?"[27] She expected her publisher to defend his writer, just as any gentleman was supposed to defend a lady.

For women, the emphasis by publishers on personal relationships involving loyalty, trust, commitment, and paternalism was important. Except for Mary Abigail Dodge, the women discussed in upcoming chapters wanted to work with publishers who generally conformed to this way of doing business. This emphasis was not at odds with women's values and experiences. After all, women had been socialized to value personal relations with family and friends, so associations with publishers modeled on that pattern were not particularly threatening to their womanhood. They were not being asked to conduct business in a totally impersonal, unknown context. Moreover, insofar as these associations called for submitting to the wisdom or care of their publishers, while taking responsibility for their own sphere of activity, women writers were also in a familiar male-female relationship. Indeed, in some ways women may have been more comfortable than men in the interactions of this marketplace that frequently put writers in a "female" position.

The relationship between Gentleman Publisher and writer, like the relationship between gentleman and lady, may have been a familiar one to women, but, like male-female relations, it perpetuated inequalities between the two, as Mary Abigail Dodge (Gail Hamilton) pointed out in *A Battle of the Books* (1870). Publishers generally had more power and more autonomy than writers, no matter what their sex. And, publishers had the final say about what would be published and about how much the writers would be compensated for their work. Moreover, publishers could rely on many books or articles to help them earn profits, while authors could only write a few in the same time period. Finally, trade courtesy and the aim of noncompetition between publishers over authors actually disadvantaged authors more than publishers by discouraging authors from seeking competitive bids in the marketplace. In short, the ideal relationship between Gentleman Publisher and author, though often personal and respectful, did not mean equality between the two.

Similarly, the emphasis on personal relationships with all authors did not guarantee that publishers would have the same types of informal interactions with female and male writers. There definitely was a male network between male authors and publishers to which women did not always have access; women writers were not invited to the Saturday Club in Boston where Nathaniel Hawthorne, Oliver Wendell Holmes, and John Greenleaf Whittier joined James Russell Lowell, James Fields, Charles Sumner, and others for dinner. Women were not invited to an 1837 banquet for authors given by the Harper brothers, nor, as stated in the previous chapter, to the Whittier dinner in 1877, though that was definitely a public relations error on Henry Houghton's part. Men's dinners were often raucous affairs; but when women were invited, the occasions, like the Fruit and Floral Festival, were much more formal. Because of social norms discouraging public show, women were not even totally comfortable with the Fruit and Floral Festival. Most women of the period, like those considered in this book, preferred to share private social occasions with their publishers in each others' homes, in the fashion of nineteenth-century visiting. This difference in the informal interactions seems to have had important ramifications for the authors' long-term reputations: same-sex friendships often resulted in male publishers, critics, and academics naming only men as the literary greats.[28]

In terms of compensation, women may have been less disadvantaged than they were in terms of literary canonization. We might expect that women writers experienced double discrimination, first as writers in an unequal negotiating position with publishers, then as women vis-à-vis men. After all, nineteenth-century society generally accepted the idea of lower wages for women, though, of course, many women's rights advocates protested that view. In the literary marketplace, however, comparisons were not (and still are not) easily made because arrangements between authors and publishers were worked out on an individual basis, often piece by piece. Based on the documentation available, however, it appears that the most successful women writers did receive book royalties at the same rate as their male peers: 10 percent and/or author's risk in the 1840s, 15 percent and upward in the early 1850s, then back to the norm of 10–15 percent from the 1860s to the 1890s; women's compensation for essays, short stories, and poems also seems to have been comparable to men's.[29]

We know that the incomes of some popular women writers, like Harriet Beecher Stowe, made them quite wealthy, while the incomes of others, like Mary Abigail Dodge and Helen Hunt Jackson, supported comfortable life-styles. Rather than the author's sex, the most important determinant of a fair income for a writer was whether he or she had enough knowledge of other people's compensation rates to demand equitable treatment. Perhaps men in their friendships with editors and publishers had more access to that knowledge, but so many exceptions of impoverished male writers come to mind that one is forced to admit that even same-sex friendship did not give male writers an absolute economic advantage. Male writers, like female ones, suffered when they became too trusting of the fairness of their publishers.

Although the most successful women writers seem to have received pay comparable to men's, women did not always express satisfaction with what they were paid—far from it. Women's correspondence in regard to their earnings could be as bitter as men's. For example, Caroline Kirkland archly wrote Carey and Hart in 1843 that her mantua-maker made more by her needle than she did by her pen. Rose Terry Cooke indignantly refused payment for a memorial article on Ralph Waldo Emerson because the sum offered was, she felt, too small. Harriet Prescott Spofford expressed great surprise that the *Galaxy* paid her so little, thereby, incidentally, bringing herself higher compensation on her next story.[30] These complaints are replicated in correspondence by the writers studied in this book. Such protests, however, do not necessarily indicate that women were not doing as well as men; men's correspondence reveals just as many.

In regard to compensation, it is important to remember that the use of standardized contracts between authors and publishers was not a common practice until after the Civil War, presumably because between friends—between gentlemen or gentlemen and ladies—honor would prevail. Or at least that is what publishers wanted authors to believe. Authors could be more skeptical, even those who appreciated author-publisher friendship. George Boker, who had not received a contract or even a written note about an agreement with his publisher, wrote James Fields in 1856, "The want of written agreements has been the cause of so many blunders and misunderstandings in my few business transactions, that I have sworn an oath, as high as heaven and as deep as hell, never to enter on any future arrangement without having the terms of the contract clearly set forth in writing. Therefore, O my Fields, do drop me a formal official note."[31] This tactful reminder apparently worked. However, the history of author-publisher relations, despite the ideal and reality of many good relations, is replete with stories of disputes: authors often complained that publishers were making too much money from their work or were not marketing their books effectively, while publishers responded that authors did not understand how unprofitable publishing actually was.

Most authors, of course, wanted a financially sound *and* personally satisfying relationship. Washington Irving's expression of loyalty to G. P. Putnam in 1852 captures that desire for friendship *and* profit: "I take pleasure in expressing the great satisfaction I have derived from all our intercourse, from your amiable, obliging, and honorable conduct. Indeed, I never had dealings with any man, whether in the way of business or friendship, more perfectly free from any alloy. That these dealings have been profitable is merely owing to your sagacity and enterprise." Similarly, the publishers Lee and Shepard received praise in the *American Literary Gazette* for being genial, courteous, and conscious of profit: "To their authors especially, they hold the attitude of steadfast friends and this interest in the success of all their publications seems inspired quite as much by regard for the author's profit as for their own." Women writers, as well as men, appreciated such friendly concern.[32]

While establishing the ethos of personal relationships with their authors was the first major aim of Gentlemen Publishers, a second important ideal was dedication to goals more lofty than commercialism. Time and again Gentlemen Publishers sounded this theme, even while their Wall Street contemporaries sneered at their naive ways of doing business. Gentlemen Publishers claimed that their business was superior to other commercial enterprises; they expressed pride in their monetary sacrifices for the noble undertaking of making the ideas of authors available to society. Some characterized themselves as intermediaries between "the immortals and the ordinary world"; others described themselves as more than "mere businessmen," as members of a profession requiring scholarly preparation and a sense of dedication above material gains. Robert Sterling Yard at the beginning of the twentieth century described the Gentleman Publisher as one who "sees many questions besides profit—questions of art, of literature, of reputation, of personality, of list dignity, of house influence." Walter Hines Page claimed that respectable publishers invested in books they knew would not yield an immediate profit because "they feel ennobled by trying to do a service to literature."[33]

Of course, publishers and editors sometimes exaggerated their monetary sacrifices for the sake of literature, especially when authors complained that publishers were making more money than they were. Horace Scudder wrote in the *Riverside Bulletin* in 1873, "When one sees the load which every book has to bear of expense before the first return begins, one is tempted to say—Go back, poor little book, into the brain of your author." Another time, *Publishers' Weekly* defended book publishing as too risky to pay even successful authors what they expected: "If the author complains that his successful book ought not to pay for others' unsuccessful books, he can get over the difficulty by taking the risk himself, and making corresponding terms with the publisher." In a similar vein, Henry Holt characterized the royalty system not as profit, but as loss sharing.[34]

There was some justification for publishers' defensiveness about their sacrifices, especially after the 1850s. Book publishing in the second half of the century did not keep pace with the growth of other manufacturing, which increased five times faster than the book trade. Furthermore, leaders in the industry could not be confident of future prosperity because they did not control major portions of the marketplace nor monopolize the selling of best-sellers. Indeed, some of the financial figures are arresting: on first editions of thirteen books published by Scribners in 1880, the most successful returned only $90 in profit; three of five books published in the 1880s, it was said, would fail. Some publishers did become wealthy —on their profitable back lists, lucrative series, best-sellers, and other specialized nonfiction. Most, however, counted their wealth in tens of thousands rather than in tens of millions as other business leaders of the time did, but that financial disparity was more apparent to the publishers themselves than to their authors, who felt a rising irritation at the profits of publishers as the century passed.[35]

The belief that the Gentleman Publisher ought to be more interested in cultural aims than profits also, to some extent, probably perpetuated lower profits in the industry. Henry Holt's view that competition should consist "simply in selecting books wisely, making them tastefully and honestly, informing the interested public of their existence and supplying them to whatever legitimate demand they might effect through their own merit" certainly did not increase consumer demand.[36] In that same spirit of noncompetition, some quality magazine publishers played down circulation figures for fear of stimulating unruly competition, which might, in fact, have increased sales and profits. Gentlemen Publishers traditionally resisted flamboyant advertising, inserting instead brief, dignified announcements of publication in the papers. And editors, like Henry Mills Alden and Richard Watson Gilder, were skeptical of trying to market to literary fads. This attitude of superiority to commercialism carried over into internal business affairs as well. Because many publishers were literary men, they preferred creating books to marketing them; for them, distribution often remained an unsolved problem. Moreover, bookkeeping at many firms, including the preeminent Ticknor and Fields, could be very informal. Indeed, *Publishers' Weekly* attributed Harper and Brothers' bankruptcy at the end of the century to its family-based organization which resisted "thoroughly modern business administration."[37]

Nevertheless, it is important to emphasize that Gentlemen Publishers never forgot that they were in business, even while insisting they had other, noncommercial aims. As historian Donald Sheehan said, publishers were "business men of letters."[38] They wanted profits from their undertakings and, in many cases, earned them; family companies of antebellum origins could not have survived into the twentieth century if they had not known how to make enough profit. James Fields, who perhaps embodied better than anyone the model of Gentleman Publisher, can also be credited with devising many successful book promotion techniques. Indeed, actual behavior in the market was sometimes less admirable than the ideal would admit. Histories of publishing record sharp bargaining, sneaky deals, and ample competition—some by publishers who did not care if they were seen as Gentlemen Publishers and some by those who did not live up to the ideals they espoused. Publishers did jump on the bandwagon of a best-seller like *Uncle Tom's Cabin*, trying to publish their own best-seller on a similar theme. Even traditional firms like Phillips, Sampson and Company sometimes tried "puffing" novels—hyping books by distributing advance copies to newspapers, making prepublication advertisements, and taking advance orders.[39]

Because publishing under the influence of Gentlemen Publishers was on the verge of becoming a modern capitalist business, it should not be surprising that precursors of modern business techniques like advertising were in use in the 1850s, 1860s, and 1870s. This did not, however, do away with attitudes toward publishing as patronage; rather, in some ways, it probably reinforced those attitudes among some publishers as a defensive reaction against the new commercial order coming into being. Profits were, of course, a motive of Gentlemen Publishers, but so, too, were more lofty aims of public service; the leading publishers were men of integrity who seem to have believed sincerely in noncommercial values.[40] The most respectable ones did sacrifice personal gains by adhering to the ideal. Still, they did not completely forego experimentation with some of the newest kinds of advertising, distribution, and sales techniques. To deny one or the other side of publishers' motivations is to misinterpret the Gentlemen Publishers.

In an interesting congruence, this second major aim of Gentlemen Publishers—noncommercialism—combined with their business skills made them a good match for many women in the literary marketplace. Economic gain was important to most women writers, whereas their socialization as women had encouraged them to value moral, spiritual, and cultural aspects of life. The result was that they often affirmed noncommercial values while competing for a good income. These seemingly contradictory motives helped women to fit into the literary marketplace, where Gentlemen Publishers also expressed noncommercial aims while needing to make a profit. Those women who thought of themselves as genteel amateurs could be comfortable in a marketplace with an ethos of noncommercialism that nevertheless gave them an ample income.

Like publishers who in the context of noncommercial aims did not neglect the techniques for earning a profit, women writers who had lofty aspirations often perfected the skills of negotiation, choosing to use one strategy or another depending on their personalities. Though some writers like E.D.E.N. Southworth said they would accept whatever their publisher wanted to pay them, most did not make a regular practice of saying that. Many, like Harriet Beecher Stowe, were not hesitant to name their price firmly upon the submission of a manuscript. Others, like Elizabeth Stuart Phelps (Ward), mentioned the prices they were being paid elsewhere as a less direct way of indicating what they thought they should be paid and as a means of stimulating some competition for their work. Many reminded their publishers what they had been paid previously or what they had heard other writers were being paid. Though some justified their requests for compensation with a litany of family and personal needs, this was not the typical or only way of negotiating with publishers. Rather, as a group and as individuals, women successfully used a wide variety of negotiating techniques. The espousal of noncommercialism in the marketplace seems, paradoxically, to have allowed for the development of some very commercial skills on the part of writers.

Just as the Gentleman Publisher strove to establish an ethos of personal relations and noncommercialism in his interactions with authors and other publishers, he also cast himself in the role of moral guardian for his society. Precedent for this role was set early in the nineteenth century when some publishers advertised themselves as the "custodians of public morals."[41] At mid-century the Gentleman Publisher was expected to have the highest personal morals, which commonly meant strong Christian beliefs, concern for others, strict sexual standards, and cultivated behavior. More than that, Gentlemen Publishers were expected to promote morality in their society. As members of the middle or upper class, they shared, as Donald Sheehan pointed out, the same sense of moral guardianship that led to the founding of the New York Society for the Suppression of Vice. Time and again publishers in this tradition referred to their role as one of ensuring that immorality did not spread in society. Thus, James Derby, who wanted to be remembered as a Gentleman Publisher, claimed that "in the long and varied experience of my brothers and myself, not a single volume has ever been sold of a doubtful moral tendency."[42] Similarly, founders of the *Atlantic Monthly* announced that the magazine would foster the expression of unbiased opinion within the bounds of dignity and morality. Publishers even judged each other in terms of moral guardianship, awarding a prize to the publisher who not only demonstrated the most advanced art of bookmaking but also did the "most to advance the principles which underlie civilization, and present the advanced state of thought and morals."[43] Even as the aim of moral guardianship faded at the end of the nineteenth century, editors and book publishers still felt compelled to express a high regard for standards of decency.

While the role of moral guardianship was certainly related to publishers' class origins and aspirations, it also reflected their assumptions about the audience of popular fiction. Publishers, booksellers, and authors would not have been surprised that nine-tenths of the spectators for the Fruit and Floral Festival were women, because they assumed women were the major portion (though not nine-tenths!) of the audience of literary readers. Thus, Gentlemen Publishers felt it was wholly appropriate to adopt the paternalistic role of moral guardian toward their readers: those readers were women and families who needed to be protected. Even the flamboyant Robert Bonner, publisher of the *New York Ledger*, had a sign over his desk saying, "Take the most pious old lady in a Presbyterian church, and any word or phrase, innuendo or expression that she would want to skip while reading a *Ledger* story to her grandchild—strike out."[44] In the same spirit, the more proper James Fields would not sell *Wuthering Heights* in the Old Corner Bookstore, declaring that customers would not accept the book because of its profanity. As moral guardians, Gentlemen Publishers always compared themselves favorably with newspaper and reprint publishers who catered, they thought, to the "vulgar" trade, which presumably did not worry about the morals of society.

This emphasis on moral guardianship affected authors throughout the industry, but it did not result in complete censorship. Publishers frequently directed authors to avoid morally offensive scenes. Even authors of the sensational dime novels received directives that said, "We prohibit all things offensive to good taste in expression and incident—We prohibit subjects of characters that carry an immoral taint." While such attitudes led to a good deal of prudery and narrow-mindedness, particularly in connection with sexuality, they did not result in full-scale censoring of controversial ideas. For example, William Appleton, though an adherent of the Gentleman Publisher's values, published Charles Darwin's *Origin of the Species* in 1860 because, as Tebbel explained it, Appleton thought "a publisher's imprint was not an absolute endorsement of a book's contents, or even an approval of its arguments and tendency, but only a guarantee that the book possessed merit and was free from immorality." Appleton's bottom line, like that of many Gentlemen Publishers, was drawn at sexual standards, not religious controversy.[45]

Along with their Gentlemen Publishers, most women writers shared the moral standards of the nineteenth-century middle class and were encouraged by their society to be the moral guardians of their families and communities. Women were expected not only to be morally pure, but also to inspire purity in those around them. Prescriptions for women advised them to be genteel and to give moral instruction to their husbands and families. Indeed, many nineteenth-century women took those prescriptions seriously, committing themselves to preserving morality at home and in society at large. In this regard, in the partnership of publishing, women's moral responsibility was united with the Gentlemen Publishers' in a way that made the literary enterprise acceptable to many women. Of course, publishers and authors sometimes disagreed about what it meant to be a moral guardian, as the upcoming chapter on E.D.E.N. Southworth will show. But one can generalize that, as writers, women were by and large dealing with people whose commitment to fostering morality in society was compatible with their own. The Gentlemen Publishers' aim of moral guardianship, like their aims of personal relationships and noncommercialism, helped to create a congenial environment for women.

The Complimentary Fruit and Floral Festival in 1855 captured the aspirations of literary business at mid-century. At that gathering the audience and guests were presented with a vision of Gentlemen Publishers who nurtured personal relations with their authors, were dedicated to the advancement of culture more than (as well as) profits, and aimed to be moral guardians for their society. At the same time, in the 1850s, nearly 50 percent of the best-selling titles were by women, any one work selling more than writings of Nathaniel Hawthorne, Herman Melville, Henry David Thoreau, and Walt Whitman combined. This success was apparently matched by equally high percentages of women submitting and having works accepted. By 1872, nearly three-quarters of American novels were written by women.[46] Was it coincidental that the image of Gentleman Publisher flourished during the era of women's greatest success as writers?

The evidence suggests that the image and values of the Gentleman Publisher provided a business environment that was relatively more comfortable for women writers than many other types of business situations would have been. One might debate whether the rise of the Gentleman Publisher should be seen as one factor contributing to the increase in women choosing literary careers, or whether publishers emphasized the "Gentleman" image because so many *women* were entering the marketplace for other reasons, such as those pointed out in Chapter 1. In either case, it seems indisputable that the emphasis on Gentlemen Publishers' values and the success of women writers evolved simultaneously and dialectically.

But the reign of the Gentleman Publisher was not destined to last forever. As an ideal it gradually faded while a more managerial, commercial orientation came to predominate in most areas of publishing at the end of the century. Even then, all the older ideas and their structural manifestations did not completely disappear. Some editors and publishers, like Alfred Knopf, still emphasized the importance of personal relationships between authors and publishers. Others, like Henry Mills Alden and

Richard Watson Gilder, continued to stress the moral responsibility of their publishing roles. Many still operated in small companies where the predominant goals were cultural and noncommercial. But such an orientation was increasingly viewed as something of the past, as out of step with the spirit and technological potential of the times.[47]

The new ideal of Businessman Publisher emphasized very different values and may have been less congenial to women writers than that of the Gentleman Publisher. In contrast to their more leisured predecessors, editors and publishers like S. S. McClure, Edward Bok, Frank Munsey, and "Colonel" Harvey (at Harpers) were workaholics who emphasized activity, energy, and time orientation. They organized their offices for efficiency and profits. They de-emphasized personal relations with writers; instead, they competed for authors, commissioned and planned authors' articles and books, then used expensive, modern advertising to sell those works. These new publishers and editors were often more interested in audience appeal than moral guardianship. They encouraged hard work, rather than style, as the route to literary success, and frequently associated their views of writing with masculinity.[48] Although the connection between literary work and masculinity was not entirely new in the Progressive Era, the increased emphasis on vigor and marketing made authorship seem more than ever to be a male activity. Consequently, while some women adapted to the professional expectations of the new era, others like Willa Cather and Edith Wharton preferred to publish with houses like Alfred A. Knopf and Charles Scribner's Sons that resisted the modern style. Chapter 7, on Elizabeth Stuart Phelps (Ward), shows how frustrating the new marketplace could be to women who retained the older, "feminine" values.

Publishers who adhered to the Gentlemen Publishers' emphasis on personal relationships, noncommercial aims, and moral guardianship were important to women, even if their values were elitist, paternalistic, and ultimately restrictive to some authors' market potential. Paradoxically, those values made it possible for nineteenth-century women to conduct literary business with some comfort and a good deal of monetary success. Because they believed in the values of Gentlemen Publishers, writers like E.D.E.N. Southworth left publishers who were not "Gentlemen" and stayed with those who were. It is to Southworth's story that we now turn.

3

E.D.E.N. Southworth

Courtesy of the Prints Collection, Special Collections Department, Clifton Waller Barrett Library, University of Virginia, Charlottesville

The Place of Gender in Business

The Career of E.D.E.N. Southworth

On December 26, 1869, the popular writer E.D.E.N. Southworth took her pen in hand to write a letter to her Gentleman Publisher, Robert Bonner:

> I have received your kind note and munificent present. It reached me on Christmas morning. I had no right in the world to expect it, but I am, if possible, even more grateful for it on that account. . . .
>
> The first day that you entered my little cottage, was a day, blessed beyond all the other days of my life. I had some genius in popular writing; but not one bit of business tact and my pen was the prey of whoever chose to seize it. When you came to my cottage, I was dying from the combined effect of over work and under pay, of anxiety and of actual privation. When my doctor told me of a diet necessary to the restoration of my health, I was obliged to reply to him that I could not afford it—and so I could not.
>
> But that same winter you came to me, . . . and from that time to this, nearly fifteen years, you have made my life prosperous and happy. Every improved circumstance around me, every comfort in my home, every attainment of my children, speak of your kindness and liberality to us. Among the pre-eminent blessings of my life, for which I daily and nightly return thanks to the Giver of All Good is your friendship for me.
>
> Heaven bless you and yours with all prosperity and happiness. And Heaven grant that this year I may be able to prove my gratitude and fidelity in deeds.
>
> Please give my love to Mrs. Bonner And the Children and believe me ever,
>
> Gratefully & Faithfully Yours, E.D.E.N. Southworth[1]

This letter illustrates much about Southworth's pursuit of a literary career. First of all, it reveals the writer's attitudes toward herself and her views of the ideal business relationship: although she did believe in women's self-reliance, generally, she wanted to be a True Woman—pious, pure, domestic, and pleasing to others, and she expressed those values in the conduct of her career. The letter also shows how personal her business association with Robert Bonner had become. Theirs was a relationship that cast Bonner in the "male" role of provider and protector and Southworth in the "female" role of less able, though creative dependent. Moreover, the letter hints at the hardships Southworth had faced in her life as well as providing a glimpse of the dramatic storytelling abilities that brought her fame and fortune. In short, as a writer, Southworth was able to express her feminine ideals and use her storytelling skills to pursue an enormously successful literary career.

By almost any measure her success was phenomenal. Acclaimed by the journal *Saturday Night* in the late 1860s as "The Queen of American Novelists," E.D.E.N. Southworth (1819–99) earned her reputation as an author of sensational fiction who surpassed many others in the quantity as well as the quality of her work. In her lifetime, she published over sixty novels, some under several different titles, all serialized in newspapers or journals before book publication. Issued in both cloth and paper in the United States, her works were also published in England and at various times were translated into French, German, Spanish, Icelandic, and Swedish. After she was established, her earnings from her writings may have been higher than $10,000 a year, giving her an income that was unusually good for a nineteenth-century writer.[2] Along with this success, she gained the friendship of many writers, like John Greenleaf Whittier and Harriet Beecher Stowe, and she was frequently subject to the attacks of plagiarists, pirates, and imitators.

Although sophisticated readers and critics increasingly scorned her work as the century passed, almost everyone read something by Southworth in the nineteenth century. Indeed, her work was a household passion throughout the nation. As an "exclusive" contributor to Bonner's family paper, the *New York Ledger*, Southworth's serials were loved by its 400,000 subscribers (and probably a million readers) in the 1860s. In public libraries her books had to be continually replaced. She was the favorite author of patrons of the Boston Public Library in 1872 and held the same position in Lawrence, Massachusetts, at the end of that decade. Her books were everywhere; in 1887 when the Woman's Hotel opened on Park Avenue in New York, the black walnut bookcases held every one of Southworth's books. She once justifiably said, "I know that I number among my readers some professors of colleges, ministers of the gospel, and senators on the one hand—school boys and girls and little street gamins on the other—& a vast multitude between."[3] In fact, Southworth claimed she had never met anyone who had not read one of her books. She probably was not exaggerating, for she was among the most popular, if not *the* most popular novelist of the nineteenth century.

Many of her books were best-sellers. James D. Hart, author of one of the major studies of best-sellers in the United States, includes *The Curse of Clifton* (1852), *The Hidden Hand* (1859—actually not in book form until 1888), *The Fatal Marriage* (1863), and *Self-Raised* (1876) (which along with *Ishmael* had been the 1863 serial, "Self-Made") in his list of books most widely read in the years immediately following publication. *The Hidden Hand*, the most popular novel ever to run through the pages of the *Ledger* (and it did so three times!), was Southworth at her best. Filled with multiple mysteries, innumerable coincidences, and moments of suspense, the novel is about the ways in which the resourceful, independent, fun-loving young woman named Capitola solves the many problems of women created by men who mistreat and abuse them. There were some forty theatrical adaptations of *The Hidden Hand*, and Southworth herself saw John Wilkes Booth in one of two renditions of the work playing simultaneously in London during 1860–61. *Self-Raised* (run twice in the *Ledger*), which Southworth sometimes claimed as her personal favorite, traces the trials and triumphs of a self-made man whose legal career is dedicated to protecting women. Through two long volumes, *Ishmael* and *Self-Raised*, the hero Ishmael climbs from low birth to the pinnacle of honor and success, all the while showing the kindness, altruism, loyalty, and religious feeling of the ideal nineteenth-century gentleman. The story first ran through the columns of the *Ledger* in 1863–64 and, when it was issued in two volumes for the centennial in 1876, sold over two million copies. When copyrights to many of her novels began expiring in the 1880s and 1890s, various publishers reissued Southworth's books for ten and twenty cents apiece, spreading her fame still wider. In 1899 at her death, her works were still selling well, although in some libraries they had been blacklisted for vulgarity. As late as 1930, the publishers Street and Smith listed over ninety volumes of her work for ten cents each.[4]

At her birth, someone interested in good omens might have predicted her future fame. Emma Nevitte was born on December 26, 1819, in the house in Washington, D.C., designed by and built for another well-known American, George Washington. Even though she was born in the very room George Washington had planned as his own, no one seems to have taken this omen of future fame seriously, and life for Emma began unpropitiously. "I was a child of sorrow," she recalled, "from the very first year of my life. Thin and dark, I had no beauty except a pair of large, wild eyes—but even this was destined to be tarnished. At twelve months, I was attacked by an inflammation of the eyes that ended in total blindness—though happily temporary. Thus it was, my first view of life was through a dim, mysterious cathedral light in which every object in the world looked larger, vaguer, more distant and more imposing than it really was."[5] Although this blindness caused only temporary problems, until age thirty her life was filled with as much hardship and despair as any of her future heroines would experience.

When Emma was three, her sister Charlotte was born. The girls were constantly compared as they grew up. Charlotte was prettier, livelier, and more sociable than the "weird little elf," Emma. Except for her maternal Grandmother Wailes, whom Emma remembered fondly from these years, everyone, including her mother Susannah, preferred Charlotte, and Emma was painfully conscious of their preference. Years later she wrote with vehement anger in *The Deserted Wife* about how much such comparisons between young girls wounded both the admired and the unappreciated. Perhaps she was talking about herself when she described Hagar, the "wild, shy" girl who, because of comparisons, developed "jealousy and suspicion of the few she loved, scorn and contempt for the opinion of others—neglect of her person as little worth attention, and a morbid desire to be loved exclusively."[6] Even if that description was not a self-portrait, we do know that the sensitive, sorrowful daughter turned to worshipping her merchant father, Captain Charles LeCompte Nevitte, feeling her life divided between happy periods when he was home and unhappy periods, sometimes lasting many months, when he was not. When he was dying in 1824, he asked that she be christened Emma Dorothy Eliza Nevitte, giving her the initials "E.D.E.N." of which she would be so proud later in life. His death plunged the family into poverty and the daughter into deeper depression.[7]

In 1826, her mother married Joshua L. Henshaw, Daniel Webster's secretary. The Henshaws opened a private academy in 1829 with their daughters among the first pupils. There, Emma discovered her intelligence; she studied the classics and became fond of reading. On the whole, however, she was not happy. "Year after year," she wrote later in life, "from my eighth to my sixteenth year, I grew more lonely, retired into myself more, until notwithstanding a strong, ardent, demonstrative temperament, I became cold, reserved and abstracted. Let me pass over in silence the stormy and disastrous days of my wretched girlhood and womanhood, days that stamped upon my brow of youth the furrows of fifty years."[8]

Several factors probably contributed to her unhappiness, but, because of her reticence, we can only guess what they were. Certainly, the invidious comparisons with her sister Charlotte must have continued to distress her. In addition, she apparently experienced a great deal of misunderstanding, if not physical abuse, from her family. Years later she told her own daughter that both she and Charlotte suffered from neglect.[9] And, because she was born with what she called a "strong, ardent, demonstrative temperament," she may have also felt, more strongly than most, the pressures of conforming to the cultural ideals of True Womanhood. In any case, of the five writers discussed in this book, her childhood appears to have been the most traumatic.

Though bent, she was not broken by her growing pains and, possibly, they helped her to develop a fortitude for later trials. In addition to her achievements in school, two other aspects of her life seem to have counterbalanced the sorrow she experienced in those years. For one thing, out of despair over her father's death, she sought and found comfort in religious beliefs that were strengthened as years passed. Baptized in her father's faith as a Roman Catholic, she was raised in her mother's Episcopal church, but she eventually developed nondoctrinal Christian views.[10] Another support came from visits to her Grandmother Wailes's home in rural Maryland. There, despite being called a tomboy, she went horseback riding as often as possible, exploring the countryside, gaining physical strength, and listening to the old people tell their stories of the past. She became fascinated by family legends, ghost stories, and other provincial tales of courage, cruelty, wonder, and fear—tales that had all the ingredients of the fantastic stories she herself would someday tell.

Emma graduated from her parents' academy in 1835. Afterward she taught school until her marriage to Frederick Hamilton Southworth on January 23, 1840. Here at last, she must have thought, was someone who would love her exclusively. They moved to Prairie du Chien, Wisconsin, where Mrs. Southworth taught school in a neighboring town until the birth of her son, Richmond. She was pregnant with her second child, Charlotte Emma, when she and her husband returned to Washington, D.C., because of his unemployment; within a short time he abandoned the family to go exploring in South America and apparently never lived with his wife again, though he tried to get money from her or her publishers until his death in the early 1860s.

The reasons for their separation are unknown; she was as reticent in talking about her unhappy marriage as she was about her growing up. But in novel after novel, she paints empathic pictures of abandoned and mistreated wives whose moral superiority to their husbands is clear. Perhaps she was thinking of her husband when she said in an autograph album that the trait she detested most in people was cruelty. Whatever the reason for their separation, she and Frederick Southworth were never formally divorced, although she made inquiries about divorce in 1850 and her editor, Robert Bonner, had a bill submitted to Congress on her behalf that gave the courts of the District of Columbia the power to grant divorces.

Like many people in antebellum America, she believed that marriage was a sacred contract and could be broken only under the most extraordinary circumstances, which, apparently, she finally decided hers were not.[11]

Looking back on those hard times, E.D.E.N. Southworth described herself as "broken in spirit, health and purse—a widow by fate but not by fact—with my two babes looking up to me for the support I could not give."[12] Her family gave her little assistance. Her sister had moved to Mississippi to live with an uncle, her maternal grandmother died shortly after her return to Washington, and her parents were busy with their school and young family. Often she was without shoes or a fire, starving for food and for love, turned out of her grandmother's home by her stepfather. Like other women raised under the popular dictates of True Womanhood, she was not well prepared to support a family, and there were not many opportunities for her to do so. After months of suffering, she obtained a teaching job, but life continued to be a struggle on her meager salary of $250 a year. Her own ill health and that of her children compounded her financial troubles. Nevertheless, she earned a reputation as an excellent teacher, fond of children and her work, and in the next few years was promoted to principal, though her salary remained low. The difficulties of this time, reflected in her continuing fears of poverty and in her many stories of abandoned wives, haunted her for the rest of her life.[13]

Finally, almost without hope, Southworth wrote her first short story, "The Irish Refugee," for the press. She sent it to the nearest literary journal, the *Baltimore Saturday Visitor*, in 1846 and was heartened by the $15 she earned. Her second story, "The Wife's Victory," also submitted to the *Visitor*, was actually published in the *National Era* when the *Visitor* suspended publication and sold its plates to the *Era*. Its editor, Dr. Gamaliel Bailey, was a kind and insightful person, who during his career supported the efforts of a number of important writers, including Harriet Beecher Stowe and Mary Abigail Dodge. The financially strapped Bailey also encouraged Southworth, but at first did not pay her for her writing. When no money was forthcoming she continued to teach, trying to supplement her salary by sewing and by an occasional publication. Then, one day, in the midst of a snowstorm, Bailey arrived at her schoolhouse door with compensation for her previous submissions and a promise to pay her $10 a column. Soon her stories were being copied from the *Era* in such places as the *Christian Register* and the *Methodist-Protestant*, and her reputation as a writer grew.[14]

Her first important literary success was her ten-part serial story "Retribution," published in the *Era* in 1849. Bailey, who had expected to receive only a *short* story, paid her fifty dollars for it.[15] The difficulties Southworth surmounted in writing this serial and her joy in its reception are best reported in the author's own words:

> I had many minor troubles. My small salary was inadequate to our comfortable support. My school numbered eighty pupils, boys and girls, and I had the whole charge of them. Added to this, my little boy fell dangerously ill, and was confined to his bed.... The time devoted to writing was the hours that should have been given to sleep or to fresh air.... My health broke down.... The child suffered and complained, the patrons of the school grew dissatisfied, annoying, and sometimes insulting me, and as for the publisher, he would reject whole pages of that manuscript.... But look you how it terminated. That night of storm and darkness came to an end, and morning broke on me at last—a bright, glad morning, pioneering a new and happy day of life.... I, who six months before had been poor, ill, forsaken, slandered, killed by sorrow, privation, toil, and friendlessness, found myself born, as it were, into a new life; found independence, sympathy, friendship and honor, and an occupation in which I could delight.[16]

If she was exaggerating here, either about her trials or the importance to her of her achievement, it was only slightly, because all evidence supports the drama of her report.

After appearing in the *National Era*, *Retribution* was printed in 1849 by Harper and Brothers in an inexpensive paperback edition. Of the book, *Graham's Magazine* said, "This work has considerable merit, and is worthy of a more permanent form than the pamphlet in which it is published." The *Saturday Evening Post* praised it as displaying "a power of characterization, a fertility of invention, and a warmth and luxuriance of imagination which are seldom excelled."[17] The poet John Greenleaf Whittier also reviewed it, comparing it favorably to the work of the novelists Charlotte Brontë and Charles Brockden Brown; having met her at Gamaliel Bailey's house, Whittier encouraged Southworth to try a writing career. Although there were also those who criticized her work, Southworth was convinced by all the praise she received that she might earn her living as a writer instead of as a teacher.

Southworth's popularity and value to publishers were increasingly apparent to everyone. Her story "The Mother-in-Law" dramatically boosted *Era* subscriptions. In 1849, while still submitting pieces to the *Era*, she began writing for Henry Peterson of the *Saturday Evening Post*, then the leading story paper in the country. Her contributions to the *Post* helped boost its circulation to 80,000 subscribers by 1855. The paper offered supplements of her stories to its new subscribers and, for some stories, published extra copies of the *Post* to satisfy public demand. After Harper and Brothers published one of her books and D. Appleton and Company three others, the highly respected Abraham Hart of Philadelphia brought out several books made from her serials and short stories.[18] By 1853, although still experiencing some financial difficulties, she had saved enough money to purchase a home overlooking the Potomac in Georgetown, just outside Washington, D.C. She owned Prospect Cottage, as she named the house, for the rest of her life.

In 1854, when Abraham Hart went out of business, the plates of her work were purchased by Theophilus B. Peterson, the major U.S. publisher of inexpensive, sensational fiction, who also happened to be a cousin and competitor of Henry Peterson, editor of the *Saturday Evening Post*.[19] T. B. Peterson remained Southworth's American book publisher until her death, printing almost all of her books and periodically issuing them in uniform editions of gilt on morocco cloth. In 1857, after troubles with Henry Peterson, Southworth became an "exclusive" contributor to Robert Bonner's *New York Ledger*, a family story paper of fiction, moral essays, and poetry. Eventually thirty of her novels appeared in its pages. In other words, within eight years after the publication of her first novel, *Retribution*, Southworth had established business connections in the United States with Robert Bonner and T. B. Peterson that would last for the rest of her literary career.

Over the next thirty years, her life and the pursuit of her career were relatively routine. On the professional side, she devoted much time and energy to writing. At the beginning, Southworth wrote as many as three novels a year; from 1862 until 1890, she produced at least one a year. To accomplish this in her early days, when burdened with many responsibilities, she wrote from noon to midnight. Toward the end of her career, in 1881, she claimed, "On Monday, Tuesday, Wednesday, and Thursday, *both day and night, until midnight,* I sit at my writing desk and write, seldom leaving it except for meals—until about half past seven o'clock on Thursday evening when I usually send off my number for the week. It takes me four days and three long evenings to write a number."[20] Elsewhere she said her habit was to write all week and send her manuscript off at two o'clock Friday afternoon. She followed such routines for years. It is no wonder that she sometimes collapsed in exhaustion for weeks after completing a novel.

Like any single parent today, however, she could not spend all of her time writing. Family obligations of various sorts also demanded her attention. She had to deal not only with the routine concerns of her children, but also with their frequent illnesses when they were young. She liked to tell others—perhaps triumphantly—that she wrote *The Hidden Hand* in 1859 while caring for three people: her son, who was an invalid; her sister, who had tuberculosis; and herself, as she suffered from bronchitis.[21] Even though she once told Bonner that the income he provided had restored health to her family, she and others under her care were periodically ill. She sometimes complained to Bonner that visitors and other disturbances in her life made it difficult to find the time and energy to write. From time to time during the course of her career she took care of and financially supported her mother, her sister, and her half-sister's family, in addition to her own children. From 1876 to 1890, for example, she let her half-sister's large family live in Prospect Cottage, while she stayed most of the year in Yonkers, New York, near her grown son and daughter. Even as an adult, her son, Richmond, was an invalid and needed some of her care. Given all of these family obligations, it is amazing that she found any time to write.

But if family and friends caused complications, they also brought joy to her life. She once reported that the "sweetest words" she knew were "life, love, light, home, heaven, and mother." In 1862 when she was ill with smallpox, her mother nursed her to health and the two of them became close for the first time in Southworth's life. Her half-sister's family loved her dearly for her generosity, and she remained attached to her grown children and their families. Likewise, the pleasures of friendship were also hers. By middle age, the lonely child had become, according to some people, a warm and outgoing person. Others knew her as a woman "of refined sensibilities, and a brilliant conversationalist, and greatly beloved in private life."[22] Her home was for many years the site of a Washington literary salon, as well as Sunday evening gatherings for thirty or forty and lively parties for neighborhood schoolboys. She was finally well loved.

Although in large measure Southworth seems to have found the happiness and respect in adulthood that she did not experience as a child, her stories continued throughout her life to focus on the mistreatment of women. Her novels are filled with tales of women who are abused, violated, mistreated, deserted, deceived, or trivialized. But, while she enjoyed imagining a heroine like Capitola in *The Hidden Hand* turning the tables on men, in fact, most of her heroines embody conventional female values—religious faith, moral purity, domesticity, and self-sacrifice—with one difference: they do not show extreme feminine docility.[23] Instead, her novels demonstrate that women could be self-reliant and powerful in their sphere. Like other proponents of True Womanhood, Southworth valorized woman's sphere; her ideal women are morally superior to men, have their self-respect, and ultimately are rewarded for their suffering, usually by a repentant male who has come to recognize the woman's worth. However, in contrast to the prescription that women should not know about, much less write about evil in the world, her heroines experience, just as she herself did, the unpleasant underside of genteel social life.

Her entries in the autograph album of one of her friends suggest the high degree to which Southworth herself conformed to the popular ideals of womanhood.[24] She wrote that her amusements were "writing, reading, and playgoing"; her occupations were "writing, sewing, almsgiving and worshipping." Although playgoing suggests a more relaxed attitude toward entertainment than some would have had in the nineteenth century, her other occupations and amusements were above reproach for a True Woman. Moreover, she reported that she thought her most distinguishing characteristic was her "love for all creatures." In men, she said, she most admired magnanimity; and in women, devotion. Her idea of happiness was "power, beauty, and the united circle," and her aim in life, she wrote, was "to excel." In these brief phrases, she expressed her acceptance of several popular beliefs of the time: the power that comes from moral superiority, the beauty of a comfortable life, the love of a close family, and the joy of personal accomplishment. From her perspective, woman's sphere could be satisfying enough.

In her desire to excel, it might seem as though she diverged dramatically from the prescriptions of True Womanhood. However, it was not a desire for public achievement that originally made her step out of woman's sphere most narrowly defined and undertake a literary career. Rather, she was in circumstances that made it necessary for her to earn a good income, and, somewhat unexpectedly, she discovered she could do so as an author. Only later did she learn the pleasures of personal accomplishment in literature; only then did she discover the importance of storytelling to her sense of self.

To Southworth, excelling was not synonymous with financial profit, although financial stability was always an important consideration in her business dealings, more so than for the other writers examined in this book. Even though for each of these authors earning an income by writing was important, Southworth was less willing than the others to deny financial needs and to take financial risks, first of all, perhaps, because she had experienced more severe poverty, and, second, because she more fully accepted conventional views of noncompetitive, feminine behavior. What excelling ultimately meant in her career was entirely compatible with her belief in woman's sphere: she would generously provide support for those whom she loved.

Just as Southworth felt her financial motives were compatible with her feminine views, she claimed that she wrote to please others as well as to promote moral good—goals that were also consistent with her views of herself and her womanhood. Thus, she said she wrote her first stories to help out the editor of the *Baltimore Saturday Visitor* who was short of copy and she continued writing to please her family and friends.[25] Throughout her career, Southworth, like many of her contemporaries, measured a novel's worth by its ability to please others. Indeed, her stories sustained reader interest and pleasure for weeks on end in the *New York Ledger*. But that interest was never aroused at the expense of her sense of morality; in her novels, right always triumphed over wrong. She thought of herself as a popular Christian novelist, once declaring, "We must teach Christian lessons in parables as our Lord and Savior did—put ourselves *en rapport* with the minds of the young as He did. The novelist—the popular novelist—has a hundred-fold larger audience than the most celebrated preacher, and, therefore, a tremendous responsibility." In "Self-Made," however, she worked harder than ever to make her moral intentions clear, though she also did not want to displease her audience. As she told Bonner, "In former stories, I have catered for [*sic*] what I believed to be the popular taste; but in this I have a higher aim—popular good. The character of this story required that I should be deliberate in developing it, and *I have* found that such deliberation might be dangerous to its popularity. . . . I can easily return to my old style, if this should not please the millions."[26]

E.D.E.N. Southworth almost always succeeded in pleasing "the millions" because she was a superb storyteller. Who could resist a story that began, as *The Hidden Hand* did:

> "The Nocturnal Visit"
>
> "***Whence is that knocking?
> How is't with me when every sound appals me?
> ***I hear a knocking
> In the south entry! Hark!—more knocking!"
> —Shakespeare

Hurricane Hall is a large old family mansion, built of dark, red sandstone, in one of the loneliest and wildest of the mountain regions of Virginia.

The estate is surrounded on three sides by a range of steep, gray rocks, spiked with clumps of dark evergreens, and called, from its shoe form, the Devil's Hoof.

On the fourth side the ground gradually descends in broken rock and barren soil to the edge of the wild mountain stream known as the Devil's Run. . . .

[Roused from his bed in a snowstorm, Major Ira Warfield, owner of Hurricane Hall, is commanded by a local parson to accompany him to the bedside of a dying woman to hear her deposition.]

"Well, then, what is it? Dying deposition! It must concern a crime!" exclaimed the old man, hastily drawing on his coat.

"It does concern a crime."

"What crime, for the love of Heaven?"

"I am not at liberty to tell you. She will do that."

. . . .

It was dark as pitch when they emerged from the hall-door out into the front portico, before which nothing could be seen but two red bull's eyes of the carriage lanterns, and nothing heard but the dissatisfied whinnying and pawing of the horses.[27]

While her storytelling ability owes much to the traditions of the folk tales and ghost stories in which she thrilled as a child, it was her own vivid imagination that enabled her to create stories ever new, though repeating many of the same themes over and over. As she described them, her plots were "adventures with a good deal of sentiment." With some pride she reported that Harriet Beecher Stowe "used to say that there were incidents enough in any one of my stories to supply a half dozen novels." Southworth rightly claimed as her own special skill making all those "incidents acceptable, as probabilities or even possibilities, and that is not easy." Overall, she was justifiably proud of the originality of her work, insisting she never got her ideas from anyone else, though many copied her: "I can challenge anyone," she asserted, "to find *anything* in my stories that ever were published in any *preceding* story; but enough in *succeeding* [italics in original] ones."[28]

Southworth never entertained pretensions about being an artist or a "genteel amateur," but she defended her work in terms of its truthfulness and her sense of a harmonious whole. In an interview in 1890, she asserted, "I have no method. I never did have. I began without knowing I could write a novel. My novels are all founded on facts. . . . [*The Hidden Hand* was started when] I happened to see in a New York paper a short paragraph in which it was stated that a little nine-year-old girl, dressed in boy's clothes and selling newspapers, had been arrested. . . . That was the origin of Capitola." At other times she justified the length of her stories by talking about the need for "harmonious proportions of the whole work." By 1855, in fact, some reviewers had come to agree that Southworth's "stylistic extravagances matched her outsized characters and brought her improbable plots to life."[29]

Though during her career she was compared with many prominent writers from Shakespeare to Harriet Beecher Stowe, she herself seems rarely to have done so. One time, however, in defense of her work, she wrote Bonner: "In regard to the postscript concerning my 'unimportant details,' I have heard Richmond and others make the *very same* criticism on Walter Scott, Charles Dickens, Victor Hugo and George Eliot. It is certainly a *feature* if not a fault in most good writers. . . . Details are necessary to the true life-like realization of scenery, character and incident. All good authors know that. *And besides, Good Gracious! a horse must walk sometimes on a long journey!*"[30] At another time in a less overt defense of her work, Southworth was quoted in the *Critic* as saying that she considered Henry James an inferior and overrated writer.

Her pride in her work is better demonstrated, however, by the anger she expressed whenever someone tried to imitate, plagiarize, or otherwise "steal" it. When she learned of someone's plan to elude copyright law and reprint *The Hidden Hand* in 1887, she described, in a letter to Bonner, her indignation as "a very unchristian state of mind for a woman of my age, so near eternity!" Another attack on her literary property involved a doctor who claimed to know a woman in California who was the real author of "Self-Made" (*Ishmael* and *Self-Raised*). In this situation, Southworth wrote Bonner, "I confess that I have been more indignant over that 'outrageous libel' than necessary, but certainly it was the most impudent and audacious thing of the sort, that I ever heard of, for that fellow, Morgan (for there *is* such a scoundrel I am sorry to say) not only claims the authorship of my largest work for his woman, but accuses *me* of stealing the authorship from *her*, and *you* of fraud in substituting *my* name, for *hers*. If this is not a case for prosecution in a criminal court, for malicious libel, I do not know what is." Before this controversy was resolved, Southworth had sent denials to several papers, as had Bonner, and she wrote the doctor himself under a disguised name, successfully convincing him to publish a retraction of his claim. Southworth believed in her work and wanted no one else to profit from it.[31]

It is not enough to say she was proud of her work; in fact, she loved it as passionately as her readers did. She often reported as she was writing a story that she was "caught up in its current." After the *fifty-second* installment of "Self-Made," she asked Bonner's permission to extend the story still further, asserting: "I know *I* am not tired of the story. I never was so much in love with any hero, that I ever wrote of, as I am with Ishmael—and that is the truth."[32] She thoroughly enjoyed her own work.

It is important to note that this enthusiasm, pride, and self-respect were expressed by a woman who had been driven to her profession as a result of victimization and financial need—experiences that might have made her unhappy about having to pursue a literary career. Moreover, we might expect that her fairly conventional feminine values would have made her uncomfortable and unsure in the literary marketplace. Yet Southworth was essentially well satisfied and comfortable in her work. This was the case because, for a good part of her career, she was able to work in a primary relationship with the publisher Robert Bonner, whose values complemented her notions of herself as a woman and as a writer. In its specific, as well as in its general features, the relationship between Southworth and Bonner demonstrates the importance of the Gentleman Publisher's ethic to traditional women who became writers.

But, as mentioned earlier, Southworth did not immediately begin working with Robert Bonner. At the start of her career she had several publishers and editors, and for eight years she wrote, often exclusively, for Henry Peterson of the *Saturday Evening Post*. While she appreciated certain aspects of her relationship with Peterson, like its continuity, she was disturbed by others. In contrast to her later, more ideal association with Bonner, Southworth's relationship with Peterson was ultimately unsatisfactory because it conformed neither to the ideal image of relations between author and publisher propounded by Gentlemen Publishers nor to Southworth's ideal of relations between women and men.

In the beginning, however, Southworth had high hopes for the association. First of all, she had been wooed by the *Post*'s praise of *Retribution* as the best of American fiction, showing, as quoted earlier, "a power of characterization, a fertility of invention, and a warmth and luxuriance of imagination which are seldom excelled. Mrs. Southworth's characters are not mere names, but (so to speak) living and breathing individuals."[33] In addition, her values made her comfortable with the *Post*'s aims as recorded on its masthead: "A Family Newspaper, Neutral in Politics, Devoted to Morality, Pure Literature, Foreign and Domestic News, Agriculture, the Commercial Interests, Science, Art and Amusement." Finally, from a financial standpoint, she may have anticipated the *Post*'s growth and economic success under the respected Henry Peterson and his partner, Edmund Deacon.

For these reasons, not long after her first story appeared in the *Post*, Southworth agreed to be called an "exclusive" contributor, that is, one who would write for no one else. In response, the *Post* made their arrangement public and continued to compliment her work. When the paper published her second full-length novel, *The Deserted Wife*, in 1849, Peterson filled his columns with praise for its good judgment, fine characterization, and moral reflections. In 1851, a prospectus of the *Post* claimed that Southworth was "decidedly the greatest female novelist of America, and, in many respects, she is superior to any other novelist in the country, of either sex."[34] Again in 1854 the *Post* lauded her brilliant dialogue, engaging narrative, graphic descriptions, and original ideas. It must have seemed to the public that the Southworth-Peterson association was a happy one.

But in significant ways, their relationship did not conform to the type of relationship that Southworth eventually found with Robert Bonner. In the first place, although both Henry Peterson and E.D.E.N. Southworth thought moral guardianship was an important attribute of literary work, they did not agree that Southworth's novels were always moral. Secondly, Peterson did not really appreciate Southworth's literary style or grant her as much autonomy as she wanted. Finally, although in some respects he conformed to the Gentleman Publisher's etiquette of personal relationships, Peterson was not paternalistic and caring but authoritarian and patriarchal.

Almost from the beginning of their association, Peterson and Southworth disagreed about the morality of her stories. On September 10, 1849, he wrote Southworth, refusing to publish one of her chapters from *The Deserted Wife*. He reasoned, "without that chapter we thought the picture a most admirable and perfect one—with it, *as a reader*, we would have thrown down the tale in disgust. We should have resented the attempt to interest us in a character who could force a young girl into a marriage against her tears and protestations. . . . As to its publication when your story is republished in book form—your own taste and popularity are then alone at stake."³⁵ Although there is no record of her response to his letter, it is clear that she did not agree with his assessment because she restored the deleted chapter when she published her work in book form.

Over the years of their partnership, his criticism of her stories in terms of their morality continued unabated. In December 1854, Peterson sent Southworth a long, closely written letter accusing her of many errors, most of which related to the expression of morality in her latest work, "Miriam, the Avenger, or The Missing Bride":

> Dear Mrs. Southworth,—This week's installment would not do without great alterations—indeed it would not. It would have ruined both you and the Post. Do not for Heaven's sake, fall into your old blunder again. That free vein of your earlier writings [alluding to his criticisms of *The Deserted Wife*] injured you as you cannot compute—and now that Heaven in its mercy has given you a second chance, do not madly throw it away.... [I]n your books you reinserted sometimes what I had omitted. For this very reason, and no other, as the Appletons told us, they would not publish for you. And now that you have a publisher [Theophilus B. Peterson, her book publisher] whose name will not uphold you in the least, you should be doubly careful what you write.... [As to the character Miriam] [t]he story will be tenfold better with her pictured as a sensible and noble instead of a weak and foolish woman.... Do keep up the able and Christian elements of the story—There is enough that is weak and sinful without that.... Jacqueline is your *best* character, in an artistic sense of the word.... [Y]ou have managed her exceedingly difficult position with admirable prudence and delicacy.³⁶

From Peterson's point of view, Southworth went far outside the bounds of the respectable woman writer, who should not know about, much less write about, human weakness and depravity.

Again, her specific response to this accusation has been lost, but we can guess that these criticisms galled Southworth, who considered herself to be a Christian woman with the best of moral intentions as a writer. While Peterson and Southworth both accepted the publishing ideal of moral guardianship, they widely disagreed about how morality should be preserved. Southworth believed that moral lessons could be taught by presenting right in contrast to wrong, whereas Peterson felt that even a hint of wrong would corrupt the reader. Southworth's life experiences had exposed her to many examples of moral failings, yet she knew she had survived with her high ideals intact. Therefore, she viewed Peterson as straitlaced, while he regarded her as indelicate. "If you read the Post," he angrily responded to one of her earlier accusations,

> you will know that it is conducted in no straight-laced system. I bear in mind of course that what I publish is to be read by wives and daughters and children—but I have yet to learn that husbands and fathers should read papers which they would not be willing to place in the hands of a girl of sixteen.... On the principles on which I conduct the Post, I should not hesitate to insert anything ever written (to my present recollection) by Scott, or Dickens, or the Miss Porter[s], or Maria Edgeworth, or Miss Martineau, or Frederika Bremmer, or Cooper, or Irving, or Miss Sedgwick—but there are one or two novels of Bulwer's, those of Eugene Sue's, most of George Sand's, which I could not publish. This is to show that our paper is not bounded by such narrow limits, that true genius cannot find room for its wings.[37]

Apparently, her adherence to her view of moral guardianship was enormously irritating to him. Finding her unwilling to bow to his arguments, he was reduced to snide remarks about her talent.

Southworth and Peterson also disagreed about literary style and authorial autonomy. In particular, Peterson took issue with the length of Southworth's stories, which always went far beyond the agreed upon number of installments. As early as 1849, Peterson insisted that she curb her creative spirit, even though, as she had told him, her friends urged her on. In 1854 he wrote, "You must know of course that the story has been spun out too much.... [T]he value of your stories is greatly lessened to us by their extreme length."[38] From Peterson's point of view, Southworth's promise of short novelettes that stretched into lengthy novels created annoying problems. The editor was caught in a difficult position between readers who wanted more of Southworth's adventure-packed stories and other authors who were dismayed when their stories had to be postponed because hers took up so much space. Southworth, of course, argued that her stories needed to be just as long as she made them to be properly told; she had her own sense of a harmonious whole. From her perspective, decisions about length were her literary prerogative.

While the disputes over morality were fought only in private, this conflict was also aired in public. In fact, the *Post*'s public praise for Southworth often included brief editorial remarks on the unexpected length of her work. The brevity of the remarks belied the seriousness of the problem, which was being more fully debated in private. Finally, Peterson's exasperation erupted in a most forthright editorial, written during the publication of "Vivia" on September 20, 1856: "We regret very much that Mrs. Southworth's story of 'Vivia' is not concluded this week, according to promise. Mrs. Southworth writes to us that the concluding scenes stretch out longer than she anticipated, and that she will not be able to finish them before another week. In the future it is our intention to adhere inflexibly to our rule of commencing no story until the whole of the manuscript is in our possession. We can then judge of its length, and of our ability to publish it in a reasonable space of time."[39] To Peterson's dismay, "Vivia" was not concluded until the thirty-ninth number, thus surpassing the length of any previous story Southworth had written. The author-publisher relationship had stretched to its breaking point over the issue of who would decide a novel's length. Southworth thought that it was the author's right and Peterson, the publisher's.

Another source of friction was Peterson's exaggerated attitude of superiority. Granted, the publisher always had more power than the author, but Peterson's attitude toward Southworth overplayed his advantage. He was far too authoritarian and patriarchal for her taste. Often, he was very condescending, delivering even praise with a tinge of rebuke. In 1854, for instance, he wrote, "By the way, [Ann Stephens] has veered around completely relative to you, and speaks of your genius in *the most enthusiastic terms*. . . . Mr. Deacon recently saw her in New York, and she spoke of your recent works in a way that I do not feel free to repeat—your bumps of approbativeness and self-esteem being already sufficiently large. You see, I remember the anecdote of the lover who flattered his betrothed to such a height that she would no longer speak to him, but cut his acquaintance." Ironically, Southworth cut Peterson's acquaintance, not because he over-flattered her, but because, from her perspective, he was ultimately unappreciative of her talents. Moreover, he often was insulting. In December 1854, after commenting on her lack of moral discretion, her poor choice of book publishers, and her inability to restrain her writing, Peterson firmly rebuked her intelligence: "Whatever you may *think* about these matters, I *know* that I am correct. I stand between you and literary perdition. . . . P.S. I think Providence will pardon you for writing on Sunday to get out of this dilemma. You have given me a deal of *trouble* and anxiety, I assure you." It was this demeaning attitude, so inappropriate to a Gentleman Publisher's relations with authors, that finally drove Southworth away.[40]

What these problems all boiled down to for Southworth was not being treated like the woman and writer she believed herself to be: moral, responsible, and worthy of respect. Her response to Peterson's mistreatment was entirely in keeping with her views of woman's honor: she covertly but firmly challenged his authority. Like a character in one of her novels, she at first said nothing that might undermine her moral superiority to him, but rather vaguely accepted his request for another novelette, having no intention of fulfilling the agreement. Assuming that he held the upper hand and that she would send him another manuscript, Peterson announced the commencement of her new story *weekly* from November 29, 1856 to April 11, 1857. She kept putting him off. In the meantime, Robert Bonner of the *New York Ledger* asked Southworth to write for him, and she assured him that she had no exclusive agreement with anyone else.

In April 1857, when Peterson finally understood he was not going to receive another Southworth story, he denounced her haughtily in an editorial. Then, Southworth spoke out on her own behalf: her agreement with the *Post* had only been verbal and conditional, and Peterson's responses to her temperate letters had always been rude. Her defense, published in the *Ledger*, concluded with statements showing how closely linked in her mind were her authorship and her womanhood: "I never purposely injured the Post, yet in consequence of this my determined withdrawal from its connection, Messrs. Deacon and Peterson in their statement in the Post have cunningly and covertly assailed my truthfulness as a woman and my reputation as a writer. Anyone may see at once the motive of the attack this pair of gentlemen have made upon one woman who never injured them unless she has inadvertently done so in leaving the Post for the Ledger."[41] In the context of the Gentleman Publisher's marketplace, her declaration that she was an innocent woman and innocent writer served as the formal announcement that publisher and author were severing their ties and that she was now engaged with Robert Bonner of the *Ledger*. As it turned out, she found Bonner's treatment of her much more in keeping with her vision of herself as woman and as writer.

Robert Bonner's first letters to E.D.E.N. Southworth were well timed and well written to take advantage of the tensions between Southworth and Henry Peterson. One wonders whether he had heard gossip of a Southworth-Peterson breakup, or whether, with his usual good business sense, Bonner simply saw another successful writer whom he wanted for his rapidly expanding paper, the *New York Ledger*. In any case, he approached her graciously: "my own belief is that there is no female author either on this or the other side of the Atlantic, who can write so excellent a story."[42] For Southworth, Bonner's unqualified enthusiasm was a welcome change from Henry Peterson's treatment. Bonner's enthusiasm was, however, but one aspect of their relationship that made their business dealings satisfying for her. In Robert Bonner, Southworth found a publisher who developed respectful and supportive personal relationships with writers, who shared her views of moral guardianship, and who could provide her with the stable income she wanted. Even though he was on the fringe of the circle of most respected publishers in the nineteenth century, he nevertheless tried to uphold many of the ideals of the Gentleman Publisher. Because he did so, he provided a comfortable environment in which she could pursue her career.

At first glance, Robert Bonner does not seem to fit the image of Gentleman Publisher. Bonner, an Irish immigrant, is usually remembered as one of the "self-made men" of the nineteenth century. He bought the *New York Merchant's Ledger* for $500 in 1851 and, having dropped "Merchant" from the title as it evolved into a family story paper, turned the *Ledger* into a $2 million asset by 1880.[43] At his death in 1899, Bonner himself was worth $6 million, an amount far beyond the dreams of most Gentlemen Publishers. In fact, he has been more often compared to the showman, P. T. Barnum, than to the other Gentlemen Publishers because, like Barnum, Bonner was exceptionally good at advertising. He tried all sorts of innovative, sometimes questionable advertising schemes, filling entire pages of other papers (he never allowed advertising in his own) with catchy phrases, sample stories, or claims that everyone, including Queen Victoria and President Franklin Pierce, was reading the *Ledger*. Perhaps the most astounding advertising feat of all time was his purchase in 1858 of the entire May 6 edition of the *New York Herald* for his advertisements. In fact, he was known to spend as much as $20,000 a week on advertising. He also lured readers by announcing that he was paying such astonishing sums as $30,000 to Henry Ward Beecher for *Norwood*, $10,000 to Edward Everett for a series on Mount Vernon, and $5,000 to Alfred, Lord Tennyson for a single poem. He proudly pointed out that Lydia H. Sigourney, Fanny Fern, and Sylvanus Cobb, Jr., were *Ledger* exclusives, and that his list of occasional contributors also included such writers as Louisa May Alcott, Harriet Beecher Stowe, and Horace Greeley. He definitely was a showman.

But the other side of his personality aligned him to the Gentlemen Publishers. Like them, his values were grounded in nineteenth-century moral idealism and didacticism. He rightly attributed his success to "integrity, combined with energy and a knowledge of one's business," for his integrity often won him friends in his career. In his private life, he was extremely upright; he never drank, smoked, or swore. Even though he owned the fastest horses in the world, he never raced them on a wager for he was opposed to gambling. Moreover, he was exact in business affairs and never allowed himself to be in debt. He was also a religious person who tried to live by a Christian code of social responsibility: "I would not ask any man," he insisted, "to do anything for me that I did not think to be right."[44] These were the moral attributes that he, like other Gentlemen Publishers, expressed in his career. Other characteristics in his dealings with authors also aligned him with the ideals of the Gentlemen Publishers of his time.

In welcome contrast to the autocrat Henry Peterson, Robert Bonner publicly as well as privately praised Southworth's work. In fact, two years before she started writing for him he had announced that he thought she was the best fiction writer in the United States and that he would be willing to pay her liberally for a story, though he understood she was currently "engaged exclusively" on the *Saturday Evening Post*. When she accepted his offer to write for him, he demonstrated his esteem for her by spending $27,000 advertising her first contribution, *The Island Princess*—more than he had paid to advertise Sylvanus Cobb's best-seller, *The Gun Maker of Moscow*.[45] He continued to praise her highly over the forty years of their association. In 1883, toward the end of her career, her publishers commented that "she has written nothing but good novels for the fireside and furnished an amazing fund of pure and healthy entertainment to thousands of readers. . . . The great secret of her hold upon her readers is, after her inventive genius, in framing the plots of her stories and in the brisk and wide-awake manner in which all details are executed. There is no time for listlessness, every moment is animated, and she is not only a popular and entertaining author, but a moral one, as she inculcates propriety both by precept and by the example of her characters. . . . Her characters are drawn with a strong hand, and actually appear to live and move before us." Even in 1885, Bonner's paper proclaimed her "the most popular authoress in this country."[46]

In private, their relationship was equally warm and personal. He generously passed on compliments he heard about her stories; when he did criticize her work, he displayed the tact one would use with a friend. But their relationship was built on more than his praise. Their families became close; they visited one another and sometimes even vacationed together. As friends, both author and publisher sometimes expressed concerns in their business letters about their families' health. Because they liked each other so well, she sometimes even teased him about his horses, other contributors, or his children. In tribute to their close friendship, she dedicated her favorite work, "Self-Made," to his son, Eddie.[47] In short, theirs was the kind of business relationship advocated by Gentlemen Publishers: a business relationship that involved personal friendship as well.

Given the nature of their association, both people accepted assumptions about the importance of loyalty and reciprocity between author and publisher. Generous in his financial support, from the beginning Bonner gave Southworth, as he did his other writers, five-year contracts that provided weekly payments for weekly submissions. Compensation to Southworth under those contracts steadily increased from $40 a week in 1857 to $150 by 1878. He was faithful in making payments promptly and, when she asked, let her draw on them in advance with no questions asked. When she was short of cash, he loaned her money, apparently at no interest. He seems to have sent generous Christmas bonuses annually, like the one that prompted the letter quoted at the beginning of this chapter, and at least sometimes paid her salary when she was resting and recovering her health between novels. For her part, she conscientiously fulfilled their contracts to provide twenty to twenty-five pages of manuscript weekly, always sending extra pages the next week if she were short on pages one week. In fact, she often sent him more than the contracted pages of manuscript. Once, she even volunteered to do any revisions on any stories he wanted as a "*free will offering* of friendship and gratitude."[48] Thus, she matched his loyalty and generosity with some of her own.

Southworth seems to have found her relationship with Bonner especially satisfying because it replicated in certain ways the attitudes and behaviors she thought were appropriate for honorable relationships between women and men. In a number of ways, Bonner's generosity as a publisher and friend placed him in a "male" role in her family's life. In the absence of a real father, Bonner was a role model for her son Richmond, who attended school near Bonner in New York. Afterward, she wrote Bonner, "I wished to tell you what I have discovered since Richmond's return home to live with me again—*the great influence that you have had upon his character* in consolidating his good, but rather unstable impulses into what I hope now is a strong integrity. Having had no father, uncle, elder brother or any male relative to counsel him, he stood greatly in need of just such guidance as you have given him.—You have done him so much good. And God knows how grateful I am to you for it."[49] Bonner assumed the "father" role at other times, too, offering to buy a substitute for Richmond if he were drafted for the Civil War and providing money to help Richmond set up a medical practice of his own. While Southworth thought of him as a "father" to Richmond, she also sometimes described him as a "brother" to her. She most openly expressed this when she thanked Bonner for taking her side in a dispute with her book publisher, T. B. Peterson: "If all men were as prompt and spirited in defending the women dependent upon them, as you are then we should not hear so much fuss about women's rights. We should all be very glad to leave our rights in the hands of our *brave, big brothers*."[50]

Accustomed to living in and writing about a world in which women were victimized by men, Southworth appreciated her relationship with Bonner because he respected her as a "lady." Like her heroines, she was not weak and helpless—in fact, she was often strong, ingenious, and self-reliant—but, nevertheless, she felt that she deserved to be defended because of her feminine qualities. Southworth appreciated an author-publisher relationship that reenacted what she most admired in the relations between men and women: magnanimity in Bonner and devotion in herself.

The metaphors of some of her letters to him betray how deeply gender assumptions permeated their relationship. In many letters she wrote him, including the 1869 one quoted at the beginning of this chapter, she described him like a hero in one of her novels who had swept into her life to protect and provide for her. His rescue made her always grateful and faithful, as any heroine would have been. Because he was her hero, she refused an offer from *Saturday Night* of $10,000 to write a single story, reassuring Bonner that "even without the [five-year] contract, honor, gratitude, old habit, and my own best interests and most sacred friendships, bind me fast to the Ledger." As if sensing he was uneasy about her faithfulness, she reassured him again: "Believe me ever, in *thought, word, and deed*, Faithfully yours." Finally, the author even promised, echoing a marriage ceremony, to "write and *write well* for the Ledger as long as we both live."[51] The loyalty that Southworth felt toward Bonner did indeed keep them together for life.

Like men and women in their separate spheres, author and publisher assumed they had separate responsibilities, and they honored each other in their respective roles. Each had a role—his to have the "business tact" and hers to display "some genius in popular writing," as she implied in the letter quoted at the beginning of this chapter. Neither tried to assume or direct the duties of the other. Bonner gave her essentially free rein in decisions about content, style, and length, stipulating only that he receive a certain number of pages weekly. Even though he was in the habit of making recommendations to other writers, he let her devise her own story ideas. While Southworth had bristled at Henry Peterson's criticisms, she told Bonner she was not "touchy" about his occasional suggestions on length, apparently because his overall attitude was not critical or demeaning.[52] On her part, Southworth occasionally made suggestions about illustrations and showed some concern about advertising, but, unlike the other authors discussed in upcoming chapters, she expressed relatively few opinions about these publishers' concerns and generally kept to her separate sphere. From time to time, Bonner sought her advice about potential contributors, other publishers, and some business affairs; she always responded confidently and frankly, but she never offered more than he asked.

While the supportive, respectful, gendered nature of their relationship was important to Southworth, so, too, were their shared views of morality and moral guardianship. In contrast to the Peterson-Southworth association, Bonner and Southworth shared a view of morality that did not preclude writing about adventure, excitement, and crime, while aiming to teach the reader sound morals. Throughout his career, Bonner responded to public pressure to conform to popular moral standards in his paper by defending his writers in terms of their morality. Of the often ridiculed Sylvanus Cobb, Jr., he wrote, "I value his writings and pay highly for them, because they are just what they are—pure in morals, honest and noble in sentiment, simple in diction, plain in construction, and thoroughly adapted to the taste and comprehension of the people." On his retirement, Bonner reported, "When I first bought the *Ledger*, I pictured to myself an old lady in Westchester with three daughters, aged about twenty, sixteen and twelve, respectively. Of an evening they come home from a prayer meeting and not being sleepy, the mother takes up the *Ledger* and reads aloud to the girls. From the first day I got the *Ledger* to the present time, there has never appeared one line which the old lady in Westchester County would not like to read to her daughters."[53]

While these sentiments aligned Bonner with the Gentlemen Publishers and made him acceptable in Southworth's eyes, other people, like Henry Peterson, were not so sure that either Bonner or Southworth had a proper moral sense. Many literary critics and social commentators did not see sensational fiction as either morally or aesthetically worthwhile, thus censoring Southworth overtly and Bonner by association. According to one reviewer, "Understanding well the craving for what is sensational and morbid in fiction, Mrs. Southworth, by a skillful use of the fascinations of crime, and by a systematic introduction of horror as an element of literary construction, has managed to cater so successfully to certain tastes that she stands easily at the head of this class of the trashy school."[54] But trashiness was neither Bonner's nor Southworth's intention (whether or not we judge that to be the result), as both make clear in public and private statements. Indeed, the moral respectability of their private lives supports the sincerity of their views. Moreover, they reacted just like many of their "moral" contemporaries did to the public controversy over whether or not Harriet Beecher Stowe should have published her article on Lord Byron's incest and marital problems (see Chapter 4): as a True Woman, Southworth was silent about the scandal created by the article; as a Gentleman Publisher, Bonner never again listed Stowe as a contributor to the *Ledger*. In essence, the relationship between Southworth and Bonner was satisfactory to her because he believed in her moral intentions as others, like Henry Peterson, did not.

Just as Bonner accepted Southworth's moral intentions, he also understood her financial needs. His first offer to her is illuminating: "*I am willing to pay you your own terms; or double as much, at least, as you have ever received from any newspaper publisher*. I am ready to make a contract to that effect."[55] Thereafter, by providing five-year contracts for the rest of her life, he guaranteed her an income as well as ensuring that loyalty and a noncompetitive atmosphere would prevail. The financial stability of the regular contracts was important to Southworth, as was the size of the payments. Under their contract for the years following 1878, for instance, she could have earned up to $7,800. With her salary, Christmas bonuses, and other kinds of financial support she was able to hire servants and to live comfortably in her fourteen-room cottage, which over the years she remodeled and modernized.

Southworth was always enormously grateful for Bonner's support because it enabled her to take care of those whom she loved. Expressing her appreciation in 1862, she wrote, "It is a striking fact that although duty and circumstances oblige me to do a great deal for other people—some whom have no claim upon me—no one in this world but yourself ever does anything for me." Twenty years later, when her salary was reconfirmed at $150 a week, she expressed the same view: "Heaven knows it is not for myself alone that I wanted to write on the same terms as lately; but for those whom it is my duty to take care of. Besides my own family, I have had my sister's large family to care for ever since 1876. I put them in my furnished cottage and give them a small income.... The terms on which I now write make it easy for me to do this—And when I go to the cottage it is warm for me. And it is *you* whom I thank for all this." Although it may seem by these statements that she did not give herself enough credit for what she was worth to Bonner, from her perspective he was giving her enough money to live up to her ideal self as a caring woman.[56]

While her financial arrangements with Bonner were to her liking, they also perpetuated inequalities between author and publisher. Lulled by his generosity, perhaps, Southworth was a relatively passive negotiator, as were most of Bonner's writers, incidentally. The contracts, of course, eliminated the need to discuss compensation, acceptance, or other details for individual pieces. Still, the contracts themselves were not really negotiated; Bonner offered them and Southworth accepted them with thanks. The only exception occurred in 1878 when Southworth expressed disappointment at not receiving a salary increase, but Bonner seems to have immediately agreed to raise the amount. Even for her first contract, Southworth did not hold out for a higher offer, though she must have been aware (because he advertised it) of Bonner's astounding agreement to pay Sara Payson Parton (Fanny Fern) one hundred dollars a column.[57] Southworth agreed to forty dollars a week. She was similarly passive about negotiating book publications. She sold the copyrights of her works to Bonner or had him sell them to T. B. Peterson, her book publisher, usually accepting the price he named without negotiating the terms of the arrangement.

One can see her potential losses as a passive negotiator by examining the financial agreement she made for *The Hidden Hand*. Southworth sold the copyright to Bonner for $1,000—actually more than she received for some of her other books sold to T. B. Peterson. If she had negotiated a royalty contract of 10 to 15 percent (a conservative but typical amount for so popular a writer) on the publication of 100,000 copies sold at $1.75, she would have made between $17,500 and $26,000. After running it three times in the *Ledger*, Bonner and Sons published the book, undoubtedly realizing a handsome profit. Though Bonner was generous to Southworth, this particular situation illustrates that he probably should have been more so. After all, he was a millionaire several times over, while Southworth was only fairly well-to-do. Helen Waite Papashvily, an early scholar of women's literature, is right to characterize Bonner as "generous rather than just."[58]

On the other hand, Southworth herself held essentially noncompetitive values. Beyond a certain point, money was not important to her. She turned down competitive offers that could have made her wealthier. As she said in a letter quoted previously, honor, friendship, and her best interests were more important to her than riches. In fact, she did earn a good living for herself and several dependents, and she gained fame and respect in her lifetime. It is also important to remember that she was not totally powerless in her dependence on Bonner. Southworth had a good deal of authority by virtue of her skills, popularity, and self-respect. Bonner did not try to reshape her work; he let her maintain control over it. But he did have the last word, even when he did not demand it, and she seems to have let him have it by failing to negotiate with him or to seek competitive bids elsewhere.

In regard to financial arrangements, as in their personal relationship, she was in a dependent "female" position to Bonner's more powerful "male" one. Rather than assertively and straightforwardly asking for a certain compensation, as someone who felt she was an equal might, Southworth used manipulative tactics to sustain appreciation of her work. For example, she told Bonner how hard she was working for him so he would know he was getting his money's worth from her. Or she told him how much she appreciated his many kindnesses to her, further encouraging such behaviors in him. She offered to do favors for him, thereby reinforcing the obligations he might feel toward her. Moreover, she sometimes mentioned the positive things she had heard about her work so he would not forget what she was worth to him. Finally, she often said she wanted to do her best for the *Ledger*, thereby implying the *Ledger* should do its best for her. Such manipulative tactics fit naturally in the structure of their relationship; they were the tactics of unequal male-female relationships.

In contrast to her relationship with Henry Peterson, Southworth's association with Robert Bonner worked to her satisfaction. As a woman of fairly conventional feminine values who excelled in the writing of sensational fiction, Southworth wanted a business situation that fit her values and needs. With Bonner, she found respect for her person and talents, honor for her morality, and financial success and stability. With him, she could maintain a feminine role. These things meant so much to her that she continually expressed her gratitude in her correspondence with him—more often and more effusively, in fact, than any other writer considered in this study. She credited him with a generosity beyond the bounds of any business expectations. His liberality had given her money to live comfortably, to educate her children, to enlarge and furnish her home, and to help her parents.[59] From her perspective, theirs was the ideal business relationship.

Since she was so satisfied in her relationship with Bonner, one might wonder why she worked so many years with Theophilus B. Peterson, who was one of the earliest and most successful publishers of cheap fiction. In contrast to her warm feelings for Bonner, Southworth seems not to have liked T. B. Peterson. Once she accused him of being miserly, and another time she described him as having a "peculiar manner of doing business and *'doing' the public* at the same time."[60] His advertising techniques sometimes shocked and dismayed her, apparently for their lack of propriety, and she suspected him of stirring up a controversy over the authorship of her book *Ishmael (Self-Made)* in order to spur sales and increase his profits. But he was very successful. Unlike many publishing companies of the nineteenth century, T. B. Peterson and Brothers experienced almost uninterrupted prosperity. They published foreign and American fiction by such people as Ann Stephens, T. S. Arthur, Charles Dickens, and Mrs. Henry Wood. Their books were popular and were often found in circulating libraries and on railroads.

Southworth's relationship with T. B. Peterson shows her willingness to let Bonner protect her. Once she started writing for Bonner, he acted as her intermediary with Peterson, selling the book copyrights to Peterson after they had been published in the *Ledger*. Consequently, she had little to do with Peterson. Again, her reliance on Bonner worked fairly well. The arrangements provided financial stability rather than risk. According to some reports, she earned royalties of $6,000 a year from T. B. Peterson.[61] By continuing to have him publish her books, she escaped the competition of the open marketplace that she also had avoided with her five-year contracts with Bonner. In book negotiations, as in other areas of her business life, "big brother" Bonner took care of her.

While most historians have assumed that the roles of True Woman and professional writer were incompatible, E.D.E.N. Southworth's career tells another story: without departing very much from popular nineteenth-century views of gender roles, women could be writers in the mid-nineteenth century without ambivalence, even with great joy. To make that point, it is worth quoting again from Southworth's reflections about the commencement of her literary career: "I, who six months before had been poor, ill, forsaken, slandered, killed by sorrow, privation, toil and friendlessness, found myself born, as it were, into a new life; found independence, sympathy, friendship, and honor, and an occupation in which I could delight." When conducting literary business, Southworth found her greatest delight in her association with Robert Bonner. No matter what drawbacks we see in the relationship, and there certainly were some, Southworth found it satisfying. It worked for her. She was able to conduct business without renouncing her feminine values or behaviors.

Southworth's experiences give a specific example of how the Gentleman Publisher's ethics affected women. Although in some ways the Bonner-Southworth relationship deviated from the ideals of the Gentleman Publisher, generally Southworth was pleased by the ways it conformed to those ideals: she was happy with a loyal, personal relationship; she was comfortable with its paternalism; and she was pleased with Bonner's sense of moral guardianship. In addition, she was grateful for Bonner's commercialism—so unlike the ideal—because she sorely needed financial success and stability. In its deviation from, as well as its conformity to, the Gentleman Publisher's ideals, Bonner's treatment of Southworth was satisfying to her.

4

Harriet Beecher
Stowe

*Courtesy of the
Stowe-Day
Foundation,
Hartford,
Connecticut*

The Impact of Domestic Feminism

Harriet Beecher Stowe's
Mature Career

When Harriet Beecher Stowe (1811–96) began her professional association with the publisher James T. Fields of Ticknor and Fields in 1860, she was already considered to be the most important American woman writer of the nineteenth century. As the author of the all-time best-seller *Uncle Tom's Cabin* (1852), several other books, and many short stories and articles, she was securely established in the publishing marketplace. Experiences before and after *Uncle Tom's Cabin* had matured her views of literary creativity as well as her understanding of business. She had been disillusioned by an earlier association with John P. Jewett and wanted the type of author-publisher relationship idealized by the Gentlemen Publishers. With Fields between 1860 and 1871, Stowe found just that: a business relationship characterized by personal friendship, loyalty, and trust; a shared vision of moral guardianship; and a commitment to noncommercial aims that nevertheless produced financial results.

In its broad outline, Stowe's relationship with Fields was like E.D.E.N. Southworth's with Robert Bonner. Nevertheless, while both Stowe and Southworth worked in the context of the Gentleman Publisher's marketplace, they behaved quite differently. Where Southworth was passive, Stowe was assertive. Where Southworth maintained her sphere, Stowe expanded it. Where Southworth was conservative, Stowe was moderately liberal. The differences were the result of Stowe's "domestic feminism"—her strong belief in the importance of applying nineteenth-century feminine values to public as well as private spheres of American life. Indeed, Stowe's faith in domestic feminism gave her the justification for behaving much more autonomously and assertively with her Gentleman Publisher than Southworth ever did. But the road to Stowe's mature self-confidence as a writer had been a long one.

Unlike Emma Nevitte (Southworth), whose family was relatively obscure, Harriet Beecher was the daughter of the well-known, controversial minister Lyman Beecher. Although the family lived in poverty in Litchfield, Connecticut, while Harriet was growing up, life in the large Beecher household was lively, with theological debates, wood-chopping contests, and recitations of the works of Sir Walter Scott, all intended primarily for the benefit of the sons whom their parents hoped would become ministers. Harriet soon understood she was not as highly valued as her brothers by her father, who wished she had been a boy because of her intelligence.[1] In other words, like Emma Nevitte, Harriet seems to have been neglected, though for different reasons and to a lesser degree than young Emma. She learned much from her father, but his forceful Calvinism and driving ambition led to self-doubts in Harriet that took years to overcome.

In the Beecher household, the foundation of Stowe's domestic feminism was laid by her mother's example and her father's religious convictions. Even though Harriet's mother, Roxanna Foote Beecher, died when Harriet was four, she lived on in the family's memory as a remarkably intelligent, selfless, and loving Christian woman. Her idealized example reinforced other messages Harriet heard in her culture prescribing True Womanhood. At the same time, her father conveyed to her a profound sense of the religious nature of life and the importance of working for right against wrong in the world. Those religious convictions, linked with the encouragement to become a selfless, loving woman, were the foundation of the domestic feminism Harriet would express in later life.

If growing up as a Beecher gave Harriet a more deeply religious and potentially more feminist orientation than Southworth had, it also shaped Harriet's imagination in different ways. Rather than being stirred by ghost stories and folk tales, Harriet's inventiveness was shaped by theological writings, sermons, and some contemporary fiction and poetry. Among the theological works, Cotton Mather's *Magnalia Christi Americana*, an ecclesiastic history of New England, was her favorite, because it made her feel that the ground on which she trod was "consecrated by some special dealing of God's Providence."[2] In addition, her father's extemporaneous sermons showed her the exciting ways in which personal experience could reveal moral lessons. *The Arabian Nights*, which she discovered in the bottom of a barrel of theological treatises stored in the Beecher attic, introduced her to the drama of storytelling, while works by Sir Walter Scott and Lord Byron gave Harriet her earliest exposure to the Romantic literary tradition. In fact, she read everything she could lay her hands on. Reading set her to daydreaming, and she developed the habit, so frustrating to others around her throughout her life, of losing herself in the scenes of her imagination.

No doubt because she had better family connections than Emma Nevitte, Harriet also received a better education. After attending a dame school in Litchfield, she was enrolled at ten or eleven in the famous Miss Sarah Pierce's Female Academy in Litchfield, where she excelled in the art of composition. In a school program, she thoroughly impressed everyone, including—to her great joy—her father, with a theological essay arguing the negative response to the question "Can the Immortality of the Soul Be Proved by the Light of Nature?" After Pierce's Academy, she attended the equally celebrated Hartford Female Seminary, founded and directed by her older sister Catharine. Catharine Beecher expected her students to master the principles of major fields of knowledge and to prepare themselves to be benevolent mothers, teachers, or nurses who could save their families and, hence, the nation through moral example and persuasion. Consequently, Harriet studied geography, history, philosophy, chemistry, and logic, as well as Latin, French, and the "female" arts of drawing and sewing. From her lessons, she developed lifelong beliefs not only in women's intellectual capabilities and the worth of a female perspective on the world, but also in the importance of family and home. Her ambitions were nurtured, too, and she began to cherish the dream of doing something in the world.[3]

Harriet Beecher's early adulthood, however, gave little indication of the personal fame that lay ahead. She was known primarily as the younger sister of the well-known educator, Catharine Beecher, and the daughter of the well-known minister, Lyman Beecher. At sixteen, while still a student, she began teaching Latin, which she had taught herself, at her sister's school in Hartford. In 1832, at twenty-one, she and Catharine followed Lyman Beecher, his second wife, and family to Cincinnati, Ohio, where he assumed the presidency of Lane Theological Seminary. There, she resumed teaching for her sister in Catharine's newly established Western Female Institute and wrote a children's geography book, which sold well when it was first advertised under the more famous Catharine Beecher name. Harriet did not complain about the book's misattribution; the self-confidence of her later career had not yet emerged.[4]

But encouragement from friends and family slowly changed her self-perception. In Cincinnati, she and her sister joined the Semi-colon Club whose members included Caroline Lee Hentz, a popular novelist; E. P. Cranch, a popular humorist; Charles W. Elliot, a New England historian; Emily and Elizabeth Blackwell, who became pioneering physicians; Professor Calvin E. Stowe, known in Europe and America as a scholar and author; and other intelligentsia and literati of the region. Supported and inspired by members of that group, both sisters began occasionally contributing to the popular gift books and annuals of the time. In 1834, Harriet won a first prize of fifty dollars for her tale "Uncle Lot," published in the *Western Monthly Magazine* by her Semi-colon Club acquaintance, Judge James Hall. Hall's magazine, devoted to "elegant literature" and "moral principle," argued for higher pay for writers and praised "those attractive attributes of the female pen, and of the female heart, pure morality and delicate sentiment."⁵ But even her success in this magazine did not launch a full-time literary career, though Harriet apparently began devoting more of her leisure time to writing. The Beecher family had, however, become convinced she was a "prophetess," and her friends in the Semi-colon Club continued to encourage her writing.

In 1836 at age twenty-four Harriet Beecher married Calvin E. Stowe, who was the widower of one of her best friends and a professor at Lane Theological Seminary. In later years, she described him as "a man rich in Greek and Hebrew, Latin and Arabic, and alas! rich in nothing else." For the next fifteen years, Harriet's life was consumed by childbearing and rearing, and by strength-taxing poverty. In her words, these were "long years of struggling with poverty & sickness & hot debilitating climate [while six] children grew up around" her. Though she had little time for anything else, she continued to do some writing for publication as a way to supplement her husband's meager salary. She reported, "When a new carpet or a mattress was going to be needed, or when at the close of the year it began to be evident that my family accounts, like poor Dora's 'wouldn't add up'—then I used to say to my faithful friend and factotum Anne, who shared all my joys and sorrows—'Now if you will keep the babies & attend to the things in the house for one day, I'll write a piece & then we shall be out of the scrape,'—and so I became an authoress." As a result, Harriet gradually assumed responsibility for more than the usual "female" share of the household: in addition to supervising all the daily activities of the home, after 1844 she took charge of family finances and contributed more and more to the family's economic well-being. Though she had not begun writing for financial reasons, earning an income became an important part of her burgeoning literary career.⁶

A chronological reading of business correspondence in these years reveals that she was also slowly gaining self-confidence as a professional writer. In 1838 it was Catharine who submitted Harriet's work for her to Lydia Sigourney, the popular poet, asking that she (Sigourney) dispose of the pieces "*more profitably* (for it is a money-making effort) than [Harriet] or I could [do] at this distance from the headquarters of literature."⁷ However, by 1843 at age thirty-two, Harriet was taking some literary matters into her own hands. After Catharine interested the publishers Harper and Brothers in seeing her sister's work, Harriet and Calvin decided that Harriet herself should meet with them in New York. The Harpers' flattery, her successful negotiations with them for a collection of her short stories to be entitled *The Mayflower* (1843), as well as positive responses from other editors in the East, raised Harriet's hopes of becoming a "literary lady" and initiated a discussion in letters home to Calvin about adopting a literary career.

Stowe's first letter home to Cincinnati reveals her emerging self-assurance as a writer in its delicate interplay of surprise at her success and confidence in her abilities:

> I have seen Johnson of the "Evangelist." He is very liberally disposed, and I may safely reckon on being paid for all I do there. Who is that Hale, Jr., that sent me the "Boston Miscellany," and will he keep his word with me? His offers are very liberal—twenty dollars for three pages, not very close print. Is he to be depended on? If so, it is the best offer, I have received yet. I shall get something from the Harpers some time this winter or spring. Robertson, the publisher here [Hartford], says the book will sell, and though the terms they offer me are very low, that I shall make something on it. For a second volume I shall be able to make better terms. On the whole, my dear, if I choose to be a literary lady, I have, I think, as good a chance of making profit by it as any one I know of.[8]

Though still not wholly convinced she could manage a career with young children to raise, she nevertheless explained to Calvin that she needed a room of her own in which to write. In fact, she had even decided which room in the house it would be and how she would furnish it. Calvin's responses were enthusiastic: "You must be a *literary woman*. It is so written in the book of fate. Make all your calculations accordingly, get a good stock of health, brush up your mind, drop the E. out of your name, which only encumbers it and stops the flow and euphony, and write yourself only and always, *Harriet Beecher Stowe*, which is a name euphonious, flowing, and full of meaning; and, my word for it, your husband will lift up his head in the gate, and your children will rise up and call you blessed." In another letter, he wrote: "It is just as I told you in my last letter. God has written it in His book that you must be a literary woman, and who are we that we should contend against God? You must therefore make all your calculations to spend the rest of your life with your pen."[9]

Yet, despite his verbal support, Stowe's scholarly, affable husband did not go very far to otherwise facilitate her risen ambitions. Their marriage, though loving, was not idyllic, and its early years were marked by conflicts over sexuality, spousal expectations, and differing definitions of personal needs.[10] As if foreseeing and justifying more years of waiting for a full-fledged literary career, Harriet published a tract in 1845 with the suggestive title, *Earthly Care: A Heavenly Discipline*. Her earthly cares before *Uncle Tom's Cabin* was written in 1851 included at least two miscarriages, the birth of seven children, the death of one in a Cincinnati cholera epidemic, the physical strain of many household cares, the exposure to the tragedy of slavery, and the gradual collapse of Lane Theological Seminary, which eroded her husband's income. Thus, in the years before *Uncle Tom's Cabin* her literary career did not flourish, although her short stories and articles continued to appear from time to time.

Unassumingly, at forty years of age, Harriet Beecher Stowe stood on the threshold of her greatest literary success. Though seven months pregnant, she had recently moved her family to Brunswick, Maine, where Calvin was to take a position at Bowdoin College after completing his contract in Cincinnati. Not counting the early geography, she had published only one book, *The Mayflower*, so far in her literary career. Nevertheless, she had written enough stories and articles to be considered by Sarah Josepha Hale, editor for *Godey's Lady's Book*, for inclusion in a forthcoming book on distinguished women through the ages. Sixteen years of hardship had, however, dampened Harriet's confidence about becoming a "literary lady," and she indicated that she did not consider herself to be equal to "the multitude of fine female writers who have appeared in our country of late years."[11] It is ironic that when she wrote those words to Hale, her serial "Uncle Tom's Cabin" was appearing in the *National Era*. But no one guessed, least of all herself, how famous Harriet Beecher Stowe would become.

A number of interrelated motives—religious and moral conviction, a domestic perspective on the slave problem, and the continued economic needs of her family—prompted Stowe to write *Uncle Tom's Cabin*. She was inspired by God, she claimed later, to write the story; but equally she was inspired by the examples of her preacher family, working for right against wrong in the world. Her years in Cincinnati had gradually convinced her of the abolitionist position, and the Fugitive Slave Law of 1850 ignited her moral indignation. *Uncle Tom's Cabin*, then, was her response to the morally unjustifiable situation. Furthermore, her belief in the feminine values of family and home gave Stowe another reason to write her powerful novel; with heartfelt passion she described the rending of mother from child and of husband from wife under a slave system that did not respect families or other feminine values. In this regard, *Uncle Tom's Cabin* was her woman's cry against an uncaring system. Finally, she wrote to make money, for even at Bowdoin, Calvin's salary was not large enough for the family of eight. *Uncle Tom's Cabin*, as originally negotiated in book form, was meant to buy Harriet at least a new silk dress.[12]

Of course, *Uncle Tom's Cabin* brought Harriet and her family much more than that. When it appeared as a serial in the *National Era* from June 5, 1851, to April 1, 1852, its popularity was unprecedented. The first book edition of 5,000 copies, published two weeks before the conclusion of the serial in the *Era*, sold out within a week. In the first year, sales climbed to 300,000 copies. Translated into many languages, *Uncle Tom's Cabin* was sold in countries around the world and may be the most popular success *ever* of any single American work. It was surely the most talked about book of its time, eliciting a flood of praise, criticism, and debate after the first month of publication. Royalties paid to Stowe from sales in the United States during the first three months alone totaled $10,000. In the months that followed publication, imitators and detractors published their views of slavery. Dramatizations, card games, and other spin-offs were measures of its success for years afterward. By 1857 the book had sold half a million copies in the United States and, by some estimates, over a million and a half in pirated editions in England.[13] Its author was lionized in both America and Europe. Seemingly overnight, Harriet Beecher Stowe became rich and famous.

Although Stowe did receive a considerable sum for her best-seller, it is generally agreed that her book publisher, John P. Jewett, made much more money from the publication than she did. It is unclear who should be blamed for this financial inequity, however. When they were negotiating the contract, Jewett had offered the Stowes their choice of either the potentially more lucrative half-profits arrangement, under which publisher and author split costs and profits fifty-fifty, or a less risky 10 percent royalty. Harriet and Calvin apparently chose the royalty for three reasons: they believed they had no money to risk on the potential loss of the half-profits system; Jewett himself told them he thought they would make more on the royalty system; and their friend, Congressman Philip Greeley, advised against risking half-profits on a *woman's* novel dealing with an unpopular subject. Because married women could not sign contracts, Calvin signed the 10 percent royalty contract. It was just one week before the book's publication.[14]

From one perspective, it is hard to believe that by March 1852, when the contract was finally signed and the serial in the *National Era* had almost run its course, Jewett did not know the book was going to be a great success. Using this line of reasoning, Catharine Beecher claimed Jewett was a scoundrel who had purposely cheated the Stowes by persuading them to accept a 10 percent royalty. But it is equally hard to justify the Stowes's acceptance of the contract, since they, too, must have known the almost completed serial was being talked about everywhere; from this perspective, they certainly appear to have been responsible for their own financial loss. In 1884, Stowe defended herself in a letter to James Derby, the publisher and editor, by saying, "I was not such a fool as [Jewett] represents—altho I confess I *was* surprise[d] at the *extent* of the success."[15] Nevertheless, the negotiations with Jewett suggest that in 1852 she was not yet the fully self-confident writer she would become.

At the time, neither Harriet nor Calvin were prepared to be business successes. Temperamentally, Calvin was uninterested in figures and is said to have sometimes kept financial records on scraps of paper. As a girl, Harriet had disliked arithmetic, and neither her education nor her early career as a teacher had done much to develop her business skills. At the Western Female Institute in Cincinnati she was not given a salary, which she would have had to budget, but was permitted to draw upon school funds as needed. This practice eventually had led to a dispute with Catharine Beecher over the amount of money she had taken, but it is unclear whether this dispute taught her to be more careful with her accounts. It was probably in managing family finances that Harriet finally had her first substantial lessons in economics; after marrying, she learned to make ends meet and hire servants on the money from Calvin's minimal salary and her own literary sales. Nevertheless, the large windfall of *Uncle Tom's Cabin* caught her and Calvin unprepared. She had never previously been paid by check, and she and Calvin knew nothing about how to deposit money in a bank.[16]

Apparently the fact that Jewett was making more money than they were only slowly dawned on the Stowes. At first, Harriet was quick to praise Jewett to others. During her triumphant visits to England, however, she encountered publishers who informed her that she could be earning a higher profit on the book. Businessmen in this country later told her the same thing.[17] Still, for two more years she continued to do business with Jewett, who published *The Key to Uncle Tom's Cabin* (1853), *Autographs for Freedom* (1853), and other antislavery tracts as well as reissuing her earlier work. In 1854, she wrote him a letter reviewing the main points of her side in what had gradually become a heated debate:

> It has never been my intention or desire to make you pay back any part of the proceeds of Uncle Tom. . . . Neither was the question whether you had done right in making more money than I—The simple question that I

wished to present was[:] Were you correct in persuading me & Mr. Stowe that a ten percent contract on books that sell as mine have is better for us than a twenty percent one? On that question my mind was once settled by . . . your representations made to me in the conversations. . . . Hearing your statements and arguments & having none on the other side & being ignorant of business, I was convinced very naturally that your opinion was the correct one. . . . Did you do right to persuade Mr. Stowe that it was best for him to take ten percent on Uncle Tom when he wished to take twenty & you had offered half profits—and to persuade me afterwards to make the same for the Key & so endeavor to persuade me to adopt this as the best rule in future works[?][18]

By this time she had come to doubt Jewett's honesty, even though, or perhaps especially because, she had been "ignorant of business." She soon severed their relationship, moving her business to Phillips, Sampson and Company.

Stowe's reason for changing publishers had as much to do with Jewett's personality and apparent moral failings as with their unsatisfactory financial arrangements. Honor and trust in business relations were important to her, not only because of her moral, religious background but also because she had come to recognize that others—the dramatists, the British pirates—over whom she had no control were making fortunes from her work. In 1852 she had written Richard Bentley, one of the British publishers who did send her some royalties, thanking him for his "fairness and generosity." In the next month she praised him as a publisher who had "transcended the mere legal & technical ideas of right & acted on those principles of honor which are in themselves inimitable."[19]

While profits were a major concern, Stowe's letters suggest that the final straw was her lost faith in Jewett's good intentions. To her brother Edward she wrote, "I must say that the general character of Mr. Jewett as developed in the whole makes me feel increasingly that he is *not* the man I wish to be in business relations with. He is positive—overbearing—uneasy if crossed & unwilling to have fair inquiries made. So, it seems to me. . . . Peace of mind is worth more than money & there can be no peace in future relations with him—founded on arrangements which are subject to such difficulties." The lost royalties had come to seem less important than the lost trust. After this episode, she would always try to choose publishers and agents with "a reputation for probity and honor." Thus, she would make agreements with some publishers who paid her only 10 percent royalties if she thought they were honorable, and she would avoid publishers who were overbearing and unwilling to recognize the importance of her point of view.[20]

In contrast to Southworth, who in a similar situation allowed herself to be rescued by Robert Bonner, Stowe began educating herself about various aspects of business affairs while the controversy with Jewett brewed. Her letters in the 1850s show she was becoming increasingly astute about business. By making inquiries of other authors about compensation, she learned that Gamaliel Bailey should have paid her at least $400, rather than $300, for the serial publication of *Uncle Tom's Cabin*. She also sought information about publishing arrangements in England and about the advantages of publishing on a percentage basis or otherwise. In 1855 she tried to figure out how to arrange copyrights for dramatizations of *Uncle Tom's Cabin*. In 1856 she planned a second trip to England in order to secure British royalties on *Dred: A Tale of the Great Dismal Swamp* (1856) because she had learned that to demand royalties an American author had to be on British soil when the copyright application was made. By 1860 it was a thoroughly businesslike author who wrote the popular British writer Mrs. Gaskell proposing joint authorship of a book on Italy. "Could we not in some way," Stowe asked, "unite our forces without interfering with each others['] individuality, secure copyright mutually in our respective countries and divide the profits[?]."[21] Although this particular arrangement did not work out, Stowe's inquiry showed a conscientiousness about business as well as literary matters.

While she assertively pursued business knowledge, other opportunities increased her confidence in herself as a writer. After the publication of *Uncle Tom's Cabin*, the outpourings of praise and adulation from millions of people, but especially from the major literary figures of her time—Charles Dickens, George Sand, Henry Wadsworth Longfellow, and John Greenleaf Whittier, to name a few—elevated her self-esteem. The *Independent*, the leading religious newspaper in the country, hired her as a columnist for its pages in order to increase its prestige and influence, thereby increasing hers. Other journals regularly sought her contributions. Although these requests flattered her, she must have been most pleased in the late 1850s to discover how important she was to the funding of a new antislavery literary magazine; Phillips, Sampson and Company said it would back the *Atlantic Monthly*, as it came to be called, only if Harriet

Beecher Stowe would contribute a serial. When she agreed to do so, she joined a company of influential, popular writers including Oliver Wendell Holmes, James Russell Lowell, John Greenleaf Whittier, and Henry Wadsworth Longfellow in launching one of the most important literary magazines ever published.[22]

Stowe's increasing self-confidence as a professional writer can be traced in a few key business letters. Having recently completed *Uncle Tom's Cabin*, Stowe said, somewhat disingenuously, that she was "a very incompetent judge of [her] own performances as to their monied worth."[23] But by 1854, even while admitting she might not fully understand Jewett's point of view, she presented herself as no longer "ignorant of business" as she had been in her earlier dealings with him. Subsequently, in 1859, though she revealed doubts about the literary quality of *The Minister's Wooing* to *Atlantic* editor James Russell Lowell, she also bravely requested his advice and criticism. By the time she began working with James T. Fields in the 1860s, her professional correspondence expresses *no* concerns about her literary or business abilities.

As a result of her own efforts and the opportunities extended to her after *Uncle Tom's Cabin*, Stowe's earlier self-doubts had been transformed into the self-confident modesty with which she approached her mature career.[24] Consequently, in her professional correspondence with James Fields in the 1860s, she never begs for compliments, disparages her own work, or questions its value. Nor does she brag about her accomplishments. Instead, she is straightforward and matter-of-fact, assured of her value as a writer and humble about her achievements. Her self-confidence had not led to egotism because of other values she held. As a writer, she believed she was doing what she was supposed to be doing—working for right against wrong, speaking as an instrument of God, and spreading feminine values—rather than doing something individualistic that would justify boasting. For Stowe, humility, like other feminine values, was important in the world. In fact, her concept of womanhood was central to the pursuit of her mature career.

Stowe's views of womanhood, like her views of business and literature, had evolved over the years. As a child, she had been socialized by her father's religious values and her mother's example of True Womanhood. When she was being educated, she encountered her sister Catharine's convictions regarding the importance of woman's role as nurturer and moral example in the world. By the time she wrote *Uncle Tom's Cabin*, she believed, as Elizabeth Ammons, a Stowe scholar, argues, "femininity—

true womanliness—means unshakable allegiance to the Christian virtues of faith, hope, charity, mercy, and self-sacrifice; purity in body and mind; ethical dependence more on emotion than on reason; submission to mundane authority except when it violates higher laws; and protection of the home as a sacred and inviolable institution. . . . [These are] the only worthwhile human [values] because they place the welfare of the group, of the whole human family, before that of self."[25] Although these were the virtues of True Womanhood as popularly understood, for Stowe, they were not a justification for passivity or a wholly private life; rather, they were an assertion of the positive worth of female values that ought to be central to all human life.

According to Stowe, the home was not a haven from the world but the center of it. As Jane Tompkins has noted, for Stowe the home was "a dynamic center of activity, physical and spiritual, economic and moral, whose influence spreads out in ever-widening circles."[26] This view was the basis of her domestic feminism, a perspective combining a strong belief in "feminine" values with some demands for greater respect and rights. Stowe's views made her a moderate on the continuum of cultural beliefs about women in the nineteenth century. Unlike her more conservative sister Catharine, Harriet saw nothing wrong with woman suffrage, though she was never the radical activist her stepsister Isabella Hooker became. At least before the 1870s, when she became somewhat more conservative, Stowe supported the drive for women's rights and believed in women's self-reliance, rather than dependence. Even in the seventies when she criticized women's rights activists, she did so in the name of preserving feminine values, which she believed were being abandoned in favor of masculine greed, opportunism, selfishness, and self-indulgence.[27]

While her attitudes were not radical, her views of womanhood were more liberal than Southworth's. Women in Southworth's view could inspire goodness in men; women in Stowe's view would be the model that men themselves should follow. For Southworth, women were morally superior to men and should be so recognized; for Stowe, feminine values were morally superior and should be embraced by all. Despite her call for self-reliance, Southworth's femininity was relatively passive, while Stowe's was more active. These distinct outlooks were also reflected in their different attitudes toward the creation of literature.

Although not wishing to lead anyone astray with her fiction, Southworth had a less didactic desire than Stowe to improve humanity with her work; Stowe, on the other hand, saw her role as that of a guiding light in her home and to the country through her fiction. In that sense, Stowe spoke from a more thoroughly Victorian perspective. Whereas Southworth's feminine values led to the creation of literary works for home entertainment, Stowe's values led to the advocacy of a literature that had a clear, ethical purpose and performed a public service. Thus, with *Uncle Tom's Cabin* Stowe said she wanted to "speak a word for freedom and humanity." She was pleased that "the use of the novel in the great questions of moral life is coming to be one of the features of the age" and argued that such literary works were like parables and should be judged as moral instruments, not simply as literary or artistic works.[28]

Stowe's domestic feminism encouraged her always to value moral and domestic goals in fiction—goals that were often synonymous in her view. So, for instance, she stressed the moral intentions of *Oldtown Folks* (1869), a work she hoped would be a "resume of the whole spirit & body of New England—a country that now is exerting such an influence on the civilized world that to know it truly becomes an object." She thought it was important for everyone to understand the strong moral fiber of New England's views. In another work, her aim was to spread women's domestic views throughout society. "House & Home Papers," written during the Civil War for the *Atlantic*, would be, she told James Fields, "a sort of spicy, sprightly writing that I feel I need to write in these days to keep from thinking of things that make me dizzy & blind & fill my eyes with tears so that I can't see the paper. I mean such things as are being done where our nerves are dying as Shaw said—It is not wise that all our literature should run in a rut cut thro our hearts & red with our blood—I feel the need of a little gentle household merriment & talk of common things." This was not escapism but a plea for the recognition of domestic values as the basis of a just society.[29]

While Stowe's domestic feminism led her to affirm moral and domestic literary aims, it also was used by her to justify her somewhat haphazard literary style. While admitting the technical faults of *Uncle Tom's Cabin*, she said she "no more thought of style or literary excellence than the mother who rushes into the street and cries for help to save her children from a burning house, thinks of the teachings of the rhetorician or the elocutionist."[30] For Stowe, style was only important insofar as it was appropriate for the writer and the message. She did not believe in trying to conform to others' sense of aesthetics; instead, she advocated cultivating a literary individuality such as she herself tried to preserve by not reading the work of others while her own was in progress. Furthermore, in an 1869 series of articles on literary work, she advised writers to tell a story vividly and dramatically, to use simplicity and concreteness in writing, and to avoid affectation and overused expressions. In these ways she thought writers could reach out and spread their moral and domestic views of the world.

Stowe's domestic feminism affected not only her views of literary goals and style, but also her attitudes toward herself as a writer. Early in her career, she adopted a line of argument familiar to "Super Moms" today. Stowe vowed "not to be a mere domestic slave" and justified her literary work as a way of earning money in order to be a better mother *and* a better person. In 1838, she wrote a friend, "I mean to have money enough to have my house kept in the best manner and yet to have time for reflection and that preparation for the education of my children which every mother needs. . . . [As a result of my income from writing] I am not only more comfortable but my house affairs and my children are in better keeping than when I was pressed and worried and teased in trying to do more than I could. I have now leisure to think—to plan—contrive—see my friends, make visits, etc. besides superintending all that is done in my house even more minutely than when I was shut up in my nursery."[31] In other words, even at the beginning of her writing career, she affirmed both her own needs and her family responsibilities. She would continue to do so throughout her life.

Even though Stowe saw writing and family as potentially compatible, the actual responsibilities of each were frequently at odds, even after the publication of *Uncle Tom's Cabin*. Her dual commitments are clearly represented in the two different types of excuses she gave for delays in the preparation of *Oldtown Folks* (1869). First, she defended the delay in terms of commitment to her writing: "Instead of rushing on, I have often turned back and written over with care, that nothing that I wanted to say might be omitted; it has cost me a good deal of labor to elaborate this first part, namely, to build my theatre and to introduce my actors." Later, she emphasized family responsibilities: "I have a long story to tell you of *what* [family obligation] has prevented my going on with my story, which you must see would so occupy all the nerve and brain force I have that I have not been able to write a word except to my own children."[32] For Stowe, the solution to the conflict created by dual commitments was sometimes to focus on writing and other times to focus on family. Unlike Southworth who devoted set times each day to writing as a method of dividing time between family and career, Stowe seems to have worked in less structured ways, sometimes devoting all of her time to writing and at other times, all to her family.

Time and again she faced situations that conflicted with her literary needs. For Stowe, writing was a process of meditation and inspiration that was easily sidetracked by household demands, children's needs, and social expectations like visiting. She explained the difficulties by saying, "the process [of creative writing] is to retire to the secret caverns & dip ones pen quietly and let the ink in ones inkstand settle *clear* & look into a drop of ink till you begin to see images & visions—but if anybody flutters or disturbs or makes an outcry—whisk away go visions & dreams & all ones little spider webs that beginning to stick are broken."[33] An alcoholic son, Calvin's ill health, Beecher family disputes, and the troubles of building a new home in Hartford were among the disturbances that slowed Stowe's mature literary work. But they did not stop it. As primary breadwinner, author, wife, and mother, Stowe juggled the demands of her profession with those of her family throughout her life and found that both activities could be exhausting. Nevertheless, economic needs as well as her domestic feminism kept her from giving up either her family or her career.

By 1859, Harriet Beecher Stowe's career was in full flower. She was considered to be the most important woman writer in America and, as a result of her royalties, was fairly well-to-do. While she wanted to maintain the high level of her income, she also aspired, as we have seen, to a role of moral guardianship in her work. Because she had been through the disillusioning experience with John P. Jewett, she was more than ever interested in working with a publisher whom she could trust. Moreover, she had adopted a philosophy of domestic feminism that justified her self-assertion and the promotion of feminine values in her career. In her business association with James T. Fields in the 1860s, Stowe found a publisher who helped her earn a sizable income while publishing literature with moral and domestic aims; who was trustworthy, loyal, and friendly; and who responded flexibly to her domestic feminism. In fact, they had such a solid relationship that there was no question of either abandoning the other in the biggest crisis of Stowe's career, the publication of "The True Story of Lady Byron" in 1869.

Ten years before that crisis, while she was on her third and final trip to Europe, Stowe met James Fields and his wife Annie in Italy.[34] They enjoyed each other's company so much that Stowe changed her travel plans in order to sail back to the United States with them. Beyond anticipating pleasant company for the trip home, Stowe undoubtedly saw an opportunity to develop a friendship with the man whom many considered to be the most important publisher of his time. As a highly respected member of his profession, Fields conformed to the ideals of the Gentleman Publisher, developing personal relationships with his writers and publishing literature with high moral and cultural aims. In addition, he was known for his charm, his good taste, and his astute sense of the literary marketplace. His firm, Ticknor and Fields, was the publisher of many of the most highly respected English and American authors of the nineteenth century. By 1859 the firm had purchased the *Atlantic Monthly* from its bankrupt owners Phillips, Sampson and Company. When he and Harriet met, then, Fields clearly was a publisher worth knowing. But so, too, was the world-famous Stowe. On the voyage home, the new friends wove good times into a warm friendship that would be the basis for their business dealings in the years ahead.

The friendship Stowe developed with James and Annie Fields was certainly one of the strongest publishing associations she ever had. Stowe corresponded regularly with them, both about business and personal matters. She was a frequent guest in their home, as were other members of her family. She did many things with them, from reading manuscripts and trying to save street urchins to attending parties and exchanging recipes with Annie. She had a high regard for Fields as friend and publisher, calling him in 1868 "my friend and pitcher . . . who has always done well by me & is an agreeable man to boot, & his wife still more so." After his death, she described him as "noble, just, kindly, upright & pure[,] . . . [a man who had a] play of humor which made him so delightful a companion."[35] For them, friendship and business were deeply intertwined: her letters to James, devoted almost wholly to business, have brief greetings at the close for Annie; her personal letters to Annie or to both of them, though social, often mention business matters.

With James Fields, Stowe had a business relationship that approximated the one idealized by Gentlemen Publishers. But her association with Fields did not fall into the same pattern as E.D.E.N. Southworth's with Robert Bonner. Stowe's philosophy of domestic feminism influenced her expectations and behavior in such a way as to give her more power as a writer and business person than Southworth had. In contrast to Southworth, Stowe had a friendly but nonexclusive commitment with her publisher. Though she accepted his generosity as a "provider," she never let him dictate the financial terms of their association. Moreover, she negotiated compensation straightforwardly and with self-confidence. In addition to assuming expertise in her own sphere, she also advised the publisher about his. Overall, she was much more assertive than Southworth in the pursuit of her career.

First of all, while their dealings were characterized by friendliness, loyalty, and trust, Stowe never carried her loyalty to Fields to the extreme that Southworth did in her exclusive commitment to Bonner. Many aspects of the Fields-Stowe relationship—such as her letting him make some of the arrangements for British publication of her work and her assuming his honesty in keeping her royalty accounts—show that she trusted him. From 1861 until his retirement in 1871, he published her major books and articles, but sometimes other friendships or the possibility of additional income tempted her to send her work elsewhere. Thus, in 1865 she told Fields that once again she wanted to make an exception to her "exclusive" contract with him, explaining, "The W[atchman] & Reflector, have been always remarkably honorable & gentlemanly in their treatment of me and are anxious to have six pieces for the coming year for which they offer so good a sum that I would like to accept thinking you would make no objections." In 1871 when the new firm, Osgood and Company, was launched after Fields's retirement, she assured James R. Osgood that her loyalty to the firm would remain the same, noting also that she expected the same freedom to occasionally send her work elsewhere: "My feelings towards the new firm are just the same as I expressed in 1869 in so far as the bulk of my works are concerned—tho[ugh] there may be now and then an exception."[36] In this way, Stowe maintained her independence and self-determination within a framework of friendly, loyal author-publisher relations. She was comfortable working with a Gentleman Publisher but far from acquiescent. In contrast to the exclusive commitment of E.D.E.N. Southworth to Robert Bonner, the Fields-Stowe association shows more flexibility on the publisher's side and greater self-determination on the author's.

Like Bonner and other Gentlemen Publishers, Fields often provided financial services for Stowe, but, unlike Southworth, Stowe accepted those services as a matter of course, rather than as an unusual favor. Among the many services that Fields often provided for his favorite authors was allowing them to draw in advance on their accounts. Stowe took advantage of this benefit by sometimes asking for money in advance or referring bills to her publisher for payment. Annie Fields complained in her biography of Stowe that Stowe overstepped her bounds when she received $10,000 in advances during the preparation of *Oldtown Folks*. But Stowe herself apparently did not think so. James Fields made a practice of generosity to keep his writers with him, and, in fact, at least two of them—James Russell Lowell and Nathaniel Hawthorne—sometimes worried about being overpaid. This was not so for Stowe. A $10,000 advance may have been extreme on Fields's part, but it was not unheard of in the publishing business. Robert Bonner gave that much to Edward Everett for his series on Mount Vernon. In the long run, *Oldtown Folks* was one of the author's most popular books and certainly recouped Fields's investment.[37]

While Stowe willingly accepted Fields's financial assistance, she, unlike Southworth, never let her publisher dictate the terms of their agreements. She was not at all circumspect in asking for what she wanted from Fields. In 1863, after describing her plan for "House & Home Papers," she said in her typical manner, "I shall want about a hundred dollars a number for them & we will talk about a book after." Similarly, in a letter to him in 1866, she concluded, "Finally dear friend let there be no doubt of the material understanding between us. I understand that you [will] pay me for twelve months to come the same two hundred per month that I have been receiving for Atlantic articles & I [will] continue my series in the Young Folks [at $50 a number]." In contrast to Southworth's passivity in accepting contracts from Bonner, Stowe never put off stating what she expected to receive, but always specified what she wanted to be paid in her first letter regarding a new project. This financial assertiveness held true with other publishers, even in the case of a proposed obituary about her recently deceased husband in 1886! Though she apparently did not sign formal contracts with Fields until 1870, she always had a clear understanding with him about payment.[38]

While her primary strategy for securing compensation was to tell Fields straightforwardly what she wanted, she used a variety of other techniques in her negotiations, some, but not all, of them as manipulative as Southworth's with Bonner. For instance, Stowe sometimes mentioned what others had offered to pay her, as a reminder to Fields of what she was worth. In one letter, she agreed that, if Fields would make up what she could earn by writing elsewhere, she would write just for him. Another time, she threatened (successfully) to accept another offer if he did not respond soon to her letter. Occasionally, like Southworth, she explained why a personal difficulty necessitated certain payments, hoping, it seems, to play on his sympathies. Her most important negotiating strategy, however, was not binding herself to exclusive commitments with Fields, thereby giving herself the negotiating power of having other opportunities in reserve. The latter strategy was in marked contrast to Southworth's avoidance of competitive options in her career.[39]

In an equally self-confident manner, Stowe always expected to be paid fairly for her work, and what she considered fair increased over time. Of course, because her regular readership was estimated at 150,000 she could demand the right price, and the records suggest that she received payments in line with other major writers of her time. In fact, although Fields paid her well, she did not simply accept his offers but continued to negotiate firmly for compensation: for *Agnes of Sorrento* (1862) she received $200 an installment in the *Atlantic*, plus half-share profits on the book. Stowe refused Fields's first offer of $6,000 outright for the serial and first-year book rights on *Oldtown Folks*, reasoning as follows: "I am just offered $2,000 by an English paper for a weekly story that should run through one year—of about half the length of this—and an American paper offers me $4,000 for the simultaneous issue in America, and then I am to have the disposal of the profits in book form in both countries afterwards. I made on *The Minister's Wooing* in America alone, $7,500, and in England, $4,000. On *Dred* I made $10,000 in England, and an equal sum in America. Now, however times may have changed, I cannot suppose but what, with a book *better* than either of the two, I may make quite as much as you offer. Is it not so?"[40] And who could argue with that? Certainly Fields could not.

Although generally well compensated for her work, Stowe, like many authors, including Mary Abigail Dodge (Gail Hamilton), had a vague dissatisfaction that she should be paid more money. Stowe told James Parton, biographer and husband of Sara Payson Parton (Fanny Fern), that she thought she was underpaid for her book *Men of Our Times* (1868), published by a Hartford subscription firm, and that she thought writers should join together to agree on compensation for their contributions to anthologies because literary people were "modest & unfit to make a bargain."[41] Though she said this to Parton, showing fellow feeling for another author, she never acted particularly "modest" or "unfit" in literary negotiations, especially with her major publisher, James Fields. The financial problems that haunted her later in life were not due to inadequate negotiating skills but rather to high expenditures on behalf of others and to her costly real estate investments in Hartford, Connecticut, and Mandarin, Florida.

The assertiveness and self-confidence that Stowe displayed in handling negotiations carried over in her attitudes toward her authorial responsibilities. Like E.D.E.N. Southworth, Stowe wanted free rein in terms of the substance of her work. With publishers, she would debate the titles of pieces, but never their content or scope. She sometimes read her work in progress to Fields, as she did to family and friends who would listen, but she did so for the praise, not for critical analysis. There are few indications that Fields gave her much criticism anyway on the content of her work. But while she thought ideas were the responsibility of the writer, she admitted being careless about punctuation and capitalization, which she expected her publisher's assistants to supply. William Dean Howells, who used Stowe as an example of great writers whose work had benefited by proofreading at the *Atlantic*, said, "Nothing was ever written into her work, but in changes of diction, in correction of solecisms, in transposition of phrases, the text was largely rewritten on the margins of her proofs."[42] In addition to assuming that such editorial details need not bother her, she sometimes expected Fields to find information for her, to correct proofs himself, or, even in the case of one 1864 "House & Home" article, to have Annie fill in missing information. Apparently, such minor items were less important to her than the message of her work.

While confident about her ability to manage her writer's sphere, Stowe was equally assertive about giving advice to her publisher regarding his responsibilities. Unlike Southworth, who did not offer Bonner much advice, Stowe felt herself knowledgeable enough about the publishing business to offer Fields suggestions about the most profitable ways of publishing her works. During her association with him, she proposed the timing of book releases, worried about illustrators, and discussed releasing new editions of her books. She also made recommendations about advertising and marketing.[43] She had always been eager that her books be marketed well; indeed, as early as *Uncle Tom's Cabin* she herself had sent copies of her book to many important people who might help make it known. Despite Fields's acknowledged expertise in book promotion, she continued the practice of strategically distributing her books when working with him. Frequently she promoted her own proposals by using arguments that would appeal to his business interests, such as creating variety in the magazine or responding to audience desires. In short, Stowe seems to have had, at this point in her career, enough confidence to tell her publisher what to do. In this case, as in her financial negotiations and nonexclusive commitment with her publisher, Stowe's self-concept and philosophy of domestic feminism had created a writer's sphere much wider and more powerful than Southworth's ever was.

Her professional self-confidence was also expressed in her relationship with her husband. By the 1860s Stowe felt herself fully capable of overseeing all aspects of her career with minimal help from Calvin. He was not involved in negotiations with James Fields, as he had been with John P. Jewett. Instead, he had become Harriet's muse, resource, and audience. Sometimes he was the inspiration for her stories. *Oldtown Folks* and *Oldtown Fireside Stories* (1871), for instance, were fictional transcriptions of Calvin's stories from his youth. At other times she asked him for theological or historical details. She used him as an audience on whom to test her work, because he "is so nervous and so afraid of being bored that I feel as if it were something to hold him."[44] At the height of her career, she was the head and heart of her marital relationship, as she was of her career.

Because Stowe's sense of autonomy and assertiveness altered the balance of power from what it would have been in a more conventional author-publisher relationship, one can imagine that Fields felt he had less control over Stowe than he might have liked. How much easier it must have been for Bonner to work with an author like Southworth, who conformed to the traditional woman's/writer's role. A less genial publisher than Fields might not have responded so willingly to Stowe's demands. In fact, he did sometimes feel annoyed. Annie Fields reports that he was especially irritated by Stowe's slowness in completing *Oldtown Folks*.[45] Perhaps Stowe's refusal to make an exclusive commitment with him was also frustrating. But their relationship was most dramatically tested when she decided to publish what turned out to be one of the most sensational articles of the nineteenth century—a piece publicly denouncing Lord Byron's incest with his half sister and his mistreatment of his wife. Before and during the "Byron whirlwind," as Oliver Wendell Holmes called it, Stowe's behavior and that of her publishers were influenced by Stowe's views of herself as woman and as writer as well as by mutually accepted assumptions about the Gentleman Publisher's responsibilities.

The chain of events that led to this test of the Fields-Stowe relationship began simply enough in a friendly meeting of Lady Byron and Harriet during her first trip to England in 1853. Their friendship rapidly developed into an intimate one, and in 1856 Lady Byron confided her husband's personal history to Stowe. As an admirer of Lord Byron's poetry, Stowe was shocked, both at his incestuous relationship with his half sister and at the way he had viciously maligned the religious and self-sacrificing Lady Byron. When one of Byron's mistresses, Countess Guiccioli, published her story of his life in 1869, portraying Lady Byron as a cold, mercenary woman who destroyed the poet, Stowe rushed to defend her now deceased friend. First she wrote "The True Story of Lady Byron," which was published in the September 1869 issue of *Atlantic Monthly*; then, after the public's criticism, she prepared a book-length defense of the story, *Lady Byron Vindicated* (1870).

The public furor that was unleashed against Stowe by her disclosures was beyond anyone's expectations. Just after the article appeared, Howells had assured Fields, "I believe I haven't got into difficulty with anyone, made you enemies or changed the general policy of the magazine." Although there were already some negative comments, he did not expect the great storm ahead. Mary Abigail Dodge, defending Stowe three years later, described the general reaction:

> It is not three years since blind rage and brutal ridicule from one end of this nation to the other were showered by men upon a woman, the latchets of whose shoes they were not worthy to unloose. And for what? For that which, at its very worst, was an indiscretion. If this woman had been herself guilty of the crime which she disclosed of another, she could not have been more severely censored ... a woman whose goodness is as sublime as her genius is brilliant, who has never touched pen to paper but for the furtherance of truth and humanity—a woman whose name is one of the brightest gems in her country's crown and whose light is gone out to the end of the earth.

Stowe was charged with scandalmongering, with bragging about her friendship with British aristocracy, and with devising sensational ways of increasing her income. Her old enemies *and* her old friends in the presses of England and the United States attacked for months. Very few papers defended her and the *Atlantic* ultimately lost 15,000 subscribers in the aftermath.[46]

Stowe seems to have been inspired to tell Lady Byron's story in the first place because she wanted to defend "respectable" womanhood from the charges of the "impure." She described Lady Byron as "a character remarkable for truthfulness, accuracy, self-control, patience, and above all conscientiousness." Stowe also seems to have felt that, by writing the article, she was rescuing women in general from uncaring men. She wrote Horace Greeley, "I consider Lady Byron's story as a type of the old idea of woman: that is, a creature to be crushed and trodden under foot whenever her fate and that of a man come in conflict." Stowe intended to save her.[47]

She had prepared her article in the summer of 1869, despite receiving many indications that there would be trouble with its publication. She did not stop work on the project even though friends in Hartford to whom she read the story were shocked that she would consider publishing it. Calvin tried to dissuade her. James R. Osgood, Fields's junior partner, told her he had some reservations, and William Dean Howells, then the relatively inexperienced acting editor of the *Atlantic*, sought the advice of James Russell Lowell and Oliver Wendell Holmes, but they disagreed about its publication. James Fields, vacationing in Europe, was told of the article by Howells, who expressed an opinion that Fields probably would have adopted himself: "It was awkwardly done . . . but I think the story is true and ought to have been told." But no matter how minimal the support, the determined Stowe would not be dissuaded. She would accept suggestions on how the article was to be written, but not on whether it should be written. To Holmes she communicated the attitude she adopted toward all: "When you have read my article, I want, *not* your advice as to whether the main facts should be told, for on this point I am so resolved that I frankly say advice would do me no good. But you might help me, with your delicacy and insight, to make the *manner of telling* more perfect; and I want to do it as wisely and well as such a story can be told."[48]

Stowe claimed she was authorized to tell Lady Byron's story because Byron had himself discussed his wife and incest in his poetry. Stowe argued that Byron "belongs to the world for which he wrote, to which he appealed, and before which he dragged his reluctant, delicate wife to a publicity equal with his own; the world has, therefore, a right to judge him." Although she agreed with most of the literary world that private lives generally should not be opened to the public, she also thought that those private lives needed to be respectable and morally pure in order to create good literature. The latter belief, in concert with her desire to defend abused wifehood, overcame her usual inclination to protect someone's private life. Her crusade became a defense of right against wrong: "When a noble name is accused, any person who possesses truth which might clear it and withholds that truth, is guilty of a sin against human nature and the inalienable claims of justice. I claim that I have not only a right, but an obligation, to bring in my solemn testimony upon this subject."[49]

Fields and his literary establishment did not abandon Stowe during this crisis because, as Gentlemen Publishers, they were expected to honor their long-term ties. Biographers report that when James Fields returned from Europe in October 1869, he was so angry he would not speak to Stowe.[50] However, the anger quickly dissipated and he never deserted her.

As senior publisher, he could, of course, have refused to publish the book, *Lady Byron Vindicated*. He did somewhat distance himself from Stowe by assigning James Osgood principal responsibility for overseeing the details of preparing the book; Fields always disliked unpleasantness, as shown in his dispute with Mary Abigail Dodge, discussed in the next chapter. Nevertheless, he read the final manuscript, debated the title, and checked the authenticity of some evidence published in the *London Quarterly*. Harriet and Calvin both wrote to him, appealing to his sympathy in the hard times. Calvin informed him about new disclosures that seemed to support his wife's case. Harriet said, somewhat apologetically, "You must all *help* lift this stone."[51] Publisher and author weathered the storm together.

A sense of moral guardianship on both sides also encouraged them to pursue their course. Originally, William Dean Howells justified publishing Stowe's article by expressing a sense of moral guardianship that Fields himself would have affirmed; Howells told his own father that Byron's story would be a great service to the world because its lesson would save pure young souls from undue suffering.[52] Stowe's impulse was also to provide a moral example: to "vindicate the fair fame of the noblest most Christ-like human being that it ever was my privilege to call friend." Even after she was so sharply criticized, she continued to insist it was a moral campaign that she waged: "You must be up and doing," she wrote her publishers, "and help me. This is war to the knife and the enemy are perfectly unscrupulous."[53] Her publishers agreed, even at the risk of financial loss.

Biographers have argued that the furor unleashed against Stowe effectively ruined her career and her long-term reputation. Investigation of that claim is beyond the scope of this chapter. In the short run, certainly, it did not matter. She published several popular books in the years following, including *My Wife and I* (1871), *Oldtown Fireside Stories* (1871), *Pink and White Tyranny* (1871), *Palmetto Leaves* (1873), and *Poganuc People* (1878), and she continued to be a popular contributor to various magazines and papers. She went on two successful lecture tours in New England and the Midwest and admirers continued to solicit autographs and interviews.

If the sensation hurt her literary reputation, it did not irreparably damage her relations with her publishers. In the year following the article, Fields published *Oldtown Fireside Stories* in the *Atlantic* and after his retirement in 1871 remained on friendly terms with her for the rest of his life.[54] Although her work did not reappear in the *Atlantic* until 1879, apparently because she made extensive commitments to the *Christian Union* edited by her brother, the successors to Fields's firm continued to publish most of her books. James Osgood, who espoused similar values and took over the firm after Fields's retirement, reissued many of her earlier books and wanted to publish all of her new ones; she chose to give some to her *Christian Union* publisher, J. B. Ford, however. When Osgood sold out to Henry O. Houghton, Houghton took over her works and purchased others from Ford, eventually publishing a sixteen-volume set of Stowe's works in 1896 (not including *Lady Byron Vindicated*). Houghton also carried on the *Atlantic* tradition of giving a seventieth-year birthday party for its major contributors by organizing one for Stowe in 1882. Though the author-publisher ties were still strong, no one alluded to the Byron affair during the festivities. The bonds of the author-publisher relationship had stretched but had not been broken in the difficulties attending publication of the Byron article.

Harriet Beecher Stowe's association with James T. Fields provides another example of the ways in which the attitudes and behaviors of Gentlemen Publishers accommodated women writers. But, while the major expectations of the Fields-Stowe relationship were similar to those of Robert Bonner and E.D.E.N. Southworth, there were important differences in the ways in which the individuals fulfilled those expectations. Though each woman had a successful relationship, they would not have been happy in each other's. Stowe needed more autonomy and independence, Southworth more protection and dependence. Stowe wanted to exert power, Southworth was satisfied exerting influence. Stowe was happy with Fields because of his flexibility in responding to her demands. Southworth was happy with Bonner because of his more structured forms of authorial support.

Stowe had a more progressive view of the woman writer's professional role than Southworth, but even Stowe's demands had their limits. While Southworth essentially accepted conventional views of gender and the woman writer, Stowe's domestic feminism gave her a more expansive sense of gender and professional behavior. But another, younger writer by the pen name of Gail Hamilton would go even further than Stowe, calling into question the ideal of traditional spheres in gender relations as well as in literary business.

5

Mary Abigail Dodge
From Gail Hamilton's Life in Letters, *vol. 1.*
Edited by
H. Augusta Dodge.
Boston: Lee and Shepard, 1901.

The Battle for a Fair Marketplace

Mary Abigail Dodge versus
James T. Fields

After her death, Mary Abigail Dodge (1833–96), known to her readers as "Gail Hamilton," was remembered in the *Independent* as "the most brilliant American woman of her generation." She had dazzled many with her informed, witty, and decisive articles on politics, religion, and women. Her sister-in-spirit, Sara Payson Parton (Fanny Fern), described her as "a lady, at whose mention stalwart men have been known to tremble, and hide in corners; who 'keeps a private graveyard' for the burial of those whom she has mercilessly slain; who respects neither the spectacles of the judge, nor the surplice of the priest; who holds the mirror up to men's failings till they hate their wives merely because they belong to her sex." Harriet Beecher Stowe said Dodge was "a trump—a real original—healthy—largehearted & simple minded & good as she can be." The author Rebecca Harding Davis called her "a thoroughly Western woman. . . . Rough, democratic, hardy, [with the] common sense [that] is the strength of western people."[1] A very different woman than either E.D.E.N. Southworth or Harriet Beecher Stowe, Mary Abigail Dodge, like the others, worked in a literary marketplace influenced by widely shared cultural assumptions about male and female spheres.

Fourteen years younger than Southworth and twenty-two years younger than Stowe, Mary Abigail Dodge was born in Hamilton, Massachusetts, on March 31, 1833, the seventh and last child of the farmer James Brown Dodge and the former schoolteacher Hannah Stanwood Dodge. In contrast to both Emma Nevitte (Southworth) and Harriet Beecher (Stowe), "Abby," as she was called by her family and friends, had the good fortune to be born into a close and relatively prosperous family, whose roots in this country were over two hundred years old. In his town her father was known as a kind husband and father, fine dancer, and lover of good company. Her mother was a good singer, a great reader, and a skillful seamstress.[2] Perhaps because she was the youngest child, or perhaps just because she was *their* child, Abby seems to have received constant love and support from her parents. There are indications that she was even somewhat spoiled; it is certain that she was the center of attention.

The Dodge home had not only enough happiness in it to instill a love of family and a great devotion toward parents in Abby, but also enough discontent in it to keep her from complacently following the usual feminine path, however honorable. From observing her mother, whom she dearly loved, toiling constantly to care for her family, Abby learned that "the mother transmits to her child not so much the tastes which she gratifies as those which she represses. I think that is why... I always liked books and hated housework, liked leisure and independence and hated drudgery with a mortal hatred."[3] Defiant and headstrong, Abby began to express "strong-minded" views about housework and woman's sphere at an early age. Her parents apparently accepted those feelings in her and let her go her own way with books, outdoor play, and verse writing. They did not wish she had been a boy, as Stowe's father had; rather, they seem to have believed in and encouraged her from her earliest years.

Her childhood, in fact, seems to have provided her with many opportunities to express herself, including, but not restricted to, what was culturally considered "feminine." Though she was raised in an orthodox Congregational church and was encouraged to study the Bible, she was not pursued by injunctions of a stern Calvinism or other cultural messages saying that she was inferior to men; instead, she came to believe that she had as much an obligation to God to develop her character and individuality as any man did. Furthermore, she was allowed, apparently even encouraged, to enjoy the freedom of the outdoors. Sara Payson Parton (Fanny Fern) claimed that Abby "was brought up as New England girls are generally brought up in the country—simply, healthfully, purely, with plenty of fences for gymnastics; ... with plenty of ... romping companions, not subjects for early tombstones and obituary notices, but with broad chests, sun-kissed faces, and nimble limbs and tongues."[4] Like so many other tomboys, she learned to run and climb, to garden, and to enjoy the natural things in life. Just as Emma Nevitte had thrived in the Maryland countryside of her grandmother's home, Abby gained a sense of independence and self-reliance and learned the joys of being physically fit.

Unlike Southworth, however, whose intelligence went unrecognized for many years, Dodge quickly impressed those around her, as had Harriet Beecher Stowe. Abby began attending school at the age of two and reportedly took up advanced geography at five and essay writing at six. She was sent to boarding school in Cambridge when she was twelve, then, the next year, to the outstanding Ipswich Female Seminary, an academy that stressed intellectual achievement and self-reliance in women. Although not comparable to a men's college, Ipswich provided a better education than most academies, on a par with the Hartford Female Seminary of Catharine Beecher. At Ipswich Seminary, Abby Dodge studied French, Latin, German, algebra, history, chemistry, and philosophy, and her friends teased her about becoming a "poetess."[5] When she graduated in 1850 at age seventeen, she was immediately hired to teach at the seminary.

Unlike Southworth and Stowe who started teaching as something to do before marriage, Dodge had planned for years to pursue some kind of profession. Her commitment to a career was partially influenced by her belief that her personal appearance made her unattractive to others. Blinded in her left eye by an accident when she was two, she always considered herself to be ugly. While in school she wrote, "The fact that I was ugly, surpassingly ugly, ugly in form—ugly in feature, has been ineffaceably impressed upon my mind." That conviction made her self-conscious and shy as she was growing up. Even in adulthood, she "never . . . could bear to be looked at," though her bright wit, noteworthy conversation, and elegant evening dresses made people less aware of her unmatched eyes. Nevertheless, she always perceived a connection between physical appearance and women's options in life, writing in 1863, "Now I maintain a woman ought to be very handsome . . . or else she ought to go to work and do something." And do something she did, with such energy that at her death the *Woman's Journal* recalled her face as "a keenly intelligent [one]. Her eyes were bright and penetrating. She looked like a bright, broad-minded woman."[6]

Although she enjoyed her students at Ipswich Seminary in the early 1850s, this "bright, broad-minded woman" soon longed for the stimulation of a larger town. In 1854 she accepted a post at the Hartford Female Seminary, founded but no longer run by Catharine Beecher. A year later she was hired by the Hartford High School. At the time, she refused to take the school board's examination for new teachers, insisting that members watch her teach, not give her a test.[7] Her arguments convinced them and they relented. As it turned out, Dodge was an excellent teacher, inspiring her students in the subjects she taught, including Latin, math, English, and physical science.

Although she was earning six hundred dollars a year—more than twice what Southworth had made as a teacher—and enjoying her students, friends, and the social life of Hartford, increasingly Dodge contemplated a full-time writing career. Her family had always encouraged her literary efforts and she flattered herself that she might one day be a highly respected author like Harriet Beecher Stowe. She knew that to be a good writer she needed time "to think and correct and alter," but she found it difficult to work on her writing while fulfilling the obligations of teaching.[8] Still, she wrote and published a few fugitive pieces. Then in January 1856, she sent an anonymous submission to the *National Era*, edited by Dr. Gamaliel Bailey, the same editor who had first published *Uncle Tom's*

Cabin and who had also encouraged the early work of Southworth. Addressing him with the humor for which she would become publicly known, she wrote:

> Sir—If you are not in a mood to be disturbed I beg you to take out the postage stamp which I enclose with this—burn the whole package, and send me word immediately that you have done so. If on the other hand, I may be allowed to occupy a half hour of your valuable time—allow me to say at once that I desire to become a contributor to the 'Era'. . . . [I do not] write entirely for money, as at this particular juncture I am tolerably well off, though an income of five hundred dollars and an expenditure of one thousand will sometimes produce embarrassment. . . . [I want to] see whether [the submission] be of sufficient merit to interest your readers, or [is] of real worth. . . . If you think the pieces worthless, you will not hesitate to say so and I promise not to drown myself.[9]

At first Bailey, who was always hard-pressed for funds, could only offer encouragement and the promise he would send her fifty dollars at the end of the year in compensation for any submissions she might make during the year. While meager, this sum was better than she had hoped for, so she agreed to send him something. She also began writing occasional pieces for the *Independent*, the most important Christian newspaper in the country, which was publishing major literary works of the time. For a couple of years she continued with great difficulty to try to balance teaching and writing activities. Meanwhile, she worked hard at perfecting her literary style and sought advice from popular writers, especially Sara Jane Lippincott (Grace Greenwood). Finally, feeling exhausted and having some savings, she decided to take a year off from teaching to try out a literary life.[10]

At this time Bailey, who had taken other writers—including Lippincott—into his home, persuaded her to go to Washington, D.C., to be the governess for his children. This proved to be a wonderful opportunity for Dodge, because it brought her into a public, political arena, introduced her to many of the nation's leaders, and gave her an opportunity to read, discuss, and write about the major issues of her time. As it turned out, her job as a governess did not consume all of her time; her letters home describe meeting political leaders at numerous social occasions. "People of mark and sense, one way or another, are in almost every evening—chiefly members of Congress. I have seen two or three *lords*," she wrote in one letter, "and played whist with a *Sir* who was once our consul at Constantinople." Moreover, she enjoyed life with the Baileys, whose marriage was "on terms of perfect equality."[11] She had time to write opinion pieces and book reviews under her pen name, Gail Hamilton, for the *National Era*, the *Independent*, and the *Congregationalist*, and political commentaries under the name *Cunctare* for the latter. On top of all this, she wrote some poems and children's stories. Although reluctant to admit publicly to being either Gail Hamilton or *Cunctare*, she thoroughly enjoyed the increasing recognition that came her way.

In 1860 Gamaliel Bailey died. Though she loved Washington, she did not feel she could stay because his wife was unable to pay her. In addition, her mother was ill and urged her to come home—away from the approaching war. Anyway, she longed to be back in the countryside and to settle down to a full-time writing career. Thus, she returned to Hamilton. Dodge's publications had already earned her such a good reputation that James Derby, editor and publisher, asked to include her in his book entitled *Women of the North Distinguished in Literature*. With that encouragement and two hundred dollars for the expenses of beginning her career from her good friend, the writer George Wood, she launched her literary career in earnest.[12]

For Dodge, authorship was a calling; it was "not a thing to be quietly chosen, as circumstances may determine. It chooses you; you do not choose it." Writing was not just something to do; it was "essential" to her happiness. "I think if a person has a strong native inclination for and facility in any one profession or employment, it is an indication that that ought to be his employment," she wrote a friend in 1859. "I do not think . . . that I am unduly presumptuous in assuming that I have a degree of facility in writing which, so far as it alone is concerned, would warrant me in adopting that as a profession."[13] Because of that conviction, Dodge was not ambivalent in her decision to pursue a literary career.

Although she did not believe that all women should have careers, she thought that having a profession gave women access to power and prestige in their society. "A clever woman," she wrote in 1863, "whether she be a painter or a teacher or a dressmaker—if she really has an object in life, a career, she is safe. She is a power. She commands a realm. She owns a world." In fact, she believed that, despite discrimination, women had more opportunities for careers than they usually perceived. Many women —she named Harriet Beecher Stowe, Harriet Hosmer, Rosa Bonheur, Mary Lyon, and others—had already blazed a trail for others to follow. Authorship was especially promising, she thought. As a career, it was particularly appropriate for women who were longing for more in their lives, who were "a little inclined to egotism and tolerably imaginative," and who had "acquired the habit of . . . [thinking about] things." She felt qualified.[14]

Once committed, she was not tempted to abandon her decision to become a recognized and respected writer. Since seminary days she had been perfecting her literary skills. Unlike Southworth or Stowe, whose early writings were primarily for economic gain, Dodge decided not to rush to make money if that would jeopardize either her reputation or her skills. "I would rather write for a *good* paper without pay," she asserted, "than for a foolish one *with*." Elsewhere she wrote, "Excellence is far more valuable to me than money. I want a reputation, but I want it to be for qualities which may commend themselves to the best people." Therefore, at the beginning of her career she turned down an offer from a tract society for $1,200 a year—a sum far greater than she had ever before earned by teaching or writing—saying she did not want to put her "brain in pawn," which would show that her "brain wasn't worth pawning." As she began her career, she vowed to write what she wanted to write, how she wanted to write, and when she wanted to write.[15] During the next twenty-six years she would pen countless newspaper articles, plus more than twenty-five books on topics ranging from the woman question to religious issues, politics and travel to rural life. While most of her writings would be essays, her works would also include three biographies, some children's stories, one novel, and some verses.

From the beginning, Dodge was determined to remain as unencumbered by family as possible. In a letter to her brother in 1860, she wrote, "I'm not married and I don't think I shall be. I can't afford the time, and besides, the men ought to be given to the women who can't get along without 'em. I can support myself, and so I think I'd better do it. Besides, I have a greater 'run' among the men themselves than if I were married. Now I am independent and every man is my 'humble servant.' If I were married I should be dependent on the caprices of one. An unmarried woman has an immense advantage over the married woman." Although Dodge could be very critical of marriage, she assumed that most women would and should marry. But she preferred to remain single and defended her choice in 1865 to Henry James, Sr.: "I have friends on every side who delight in me, men and women who come to me for joy, and solace, and strength . . . because I have never been overborne by hard physical labor, nor undermined by the unspeakable disappointments of marriage. God has suffered me to keep my life in my own right hand." She also understood the advantages for a writer of remaining childless, so she turned down a request to raise one of the Bailey's children after the editor's death. Still, she was not totally free of family responsibilities, for she dutifully cared for her aging and ill parents in the 1860s.[16]

Instead of marriage and childrearing, Abby Dodge's adult life included the advocacy of various causes, continued involvement with politicians in Washington, and sustained literary and journalistic work. Indeed, the causes she championed often brought her national attention. The most famous ones included defending a midshipman accused of sedition, confronting the publisher James T. Fields over royalty payments and problems in author-publisher relations, debating the woman question, criticizing civil service reform, and working to release from prison an American accused of killing her English husband. Early in life, Dodge expressed the sentiment that seems to have motivated her throughout: "I hope that when my life is closed, it may be said that the world is better for my having lived in it."[17]

Although Hamilton, Massachusetts, was her permanent home, after 1871 she divided her time between Hamilton and Washington, where she spent her winters with the politician James G. Blaine and his wife Harriet Stanwood Blaine (her cousin), writing and helping them entertain guests and care for their seven children. When Dodge was in Washington, the writer Harriet Prescott Spofford recalled, she interacted with "senators, cabinet officers, diplomats, the titled Englishmen of the High Commission, [and] the President himself." Her advice was sought in regard to many matters of state, and much attention was paid to the editorials she wrote for the *New York Tribune* and other papers. As the *Woman's Journal* said, "her entire literary career has been an object lesson in woman's capacity as a political thinker and writer." Dodge spoke out in support of Blaine's political views, aided him in the preparation of his two-volume work, *Twenty Years in Congress*, and was embroiled in the civil service controversies of the 1870s because of him. Her more conservative political views at the end of her life have been attributed to his influence on her, but he was equally influenced by her.[18]

When in Hamilton, she lived with her sister Augusta, who was also sometimes her companion on travels and visits. The two shared a distaste for housework and a love of literature. Harriet Prescott Spofford said Abby Dodge was, "after all the excitements and flatteries of Washington, ... entirely happy in Hamilton with her adoring sister Augusta, who, in spite of a keen intelligence and dry humor, never showed for what she was worth, because, as a friend said, 'she always stood round admiring Gail [Mary Abigail Dodge].'" Their bonds were quite strong. Dodge dedicated her last book to her sister, quoting in tribute a poem by Spofford: "Your life and mine, O constant heart, have glided / Like two streams into one, / We flow along, and now our way is guided / In shade, and now in sun." When Abby died in 1896, Augusta prepared her sister's letters and a book of her poetry for publication.[19]

During her writing career, Dodge built a solid reputation for intelligence, versatility, and courageousness in addressing issues and became a role model for other Washington journalists. The *Woman's Journal* eulogized her in 1896 as "one of the wittiest and most forcible writers of her day" and, as stated earlier, the *Independent* recalled her as "the most brilliant American woman of her generation." Yet she also created controversy and was sometimes viewed as a "public scold." E. P. Whipple, a contemporary literary critic, well expressed the ambivalence many felt toward her: "Miss Mary A. Dodge (Gail Hamilton) might be styled an essayist, but that would be but a vague term to denote a writer who takes up all classes of subjects, is tart, tender, shrewish, pathetic, monitory, objurgatory, tolerant, prejudiced, didactic, and dramatic by turns, but always writing with so much point, vigor, and freshness that we can only classify her among 'readable' authors." The passage captures the public and critical ambivalence that was frequently expressed toward Dodge.[20]

At least some of that ambivalence was the result of Dodge's unwillingness to conform to her culture's expectations of women. In this regard, she was much more challenging to cultural norms than either Southworth or Stowe. In her essays, she more straightforwardly criticized her society's views of women than Southworth ever did with stories of women's victimization and superiority or than Stowe did with her writings praising feminine values. In tone, Southworth was generally conciliatory; Stowe, still feminine, was assertive; but Dodge was often combative. Southworth, writing in the context of duty to her family, and Stowe, writing in the context of serving others, stayed within the expectations of woman's sphere. In contrast, Dodge wrote in the context of duty to herself—a duty more often expected in men than women of her time.

The guiding principle of Dodge's life was the Victorian belief that each person has a responsibility to God and self to develop one's character fully. To do so, Dodge thought, people needed to develop their capabilities beyond the narrow social prescriptions of male and female spheres, by expressing those aspects of themselves that were usually viewed as typical of the other sex. She wrote:

> A man who has not in his soul the essence of womanhood is an unmanly man. A woman who has not the essence of manhood, is an unwomanly woman. It is woman in man,—gentleness, guilelessness, truth, permeating strength and valor, that gives to man his charm: it is man in woman,—courage, firmness, fibre, underlying grace and beauty, that give[s] to woman her fascination. . . . God . . . is in himself type of both male and female, and only in proportion as all men are womanly and all women manly, does each become susceptible of the love and worthy of the respect of the other. Neither is the man superior to the woman, nor the woman to the man, but they twain are one flesh.[21]

In other words, she assumed the two sexes were of equal worth. She also believed that there was an essence of womanhood—gentleness, guilelessness, truth—and an essence of manhood—courage, firmness, fiber—but that both sexes benefited by becoming what today we would say was more "androgynous."

This view of women and men distinguishes Dodge from the other two writers we have studied. Southworth believed that women could survive with feminine values and some self-reliance, and Stowe felt that men should conform to women's values, but neither advocated that women consciously work to develop their "masculine" selves. Southworth was content to argue woman's natural moral superiority, and Stowe to assert the social worth of feminine values, but Dodge held that women need to adopt some masculine traits: they need to strive to be "active, self-helpful, self-reliant, alert, ingenious, energetic [and] aggressive." While all three women agreed in different ways with the idea that motherhood was sacred, in Dodge's opinion women were not automatically morally superior, as Southworth and Stowe believed, but had to work vigorously to develop their superiority through "struggle and growth."[22]

Dodge's attitudes toward womanhood fall on the continuum of nineteenth-century views of womanhood nearer the Vision of New Womanhood, as discussed in Chapter 1, than those of the other two writers. Although she felt women always would have a natural preference for home and privacy, she also felt that every woman should have a choice about how she lived her life: "What she chooses to do," Dodge wrote, "she has a Divine right to do, subject only to Divine limitations." In all cases, Dodge wanted women to be strong, brave, and self-poised; to be educated morally, mentally, and physically; and not to be submissive or inferior. Like other proponents of a New Womanhood, Dodge wanted women to develop their characters for themselves and God, rather than to be pleasing to others. She was highly critical of men telling women what to do with their lives, but equally critical of women who did not develop their own capabilities. She thought that in either career or marriage a woman needed to improve herself; in fact, Dodge thought, a woman might do so most fully if she did not also have to earn a living.[23] It was not career but character that was most important.

Although she sided with women's rights advocates in support of occupational and educational opportunities for women, Dodge opposed the call for the vote because it was "a move too far in the right direction, or rather an injudicious means to compass worthy ends." Perceiving much discrimination against women by men, she, nevertheless, felt that the vote would not significantly improve woman's lot; according to her, the vote would not automatically give women more educational or occupational opportunities. Nor did she think it would significantly improve society's morality, as some advocates said. She also argued against suffrage because it would add another responsibility to women whom she believed already were carrying more than their share of the load. Finally, if women won the vote, she feared that they would sacrifice their own values and become like men, who did not, as she said in another context, have "the self-restraint, self-denial, high dignity and purity and conscience that women have—take them in a mass." What was more important than the vote, Dodge thought, was the power to change opinions; in that regard, she believed, women already were influential.[24]

Dodge's views of the ideal woman—androgynous, self-directed, influential—matched her expectations of and attitudes toward herself. In 1865 she wrote,

> I shall not confine myself to my sphere.... I like everything that is outside of it,—or better still, my sphere rounds out into undefined space. I was born into the whole world. I am monarch of all I survey. Wherever I see symptoms of a pie, thither shall my fingers travel. Wherever a windmill flaps, it shall go hard but I will have a tilt at it.... And pray, Gentle Critic, do not tell me that I must be content simply to amuse, or must anything else. Must is a hard word; be not too confident of its power. I feel a grandmotherly interest in the world and its ways; and much as I should like to amuse it, I shall never be content with that.[25]

Like Ralph Waldo Emerson and Don Quixote she wanted to examine, to improve, to be part of the whole world. As a result, the central issue of her life and career was how to be such a woman in a society and business that divided themselves into "spheres."

Part of the problem she and other writers faced was the view that women really did not belong in the literary sphere. She herself acknowledged that "a certain prejudice against female writers 'still lives.' It is fine, subtle, impalpable, but real. It is like the great ocean of air that wraps us round. A little of it cannot be seen; it is only in mass that it becomes visible. It is like a far-off star; look straight at it, and it is not there; look askance, and it twinkles and winks at you again." One example of discrimination she pointed out was in critics' complaints that women's poetry was not enough like men's, "not Miltonian, nor Spenserian, nor Virgilian, nor Dantesque; it is not written according to the rules of high art." She thought another example of discrimination was to be found in any "half-flattering, half-contemptuous, and wholly contemptible notice, whose compassionate blame and condescending praise are alike insulting." Other times, she claimed, discrimination took the form of "disinterested counsel, paternal and affectionate advice . . . [such as] 'If you must write, write cheerfully.'" According to her, it was only the exceptional man—"large-hearted and large-brained"—who was able to evaluate women's work apart from her sex. Indeed, Dodge herself was often the subject of criticism that could not ignore her sex. For example, Henry C. Vedder wrote in *American Writers of Today* (1894), "Her championship of her sex and its cause has been aggressive, defiant, one might add blustering if she were a man."[26]

What Dodge wanted was criticism that was "just and generous . . . which discriminates between the evil and the good, condemns the one without rancor, and applauds the other without servility." She concluded that the only way for women like herself to get fair treatment was to be ready to have their works compared to men's. In any business, if a woman does what is "man's work . . . she must do it in man's way or suffer the consequences," Dodge claimed. "The products of her toil, the value of her labor, must be brought into direct comparison with those of man, and be judged solely by their worth, not by the weakness surmounted in the doing." This was the dilemma then: how was a woman to write if critics perceived women's writing either as weaker because it was like a woman's or exceptional for a woman because it was like a man's?[27]

Aspects of Dodge's career suggest that she did not want to choose between writing like a woman or writing like a man; she struggled to be unconfined to either female or male spheres. She sought a language, a style, a literary approach that "rounds out into undefined space." For instance, she despaired that women's language was limited to civilized talk: when women used the language of men, "tabooed expressions . . .

are informed and vivified with feminine sweetness, brawny vigor, strength of imagination, the play of fancy, and the flash of wit. Translate them into civilized dialect,—make them presentable at your fireside, and immediately the virtue is gone out of them." Just as the best character was androgynous, the best language, according to Dodge, was a combination of the "masculine" and the "feminine." Thus, she cultivated what she considered a reputable masculine style without wholly abandoning the feminine. As she wrote, "There is about my serious style a vigor of thought, a comprehensiveness of view, a closeness of logic, and a terseness of diction, commonly supposed to pertain only to the stronger sex. Not wanting in a certain fanciful sprightliness which is the peculiar grace of woman, it possesses also, in large measure, that concentrativeness which is deemed the peculiar strength of man. . . . [Yet] I make the unmistakable assertion that I am a woman." Dodge would not be confined to woman's sphere but she would not deny her womanhood either.[28]

In other ways, too, she expressed the desire to be unconfined to spheres. She thought women had difficulties with careers because of their "lack of perseverance" and "unwilling[ness] to bestow upon a trade or a profession the study and thought which are necessary to insure skill." By contrast, she characterized herself as disciplined, a trait associated with masculinity in the nineteenth century. In a blunt letter from 1885, probably written to her sister Augusta, Dodge asserted, "Nothing that you, or probably any other member of the [literary] club, should write about Mrs. Browning would be worth reading, because writing that is worth reading can no more be done by an amateur in a fortnight than can a statue or a temple, or a picture. Not that you could not have made the best of writers, but nobody can write without practice, anymore than he can speak French." She claimed to have the perseverance other women lacked.[29]

Although she was willing to commit herself to hard work, she was not willing to lose herself in her career—another clue to her attempt to be an androgynous, unlimited self. It was her habit to devote long mornings to her writing and the rest of the day to other activities. She shared with Stowe and Southworth the belief that there were other things in life besides work, and those things related to women's more traditional lives. She wrote her friend George Wood in 1862, at the beginning of her career, "I do not expect immortality from literature and I do not design to devote myself to it with an ardor so warm as to scorch up my womanhood. What would be excellent for me as a writer might be positively injurious to me as a woman—and I do not mean to sacrifice myself for or to anything. . . .

I retreat [?] from doing anything which the most commonplace woman may not do. I am not of the Stuff of which martyrs are made. I have no manner of desire to lecture, or to parade, or to vote . . . or to do anything *public* anyway that shall interfere with my personal comfort or personal privacy."[30] Ironically, her writings in subsequent years often brought her into the public limelight, and even her desire for privacy did not suppress her enjoyment of fame. Somehow she wanted both.

Nothing better embodies Dodge's attempt to be unlimited by spheres than her use of her pen name, Gail Hamilton, taken from her middle name Abigail and her hometown Hamilton. Unlike the male pseudonyms of some other women writers, her pen name never hid her sex. Besides the obvious fact that it was a woman's name and not a man's, Dodge freely and even defiantly admitted her sex in her first book: "I am a woman. . . . I am aware I place myself at signal disadvantage by the avowal. I fly in the face of hereditary prejudice. I am thrust at once beyond the pale of masculine sympathy. Men will neither credit my success nor lament my failure, because they will consider me poaching on their manor. . . . I could easily deceive you, if I chose."[31] Though writing in a masculine style, she would not deny her sex with her pen name.

Clearly not wanting to be thought of as a man, she nevertheless believed that having a pen name gave her the freedom to speak her mind that she might not otherwise have had. Her pseudonym, she wrote an inquirer, was "given for the sole purpose of a lightning conductor—to catch all the flash and crash of the outside electricity, and leave the inner home of privacy unharmed, untouched." She claimed to work at a disadvantage when her name was known, and throughout her career she insisted on the privacy of her personal life. An essentially shy person, Dodge wanted none "of those impertinences which are so common in newspapers," none of the "gossip that detracts from literature." She felt so strongly about maintaining her privacy that she never provided biographers with personal details of her life, she insisted on appearing in reference works under the H's and not the D's, and she sometimes told strangers that she was not "Gail Hamilton." It was with fervor that she told Sara Payson Parton (Fanny Fern), "So much of the woman as appears in an author's writings is public property by her own free will. All the rest belongs to her reserved rights."[32]

Choosing a female pen name and hiding behind it to preserve the privacy of her personal life was one way in which Dodge dealt with the gender expectations of the literary marketplace. Of course, male writers also desired to keep their personal lives from public scrutiny; Henry James seemed to echo Dodge when he said, "A man has certainly a right to determine what the world shall know of him and what it shall not; the world's natural curiosity to the contrary notwithstanding."[33] But female writers were usually more at risk in this regard; their lives as "unnatural" women were more closely examined than men's and a judgment of their femininity was frequently made part of the evaluation of their works. Dodge felt she did not want to deny her womanhood but she needed a strategy to resist those who would evaluate her work on the basis of her sex. Therefore, she worked hard to hide the information about her private life but used a female pen name. The androgynous implications of her strategy are clear when seen in contrast to Southworth, who was much more inclined toward "being feminine," and who therefore insisted on signing her works with the feminine title and initials, "Mrs. E.D.E.N. Southworth."

Because Dodge associated a preference for privacy and home with women, some have seen her use of a pen name as a way to compartmentalize her life into masculine and feminine realms. But actually her case is more complex and reveals the struggle of an androgynous self-concept in a world of divisions based on sex. A pseudonym, which kept her private life from public scrutiny, was a means of forcing evaluation of her writing on the basis of that writing, not on the basis of her personal life. But at the same time, it was not a denial of her womanhood: she claimed it and valued it. Given that she never hid her identity from editors and publishers and that most people eventually discovered who she was anyway, her continued insistence on the use of her pen name must be seen as a statement of values, not a disguise. She wanted to be unconfined by spheres that would limit appreciation of her work.

It was never easy for Dodge to maintain an androgynous position in a literary world that divided itself into spheres, valuing men and masculine qualities most highly. Sometimes she was tempted to play up to men, as in the following passage: "I don't look to school-girls for my audience—I expect them to like me, I know them well—but if I do not secure the ears of men—men who are sensible and literary, and educated and accomplished, and substantial, I shall consider myself to have failed—I like women and girls, but it is men that give the stamp of success—not such men either as one dolt and dunce of a minister in this vicinity who got himself introduced here, and dares to write letters beginning 'my precious sister.'"[34] Such a comment reveals the tensions of a person who feels "different," like a token in a group, and who wants to be seen as good, even exceptional. Any token is tempted to play up to those in power (men) and to condescend to those who are not (women). Dodge was not free from this fault. This, however, was not always her approach. Although she sometimes chose a male audience, her works on women's rights were addressed to women, and sometimes she even enjoined men not to read her work.

It was Dodge's behavior as an androgynous woman that ultimately brought her into serious conflict with the publisher James T. Fields. At first it is hard to understand how Dodge could have become so thoroughly dissatisfied with Fields. To be published by Ticknor and Fields, later Fields, Osgood and Company, was the hallmark of literary success in the nineteenth century; many authors chose the reputation of the Fields imprint over the greater pay they might have commanded elsewhere. Moreover, James Fields embodied the philosophy of the Gentleman Publisher that was, as demonstrated earlier, amenable to supporting and encouraging women writers. While Fields's prestige and publishing philosophy initially appealed to Dodge, as it had to Harriet Beecher Stowe, his paternalistic approach to writers was ultimately incompatible with her desire for equitable treatment in the marketplace as an independent, androgynous woman.

Unlike Stowe, who came to Fields as a mature and prominent writer, Dodge had just begun her full-time writing career in 1860 when her work first appeared in the *Atlantic*, "the best monthly," she thought, "that has ever been published in this country." In 1862 Fields published her first book of collected essays, *Country Living and Country Thinking*, and over the next six years he brought out seven more of her books on travel, rural life, and women's rights—some more popular than others, but all well received. Overall, Fields was very pleased with her work. He praised it lavishly, though he would criticize particular contributions that he did not like. He warned her about spreading herself too thin and in 1864 urged her to write exclusively for him. Because he thought so highly of her, he paid her five hundred dollars for the use of her name as a contributing editor—with Lucy Larcom and John T. Trowbridge—of *Our Young Folks* magazine in the mid-sixties. In 1868, he published her *Woman's Wrongs: A Counter Irritant*, a book Stowe recommended to Sara Payson Parton (Fanny Fern) as "decidedly the brightest, cleverest, healthiest, noblest kind of a book." All should have been well.[35]

However, late in 1867, while reading an article on "Pay for Authors" in the newspaper *Congregationalist*, Dodge discovered that most beginning writers earned 10 percent royalties on their books. She calculated that she was receiving between 6⅔ and 7½ percent on hers. To her friend George Wood she sent the following report of her subsequent actions:

> I have had a little experience of ["Boston infidelity"] in one shape lately. I discovered quite accidentally that ten per cent on the retail price of books is the minimum price paid to authors. As my books have brought me only from six and two-thirds to seven and one-half per cent. I laid the case before a lawyer friend, who has made investigations among the book men, which results in a conviction that I have been underpaid.... Where I have been on terms of such intimate friendship I cannot come down to mere business relations. Mr. [Fields] had the matter entirely in his own hands. I never questioned, or proposed, or bargained, and that he should have gone on, year after year, paying me less than a new author has . . . is not a thing to be overlooked.[36]

Her discovery initiated a long dispute with her publisher, which was never settled to her satisfaction and resulted finally in her thinly veiled chronicle, *A Battle of the Books* (1870).

Before their dispute, Dodge expressed deep affection both for James Fields and his wife, Annie. During their early association, Dodge reported that Fields was "not only a handsome man, but one of the nicest men in the world, straightforward, genial, simplehearted, though in the thick of the city. I like him very much, and he has the sweetest wife, and beautiful, too, and they are as happy as can be." After their dispute she avoided him on the street and described him as having "a mean face and ophidian eyes and puny voice uplift, who would have pulled the thunderbolts of Jove down upon me and did not see that they were knitting-needles forged in his own small smithy, and back-acting machinery at that. *That* is not the man I cared for at all. . . . I did not think he was a lion, but I did think he was a sprightly, agreeable, amusing, and friendly and virtuous beast. When he began to bleat, I found he was a jackal."[37]

When Dodge discovered the discrepancies in pay, she wrote Fields a letter, expecting he would immediately set her mind at ease with details she did not understand. What she knew was that for her first book she had been paid a 10 percent royalty, but for subsequent books Fields had offered her 15 cents per copy, claiming hard times and saying a set amount was the safest arrangement to protect her profits. While 15 cents had given Dodge a 10 percent royalty on her $1.50 book, it did not on any book that sold at a higher price. Since her books were currently retailing for $2.00, her percentage had dropped. Unfortunately, the change in the rate of compensation had been accomplished without a contract, in the rather haphazard way things are done when everyone is supposed to trust each other. At first, when Dodge stopped to figure out what her percentage actually was, she became confused, and Fields probably was, too. Oddly enough, he did not move quickly to rectify the discrepancy.

The story of their dispute, retold carefully from Dodge's point of view in *A Battle of the Books*, is a dramatic one. First, Fields brushed off the complaint, saying they would straighten it out the next time she came to town. Then, he tried to argue that, because her books were more expensive to publish than most and he spent more to advertise them, she deserved a lower percentage. Still unsatisfied, she consulted other publishers in Boston and New York and learned that, by their calculation of costs, she was being underpaid and Ticknor and Fields were probably making exceptional profits on her work. Finally, after asking other writers about their payments, she concluded that Fields pays "less than other publishers, and, secondly, pays me less than he pays other authors, and is thereby guilty of a breach of faith." It is not clear why he did not mend the breach; increasingly, he seemed not to be the ideal publisher she had always thought he was; his action, she wrote, "has been ungentleman-like, unfriendly, and calculated to arouse instead of allay suspicion."[38]

For months the argument went nowhere. She was ready to give it up when her anger was rekindled by the discovery that Fields seemed to be cheating Nathaniel Hawthorne's widow out of royalty payments as a result of a situation that sounded very much like Dodge's own.[39] Apparently Hawthorne's royalties were meager because his compensation had also been changed from a percentage to a lower fixed sum, and Mrs. Hawthorne had no contracts to clarify the situation. Because they were friends, Mrs. Hawthorne knew about Dodge's complaint and decided to inquire more closely about her husband's royalty agreements. She also became suspicious of Fields and sought Dodge's and her lawyer's advice. Although Elizabeth Peabody, Mrs. Hawthorne's sister, eventually examined Fields's books and could find no evidence of legal fraud, Mrs. Hawthorne and her children always believed that the now-deceased writer had been treated unfairly. In the Hawthornes' troubles, Dodge found further justification for pursuing her case.

Dodge renewed her skirmishes with Ticknor and Fields by suggesting arbitration. At first, the firm turned down the proposition and instead offered to sell her her plates and stock. Fields tried to charm her with a visit, but, when charm did not silence her complaints, he reported that she was "in an aggressive, unwomanly frame of mind."[40] Howard Ticknor, taking the publisher's side, ousted her from her position as contributing editor of *Our Young Folks*. James Osgood was dispatched to Hamilton, Massachusetts, to try to calm the author and show her the publisher's figures, but she remained unconvinced. Over the next several months Fields and Dodge moved slowly toward an agreement on "friendly, not formal" arbitration, preparing their respective defenses and disagreeing on the number and composition of the board of referees. Fields tried to exhaust her patience by inaction. Like political opponents today, both sides were unwilling to accept the other side's suggestions on referees without adding their own stipulations.

At the same time, the warring parties solicited both public and private support for their own positions in the controversy. Ticknor and Fields launched a public relations campaign in newspapers to convince the public that authors did not understand the publishing business. They also began spreading rumors that Dodge was difficult to work with, in an attempt to show, as she said, "how hard it is to climb Fame's rugged steeps without their helping hand."[41] On her side, the author initiated a letter-writing campaign inquiring of innumerable writers how much they were paid and whether they were satisfied in their association with James Fields. Her inquiries ultimately cast doubt in many people's minds about his policies.

Finally, the dispute went to arbitration. Though she had consulted with a lawyer throughout the disagreement, Dodge, who claimed to know little about business, defended herself because the firm wanted to keep lawyers out of the arbitration. The logic and weight of the evidence she had compiled in her own defense, however, was staggering. After a lengthy presentation of her argument, including the reading of copies of correspondence to verify her view, she claimed back payments on books for which she had not received 10 percent royalties, plus 7 percent interest on that amount due her. She also claimed expenses of $3,000 in preparing her case. Two days later the referees awarded Dodge only $1,250 and ordered that thereafter she was to receive 10 percent on the retail price of her books. James Fields noted in his memoranda book: "The Referees regarded the case as one of unfortunate personal disagreement arising out of business arrangements rather loosely made, but in which they discovered no evidence that either party intended to defraud the other." Believing that she had not received what was due her and that she had not been understood, Dodge wrote and published at her own expense what she called the "history of my Holy War," *A Battle of the Books*. This slightly fictionalized account of the dispute went through three editions of five hundred copies each and she lost $750 on the publication. Soon she began working with new publishers. She reflected later, "Though quarreling with your publishers may be very good as a crusade, it is a very poor way of getting a living."[42]

How justified was her complaint about pay? It seems to have been well founded. Evidence in the published cost books of Ticknor and Fields (only to 1858, unfortunately) and from other sources substantiates Dodge's claim that most authors were drawing 10 percent royalties on the retail price of their books; few were paid less. Variations above 10 percent seem to reflect Ticknor's and/or Fields's judgment of an author's literary merit or popularity. Friendship also must have played a role. Grace Greenwood, Dodge's mentor, fellow journalist, and good friend of William Ticknor, usually received 13.6 percent on her essay collections and 10 percent on her poems. Other favorites also obtained higher amounts. Alice Cary earned 15 percent on her poems, whereas Oliver Wendell Holmes and John Greanleaf Whittier were paid 10 percent on their work. Nathaniel Hawthorne received 15 percent in the early 1850s, but later the figure sometimes dropped to 10 percent before it was finally changed to a set amount per volume. Henry David Thoreau was given 15 percent on *Walden*. Emily Judson made 15 to 20 percent on her books, and the actress Mrs. Anna Cora Mowatt got 15 percent on her autobiography. Harriet Beecher Stowe often received half profits. In comparison with these figures, Dodge was being cheated. Her work was as good as Greenwood's and Judson's. Though not a Thoreau, Dodge was an enjoyable, thought-provoking writer who deserved at least 10 percent royalties.[43]

So why was she paid less? Perhaps she did not think or behave in ways Fields understood; she threw him off guard. Although he supported the expansion of women's rights, including woman suffrage, his attitude toward women and all writers still was that of a benevolent patriarch. Such a view led him to accept and encourage the writing of women, but not the individuality displayed by Dodge. Fields was a warm, genial man, but the views of women and the world she espoused were not always amenable to his kind of geniality. In the mid-sixties, even before their quarrel, he called Dodge "eccentric, a queer bird with plenty of cleverness in her beak and wings . . . not a pretty warbler. . . . [Still] she has one good eye."[44] Little did he suspect that five years later she would have seen through him and pecked an irreparable hole in the fabric of nineteenth-century author-publisher relations.

More than simply a quarrel over compensation, the Dodge-Fields dispute was a battle over the philosophy of author-publisher relations under the reign of Gentlemen Publishers. In *A Battle of the Books*, Dodge changed the names of those involved and described the dispute as if it had taken place a hundred years earlier during the "age of barbarism when author and publisher were natural enemies." With tongue in cheek she said the story could not take place at the present time because now the publisher "woos [the author] to receive his dues, wins open with gentle urgency the hand . . . modest and reluctant, and presses into it the crisp, abundant bills." Of course, this was the view of author-publisher relations that Gentlemen Publishers like Fields propounded. Such a publisher was supposed to care for all the authors' needs, knowing exactly, as Fields assured Dodge, what was best for their "reputation and pecuniary interests in the long run." Ticknor and Fields claimed the ideal of publishers' benevolence as their own. In an article they planted in the newspapers during the dispute with Dodge, it was reported that "they have dealt with authors of all lands upon the broad ground of mutual benefit, and have never sought to make bread out of other people's brainwork and leave the worker without fair compensation." Many of Fields's authors felt, in fact, that he came as close to that ideal as any publisher could. They praised his graciousness and fairness, partly because he often provided them with many literary and personal services and partly because they were comfortable with his view of author-publisher relations.[45]

Dodge, however, became increasingly uncomfortable with the view that presupposed the author would be cared for by a benevolent publisher. As she wrote Mrs. Hawthorne in September 1868, "For my part I am altogether tired of the friendly and familiar style of doing business and should be well content to exchange it for a little hostile and formal accuracy. . . . I should suppose that between man and man there must be some proper mode of transacting business, so that one could at *any time*, or at least at certain *set* times, know whether or not everything was going on correctly."[46] "Friendly and familiar assurances" seemed to Dodge too much like a "feminine" way of doing business.

From Dodge's perspective, the friendly approach to business arrangements created a dependence of authors on publishers that was as wrong as the dependence of women on men. Like women who idealized their own spirituality and moral superiority, authors who viewed themselves as above commercialism by virtue of their artistic temperament were bound to be hurt by that view:

> The confidential, friendly way of conducting affairs is pretty and sentimental, grateful to one's indolence and vanity and over fastidiousness, and confirmatory of one's conviction that he is too dainty and delicate to touch a bargain with the tips of his fingers.... You run well for a while, but a day of reckoning is almost sure to come. The thriftless, haphazard way of bargaining or not bargaining, common among literary people, is the fruitful parent of uneasiness, anxiety, disappointment, and bitterness, before which delicacy must be rudely and ruthlessly brushed. It is the same with women as with men, for in literature as in the gospel, there is neither male nor female.[47]

To guard against being "rudely and ruthlessly brushed," she advised writers not to behave "like women." Writers needed to learn to deal with the marketplace using what people usually supposed were "masculine" characteristics; or as she said, "Let writers deal with publishers, not like women and idiots, but as business men with business men.... Had I but used the ordinary care and caution which a lawyer, or a merchant, or a marketman brings to his business, this trouble doubtless would never have happened." Just as she thought women had enough duties without adding the vote, she did not think authors needed to do publishers' jobs, that is, publish their own books, because clearly that took "the vitality, the invention, the thought" that should be devoted to writing. Rather, authors as well as women needed to "be exact, prompt, methodical, and intelligent so far as possible" in the fulfillment of their duties, so that publishers would be encouraged to be fair in theirs.[48]

A fair publisher, according to Dodge, would act in honest and open ways that would instill trust in the author. Such a publisher would be straightforward, not necessarily flattering about the author's work, and would credit a book's value to the author, not to his own skills in "puffing" it. If he encouraged the author to write exclusively for him, as Fields had encouraged Dodge, the fair publisher would feel an obligation to treat the author as well "as any other house would do."[49] Dodge did not deny that status and prestige were valuable things for an author to attain through relationships with particular publishers, but she had come to believe that true fairness finally could be measured only by money—by whether or not the publisher paid as well as other publishers and whether he paid each of his authors equitably.

Since the beginning of her literary career, Dodge's attitudes toward compensation had changed. Although in the early 1860s she had been willing to sacrifice high pay from a tract society in order to nurture her talents, as her reputation became more secure during the 1860s she more fully equated the money offered her with her reputation. Compensation, according to Dodge, provided the crucial measure of an author's value compared with other authors and was an index of the relative power of author and publisher. No amount of risk or expense on the publisher's part justified a publisher earning a larger profit on a book than its author. The greater the publisher's profits in comparison to the author's, the more authors were in servitude to publishers. Because she thought authors' profits were too low, Dodge saw her fight for fair compensation as a sort of Declaration of Independence for writers, like the patriots' revolt over a tax "on tea which produced George Washington and the great American Republic." In money was power and freedom; or, as she put it, "there is no such thing as independence, or dignity, scarcely honesty, without money."[50]

Though writers generally wanted to deny the centrality of money, Dodge insisted on its importance: "In fact, we all do take money for our work when we can get it; we want just as much money and money just as much as other people—rather more—and, in sober truth, the friction, the sacrifice of delicacy in keeping your money affairs straight from day to day, is not for a moment to be compared to the delicacy which may be sacrificed by leaving them at the mercy of others." In her own case, she had sacrificed months of writing time to pursue her argument. "The very instrument that he uses in defending his works," she wrote about the author making claims like hers, "is the instrument which he ought to be using in producing them."[51] She had learned that, if in the first place she had operated with less trust and more business sense, in the end she would have had to devote less energy to her problem.

But even if compensation were fair, Dodge thought publishers would always have the upper hand. For instance, in the midst of a dispute with an author, a publisher's work, unlike the author's, could still go on. Publishers had a particular advantage in their connections with the media, which made it "the easiest thing in the world to give public opinion a tilt in the desired direction without the least suspicion on the part of the reader." Having learned from her own experience, she concluded: "Whenever I see in the newspapers a fresh ascription of praise to the liberality of this [publishing] house, I immediately infer that the screw has been given another turn on some unlucky author."[52]

This was the world that the woman who wanted to be unlimited faced: a world in which Gentlemen Publishers wished writers to behave like women, though for authors' well-being they needed to behave like "business men with business men." In Dodge's passionate conclusion to *A Battle of the Books*, the fates of women and of writers merge, so it is no longer clear when she leaves off talking about *women* writers and when she starts talking about all writers:

> It is the same with women as with men, for in literature as in the gospel, there is neither male nor female. When a woman does any work for which she receives money, she becomes so far a man, and passes immediately and inevitably under the yoke of trade. She has no right to demand a favorable judgment of her work because she is a woman, nor has she the least right to require that chivalry shall come in to help fix or secure her compensation. Trade laws know no more of gallantry than trade winds—and it is well they do not. Individuals and societies wheedle and flatter and threaten and torture according to the fashion, or passion, or panic of the hour, but under it all, the great, pitiless, unseen, inexorable law of the world holds from age to age, never relaxing its grasp, never revoking its decree, deaf to the wail of weakness, dumb to the cry of despair, forever and forever teaching with unrelenting persistency, *by* unrelenting persistency, the good and wholesome lesson that will be taught no other way. Under this law there is no sex, no chivalry, no deference, no mercy. There is nothing but supply and demand. Nothing but buy and sell. To him who understands it, and guides himself by it, it is a chariot of state bearing him on to fame and fortune. To him who does not comprehend it and flings himself against it, it is a car of Juggernaut, crushing him beneath its wheels, without passion, but without pity.[53]

In other words, while the philosophy of Gentlemen Publishers might encourage writers to expect care, guidance, or chivalry, in fact, in publishing no such consideration could be counted on by women or by men. Supply and demand were all. Behavior limited by the expectations of the women's/writer's spheres was no more appropriate in this business than in people's daily lives. Each woman/writer needed to develop "masculine" capabilities in order to survive in the Gentleman Publisher's marketplace.

Whereas in *A Battle of the Books* she argued for all writers, in her next book, *Woman's Worth and Worthlessness* (1872), Dodge refined some of the implications of her views for women. First, she argued that women deserved equal pay for equal work in all areas. But even if they deserved it, women needed to demand high prices for their work, not only for their own benefit but also for the precedent it would set for every other woman's work. Women could enforce equal pay by uniting together in making their demands, not by expecting equal pay from compassionate men. Finally, she wrote, "If a woman writer gets the same pay as a man, it is not because she reasons with her publisher about her board bill and stationery, but because, if his price does not suit her, she takes her wares to the publisher over the way. Unless she can do this, and until she can do this, she is in precisely the condition of the teacher and seamstress—she must take what is offered. Against this horrible necessity no law can be framed to protect her."[54] Because Gentlemen Publishers could not be counted on to be fair, women needed to take care of themselves.

Public reactions to Dodge's charges against publishers were mixed, depending probably on the degree to which the person believed in the image of the Gentleman Publisher. Fields's new company, Fields, Osgood and Company tried to undermine the impact of her charges and of her book by well-placed articles pointing out the high quality of the authors who were published by Fields. Other articles viciously attacked Dodge. The latter type she herself parodied in *A Battle*: "[Gail Hamilton] once more famous than now, had a little 'unpleasantness' with her publishers [Fields, Osgood and Company]. In plain words, she accused them of cheating her out of some thousands of dollars by making false returns of sales of her books. Like many authors, she had become inordinately vain, and had extravagant ideas of the popularity of her books. . . . She had a quarrel with them of eighteen months standing, but they would not even appear in self-defense; what man would want to have an open quarrel with a woman? . . . [Fields, Osgood and Company] are above the taint of suspicion."[55] It is significant that, even in a conflict like this, the publishers should mention her sex. It was not Dodge's imagination that made her see the need to eliminate expectations about women and men in all aspects of publishing.

Her outspokenness made other publishers wary of her. Robert Bonner may have been the newspaper publisher to whom Dodge referred in this story she told James Parton, husband of Sara Payson Parton (Fanny Fern):

> One New York newspaper Publisher, some time in February applied to me to become a contributor to his newspaper. Of course I have had many such applications but Mr. Fields had always enjoined upon me the desir-

ableness of writing only for them and I had been only too *happy* to do so and so had turned a deaf ear to all other charmers. But about this time I began to question whether another course might not be best. Accordingly, instead of declining at once, I named my price and with Fanny Fern in my mind set it at a hundred dollars which is exorbitant enough—but I did not particularly care to make the engagement and thought I would err this time on the safe side. The gentleman recalcitrated a little but as I was indifferent I had the advantage and he very soon started to come to Hamilton and make the arrangement. On his way down, he stopped in Boston as the guest of his friend Hon. A. H. Rice—who had sometime before accepted the office of referee *in re* G. H. & F. O. & Co. and heard *in Boston* that I was not so popular as I had been and therefore he was not willing to pay the price—It was a matter of no importance to me but the incident shows how these things are worked—Whether I am or ever was popular I do not know but all that I have heard of this *sort* has come since my trouble with F. O. & Co. began.[56]

Whether or not this was Bonner, any publisher sharing Fields's philosophy would have been put off by the self-confidence of her demands, which presented a striking contrast to Southworth's feminine appreciation or Stowe's feminine assertiveness.

Reviews of *A Battle of the Books* varied. Dodge rather optimistically described them to a correspondent:

I don't see but that the book has had its full share of attention, but it amuses me to see how constrained and guarded most of them are. Nearly all speak of it as bright, witty, piquant, sharp, etc. Many design to wait and hear the other side before judging, a few question the taste or propriety of such a publication, which, considering the marvelous sense of propriety in newspapers, is touching! Not one accuses me of garbling, misrepresentation, or any false statements. Two or three—one of them from a "religious" newspaper—are coarse and brutal. Otherwise they are not bad, no more unfair than is to be expected, and some of them are quite fine. The book has gone to a third edition.[57]

But three editions totaling 1,500 books did not make a best-seller, and, as noted earlier, Dodge actually lost money on the sales.

It is difficult to assess the importance of this particular battle in bringing changes to the literary marketplace under Gentlemen Publishers. The subsequent history of publishing testifies that changes occurred but, as in all historical processes, many circumstances contributed to that outcome. Other works—essays, novels—had criticized the traditional assumptions about author-publisher relations, though none was as pointed as this, none so clearly directed at a living ideal of traditional publishing like James T. Fields. Consequently, many people thought about Dodge's charges. Though there was not a wide-scale bolting from Fields's firm, her accusations certainly prompted many authors to discuss their views of compensation with each other, if Harriet Beecher Stowe's and Fanny Fern's letters are at all representative. After the dispute, the Hawthornes never returned to Fields's fold, and Julian Hawthorne made no mention of James Fields in his father's biography. Fields himself, in ill health and probably distressed by these charges as well as the Byron affair, retired a year after *A Battle of the Books* was published to spend his remaining years writing and lecturing about his more pleasant friendships with writers like Harriet Beecher Stowe and Charles Dickens.[58]

In the short run, author-publisher relations remained much the same as they had been. The "queer bird" had ripped a hole in the Gentleman Publisher's clothes, but few apparently wanted to see the nakedness underneath. Years later James Russell Lowell would refer to Dodge as the "pestiferous Gail Hamilton" and John Greenleaf Whittier, who still claimed Dodge's friendship, would reassure Annie Fields that Dodge's book "fell dead from the press," while everyone remembered and was grateful for James's "warmth and brightness." In some ways, Whittier's assessment was the most prophetic because the controversy did little to tarnish the image of Fields in historians' accounts of him, whereas Dodge is often characterized as an unreasonable *woman* who should have been more understanding and accepting.[59]

The impact of the battle on Dodge herself was profound. In the midst of her quarrel, she wrote Mr. Pettingill of *Hearth and Home*: "Your letter seems friendly and generous and I am myself very much inclined to write for your paper. But the consequences of trusting apparent friendliness have been to me so disastrous that I do not henceforth take a slice of bread and butter without legal counsel! I therefore at present only acknowledge the receipt of your letter and the check for one hundred dollars. I will give you a definite answer in a few days."[60] No longer would she trust the motives of editors or publishers.

Of course, she published no more books with Fields or his associates, nor articles in the *Atlantic Monthly*. Estes and Lauriat, which purchased the plates of her early books in 1876, and Harper and Brothers, a more commercial, less personal firm than Fields's company, published the rest of her books. Dodge welcomed her association with Estes and Lauriat because "they seem to be frank and honest and they make no pretensions to magnanimity, or culture, or literature."[61] She must have appreciated the same qualities in the Harpers, who paid her 10 percent royalties. The *Congregationalist* and the *Independent* continued to accept her work, as did the *New York Tribune, Harper's Bazar,* and the *North American Review* in the mid-eighties. In 1872–73 she served as an editor of *Wood's Household Magazine*, but that experience apparently did not please her and she returned to what she loved best—writing.

Dodge took to heart her advice to writers, always presenting herself in her correspondence in as independent a stance as possible. There are no instances of submissiveness toward an editor after the Fields affair. She simply would not bow to a publisher's or an editor's wishes about what she should write. As a professional, she demanded the autonomy to write what she wished, not what others expected her to write. Thus, she bluntly told James Redpath of the *North American Review* that he should not try to get her to modify her views in order to satisfy his critical readers: "I wonder if in the Heaven to which I hope my way leads, I shall have to argue and beg for leave to speak as I do in this world. I not only, you see, have to write my articles to suit myself but I have to reason and wrestle with the Editor to force him into the belief that it suits him!"[62]

Dodge conducted the rest of her career asserting the importance of money. "One ought not to *write* for money," she claimed, "but I consider it a first duty after one has written to exact the highest possible price." Though she sometimes mocked herself as "mercenary" and "cold-blooded," she still demanded fair pay. She turned down requests when she did not think the compensation was high enough. In 1877 she wrote Mr. H. L. Ensign, managing editor of the *Alliance*: "The only reason that I cannot form an alliance offensive and defensive with you is because you are poor, and I am a saint and martyr to the one fixed principle never to write except for the highest price.... As long as you cultivate literature on a little oatmeal, bless you, my children, bless you, but leave me my fatted calf! With heroic self-denial, Always truly, M.A.D." At other times, sounding even more forthright than Harriet Beecher Stowe, she boldly set the amount: "Two hundred dollars an article, without limit as to length. Free range as to themes over this world and the next." In fact, only once in a while did she demur from setting a price, asking the editor to give the market value instead of expecting her to name a price that might be below what she was worth.[63]

Though after the Fields controversy Dodge paid much more attention to the price she was paid for pieces and was angered by mispayments, she never again tried to pursue a grievance publicly. But in private she could be fierce. In frustration she once snapped at Miss Booth, editor of *Harper's Bazar*, about the Harpers when they did not pay her promptly: "Please represent to gold-encrusted and bloated bond-holding brothers that I could not pay for two dozen eggs I bought this morning and in view of that fact, ask them if they don't think it would be humane to send me some money." She did not pursue her complaints further because she well understood the costs. As she remarked to a friend in January 1881, "The publishers of 'Divine Guidance,' like all publishers here, take their own sweet will to finish, but turned up prompt and plump with their bill for plates and pictures. . . . But if we make a fuss about it they can, of course, ruin the sale, so I advise only perfect tranquility."[64]

Although she was often bitter, Dodge masked her feelings with humor. Accumulated grievances against the *Independent*, for instance, spilled out in this letter of 1879:

> As to the compensation, I remember once a stranger clergyman in a neighboring pulpit, giving out a hymn to be sung with a specification of the verses to be omitted. The choir forgot his directions. The second hymn he also specified in the same way and the choir again carelessly disregarded his directions. After he had read the third hymn, he simply remarked, "The choir will omit such portions as they choose." Similarly I say to you that you will pay me exactly what you choose. You asked me last winter what you should pay me for the Caroline Herschel article and I said $100. You paid $75. You will remember that I made no comment. You say you have paid me $25 regularly—your highest rate. I am obliged to contradict you. You first paid me $30, then $25 until Jan. 1, 1876 when I received from you $20. as henceforth your highest rate. From that time until April 30, 1879, I never received $25 from you, either as a regular or irregular rate. It is true that I have written very little for you during that time. . . . I should not have sent to you anything at all, had I not supposed that $20 was your highest rate. I am indebted to your last letter for the information that $25 has been your highest rate all along.[65]

Letters like this one reveal the psychological cost to Dodge of inequities in the literary marketplace—and of her inability to do much about them. After *A Battle of the Books*, she complained about what she was being paid and how she was being treated, but only so loudly. Her options were limited: she could either refuse to publish without fair pay or continue to chaff under inequities in order to publish in well-respected places. In many ways, Dodge's letters suggest she made the latter choice.

Once, however, Dodge tried role-reversal in dealing with editors, giving herself the upper hand. She submitted one article to two editors, hoping to get one to outbid the other and more speedily publish the work. She justified the action by joking, "I don't suppose it is customary for a man to offer himself to two girls at the same time and thus constitute himself a contingent fee—but my excuse is that time is in this case more valuable to me than—choice of girls!"[66] It was an appropriate metaphor for someone who understood how much male-female relations resembled publishing relations. The strategy worked, though less speedily than Dodge had hoped; she never used it again.

As all of this suggests, Dodge never again expected kindness or chivalry from publishers. As the years passed, she felt like a martyr to the cause of better opportunities for writers. In 1891, when asked to join the Society of American Authors and become a vice-president, she said, "I will do a great deal better for you than that. I will send you a 'Battle of the Books' which will show you that I was fighting for your Author's Club while you were all rocking in your respective cradles. . . . I admit that I am skeptical of results. I have lately published a book. . . . Yet, speaking as a wise man confidentially to Authors, I confess that in spite of your efforts and mine, I shall be surprised if the author receives as much money for the brain-work of the book as the publishers receive for the de luxe work."[67] Apparently, many in the authors' society had come to share her views of the publishing industry.

In many ways, Dodge's experiences could have wholly discouraged a weaker person. Dodge persevered because of her strong sense of self—androgynous, self-directed, influential—and because of her generally combative approach to life. She made a significant contribution to the history of professional (women) writers, and she exposed the Gentleman Publisher's market for what it really was: a relationship based on power, even when conducted as friendship. "My strength," she had written Henry James, Sr., in 1864, "is that I see [things] as they are, and not as tradition, or prejudice, or popular opinion, represents them."[68] She may have overestimated her own abilities but in this case not by much. She could see that, as in a traditional male-female relationship, economic power was in the hands of the (male) publishers, not the (female) writers. That power, like the power of males, seemed always to outweigh the power of women/

authors. Nevertheless, she believed women/authors could gain relatively more control over their own destinies, depending on their commitment to developing themselves unconfined by their spheres. *A Battle of the Books* was also a battle to get the "male" and "female" spheres out of the literary marketplace.

6

Helen Hunt Jackson

Courtesy of the Prints Collection, Special Collections Department, Clifton Waller Barrett Library, University of Virginia, Charlottesville

"Very Serious Literary Labor"

The Career of Helen Hunt Jackson

In the 1870s and 1880s, when the Gentleman Publisher's views of the literary marketplace were giving way to more avowedly commercial aims, Helen Hunt Jackson (1830–85) earned a reputation as a major poet, essayist, short story writer, and novelist. Yet she remains in many ways as much an enigma as her more well-remembered friend, Emily Dickinson. Jackson started her career almost by accident as an expression of personal grief; she finished it speaking out for American Indian rights. She began her professional life as a protégée of Thomas Wentworth Higginson; she ended it encouraging Emily Dickinson to publish her poems. Clinging for most of the time to publishing's oldest habit—anonymity and pseudonymity—she simultaneously asserted its newest value—commercial worth. Choosing to write for Gentlemen Publishers, she nevertheless built her career, not on personal relationships with them, but on more "progressive" views of hard work and attention to details. Hers was a vocation of paradoxes and purpose, symptomatic of encroaching changes in the literary marketplace.

But for over thirty years of her life, a literary career was far from Helen's mind. Her parents certainly did not expect such a profession for their daughter Helen Maria Fiske, who was born on October 14, 1830, in Amherst, Massachusetts, two months before the birth of the other famous Amherst daughter, Emily Dickinson. Helen's father, Nathan Welby Fiske, was a professor of languages at Amherst College, where he taught Latin, Greek, and moral philosophy. He was the author of several books, including the widely used *Manual of Classical Literature*. Like Emily Dickinson's father, Helen's was apparently of the "unbending Calvinist mold," while her mother, the former Deborah Waterman Vinal, was known for charity, goodwill, and hospitality to her husband's students. Deborah Fiske also was a good storyteller and witty; in fact, years later Helen published one of her stories, *Letters from a Cat* (1879), which Deborah had written for Helen as a child. Though Helen undoubtedly acquired some of her literary abilities from her parents, she claimed, "I inherited nothing from either of my parents, except my mother's gift of cheer."[1]

In many ways, it did seem as though the rambunctious daughter was not of the same stock as her more restrained parents. A boisterous baby, as she grew she enjoyed playing tricks on people and dressing up in odd clothes. At six, she and another professor's daughter walked through the woods to the town of Hadley, about four miles away, making not only her family but also everyone else in Amherst frantic about their fate until ten o'clock that night when she strolled into her house, announcing, "Oh, mother, I've had a perfectly splendid time." Unlike her younger sister Ann, Helen was not always completely honest or affectionate; in fact, she was often almost unmanageable. A young neighbor compared the sisters by saying that "Annie was a tender little girl but Helen was tough & hardy & would wrestle or fight at almost any time or any body."[2]

The madcap Helen worried her parents. When she was six and a half, her mother reported to a cousin that "Helen learns very well, but I do not drive her very much to make her very literary [that is, knowledgeable about literature]—she is quite inclined to question the authority of everything; the Bible she says she does not *feel* as if it was true."[3] At Nelson's School for young children, she received "bad reports" on her behavior because she was too busy having fun. The Fiskes transferred her to Amherst Academy but then removed her from there as well after deciding the discipline seemed "too lax to risk sending Helen fulltime." Deborah's illnesses and self-doubts about being able to manage her eldest daughter led her and her husband to try several more schools away from Amherst in search of an education and discipline for Helen. But nothing suppressed her high spirits. Furthermore, since she was often away at school, Helen was both of and not of Amherst, an acquaintance of Emily Dickinson but not a close friend.

Helen's mother died in 1844. Two years later Helen entered Ipswich Female Seminary, where she must have met Mary Abigail Dodge who was also there. A persuasive young woman, Helen had talked her father out of sending her to Mt. Holyoke where she thought girls spent too much time making hasty pudding, cleaning gridirons, and washing floors. But Ipswich did not please her, even though one of her mother's old friends was the director; once again, she hated the discipline. After her father's death in 1847, she transferred to the Abbott (later Springler) Institute in New York at the invitation of John Abbott, the brother of one of her father's friends. In New York she encountered a more sophisticated world of art, music, and drama than she had previously known. Moreover, at last she had found a school that used a more "progressive" approach to discipline. Here, she earned the reputation of being a "scholar" and in 1850 she began teaching a section of younger students. Her own haphazard education, then at an end, had included languages, mathematics, science, and philosophy.[4]

Helen was not destined to continue teaching at Abbott Institute, though she loved it, nor to begin a literary career in the 1850s, though as a schoolgirl her compositions had impressed her classmates and as a teen some of her verses had appeared in the Boston *Press and Post*. Instead, on October 28, 1852, she married Army Lieutenant Edward Bissel Hunt, a young mathematical physicist, whom she had met while visiting in Albany in 1851. Helen was passionately in love, although temperamentally she and Edward were quite different. She was spontaneous and lively; he was more serious and reticent. She tended to be argumentative; he disliked arguments of any kind. She was very emotional; he was much more stoic. Nevertheless, they were, from all reports, happy together, though his military career meant frequent moves and separations.[5]

During their eleven-year marriage, Helen Hunt conscientiously fulfilled the role expected of the wife of a rising army officer and increasingly prominent scientist. Despite her outspoken nature, she became supportive, even submissive, willing to forego, for instance, defending the views of Harriet Beecher Stowe in the presence of Edward who hated all abolitionists. Still, she did not totally efface herself. By all accounts, she was a fascinating woman with blond hair and blue-green eyes. "She was highly educated, brilliant, and sometimes satirical in conversation," the writer Moncure Conway recalled of their first meetings in Washington, D.C. She "dressed with elegance, and, while laughing at the world of fashion, entered it with an eagerness that suggested previous repression." Though she attended scientific meetings with Edward and impressed his associates with her intelligence, she, nevertheless, maintained more literary than scientific interests. Although not particularly widely read, she liked to test, Conway wrote, "the intellect or heart of any acquaintance by inducing him or her to read one or another of Hawthorne's tales, and afterwards discovering what they thought of it."[6]

Unknowingly, as she and Edward moved around, she made friendships that would be important to her in her later literary career. In Providence, Rhode Island, at a scientific meeting in 1855 she met her future mentor, Thomas Wentworth Higginson, as well as the literary hostess Ann Botta, who invited Helen to attend some of her (Botta's) gatherings of literary, artistic, and intellectual people in New York. In New Haven, Connecticut, she cemented her lifelong friendship with Sarah Woolsey, who would someday write under the name "Susan Coolidge." In August 1860, Helen and Edward attended commencement in Amherst and briefly visited with her old acquaintance Emily Dickinson, who gave them no indication that she was writing poetry; at this time, Helen may even have shared her husband's view that Emily was "uncanny."[7] As for Helen Hunt, no one, least of all herself, suspected that she would someday be a prominent writer.

In the meantime, she poured out her energy and her imagination onto her family. Her first child, Murray, was born in 1853. His death of a brain tumor the following year left her devastated for months. Her second son, Warren Horsford ("Rennie"), was born in December 1855. Helen was devoted to Rennie, using the same progressive childrearing practices on him that she would advocate years later in *Bits of Talk about Home Matters* (1873). She opposed corporal punishment, favoring instead positive reinforcement and a loving home atmosphere for nurturing children. Helen Hunt seems to have thoroughly enjoyed being a wife and mother, but this phase of her life ended abruptly in October 1863 when her husband was killed in an accident while he was experimenting with a submarine. A year and a half later, in April 1865, Rennie died suddenly of diphtheria. "And I alone am left," she wrote a friend, "who avail nothing."[8]

Prostrated with grief, she shut herself up in a room in the Abbotts' home, now in New Haven, Connecticut, and saw no one. Out of her anguish, however, she wrote a poem, "The Key to the Casket," and sent it to a friend whom she had met at Ann Botta's salon in New York, Parke Godwin of the *New York Evening Post*. The poem was published on June 9, 1865, attributed to a new author "Marah." A month later at Godwin's suggestion, she submitted the sonnet "Lifted Over" to the *Nation*. Then, one day in July she emerged with some of her old vitality from the room where she had been mourning and declared that she was going to travel around New England. Exploring place after place, she finally settled into an inn in Bethlehem, New Hampshire, and on an impulse wrote an article about the region and sent it to Godwin. It, too, was published but this time under the initials "H. H.," which would become so popular to readers in the years to come.

At age thirty-five, with a very different background than that of the other writers already discussed, Helen Hunt was embarking on a writing career. Unlike Mary Abigail Dodge, she had not aspired from girlhood to becoming an author, nor was she as desperately searching for a way to earn money as E.D.E.N. Southworth was when she began to write. Unlike Harriet Beecher Stowe, she had not been intellectually stimulated as a child; neither was she as creatively driven or as intellectually gifted as her Amherst acquaintance Emily Dickinson. Rather, Helen Hunt began her career out of the coincidence of grief and a natural facility with and enthusiasm for words. Early success encouraged her, and soon she was earning her livelihood as an author.

With determination and a surprisingly modern practicality, Helen Hunt decided that to establish a writing career she needed instruction from Thomas Wentworth Higginson, one of the major literary craftsmen of the day. Unlike Emily Dickinson, who coyly sought Higginson's advice by letter in 1862, Helen Hunt decided to move to Newport, Rhode Island, in 1866 and to rent a room at Mrs. Dame's boardinghouse where Higginson and his wife lived. When she arrived, Higginson noted in his journal that "Mrs. (Major) Hunt ... is in deep mourning ... & I fancy has private depression to correspond with her high spirits in the family.... She seems very bright & sociable & may prove an accession."[9] Indeed, Helen quickly won a special place in the literary and artistic circles of Newport, but she waited a month before she showed any of her poetry to Higginson. When she did, he agreed to help her revise her work and soon encouraged her to submit pieces to the *Independent* and the *Atlantic*, as well as to the publications—*Nation*, *Galaxy*, and *New York Evening Post*—already accepting her work. As it turned out, Higginson was in many ways a good choice as a mentor. Later he acted as the agent for her work when she was in Europe, from time to time throughout her career he helped her with her proofs, and he consistently praised her publicly and promoted her work.

In the early days of their association, Higginson and Helen Hunt discussed not only their own work but also that of other writers of the day. In 1866 he asked her if she had any knowledge of Emily Dickinson from Amherst and showed her some of Dickinson's poems. It was the first of many times that Hunt and Higginson would share their impressions of Dickinson's poetry. No one knows whether it was Hunt or Dickinson who subsequently initiated the process of reacquainting themselves, but by 1875 they had developed a deep regard for each other and for each other's writing. In 1876, Helen wrote her friend, "You are a great poet—and it is a wrong to the day you live in, that you will not sing aloud. When you are what men call dead, you will be sorry you were so stingy."[10]

Helen Hunt herself was far from stingy with her words. According to Higginson, "from the beginning she composed with great rapidity, writing on large sheets of yellow post-office paper, eschewing pen and ink, and insisting that a lead pencil alone could keep pace with the swiftness of her thoughts."[11] In the next several years, the quality, quantity, and diversity of her writing grew dramatically and she firmly established herself in her field. She experimented with translating poetry and writing stories for children while continuing to publish poetry that was both popular and well respected in the literary community. In 1870 Fields, Osgood and Company published on a half-profits contract H. H.'s first collection of

Verses. In various magazines, including the *Atlantic*, she published travel articles from Europe and around the United States. For the *Independent*, she wrote poetry, articles, book reviews, and editorials. In 1871, using the pseudonym "Saxe Holm," she submitted her first short story "Whose Wife Was She?" to the new magazine *Scribner's Monthly*; she would publish others under the same pen name in the years ahead. In 1873 she began a long and profitable association with the publishers Roberts Brothers of Boston; the firm eventually published twenty-two of her books.

In spite of her increasing literary and financial success, before 1875 Helen Hunt did not have a permanent home. Restlessness and illnesses often motivated her to search for new surroundings and healthier climates. She subsidized her travels by writing articles contracted in advance of her departure with various newspapers and magazines. In 1873, however, it was not a literary contract but a doctor who sent her to Colorado Springs as a last resort to cure a serious bronchial infection. While recuperating, the widow Hunt sat across the boardinghouse table from William Sharpless Jackson, six years her junior, a banker, railroad man, and financier. As she recuperated, she fell in love with the beauties of Colorado but did not quickly reciprocate Jackson's romantic interest in her. She wrote enthusiastically to her literary friends on the East Coast about moving there, though she turned down Jackson's persistent marriage proposals until 1875.

Like many before and after him, Will Jackson was captivated by Helen's charismatic, mercurial personality. He may not have shared Emily Dickinson's view that Helen Hunt was "deified," but he knew he had fallen in love with the woman whom another described as "a charming, brown-haired woman with thoughtful blue eyes, frank of speech, with a merry laugh, and a warm heart for those she liked." He probably admired her generosity toward those in difficulty and was captivated by what Sarah Woolsey described as "something all her own—Sadness and mirthfulness, a chorded strain, / The tender heart, the keen and searching brain, / The social zest, the power to live alone." Apparently, he was also smitten, as some others definitely were not, by her strong individuality. Over the years that quality angered as many people as it fascinated; so characteristic were her unpredictable opinions that years later most obituaries would comment on that aspect of her personality. But William Jackson was threatened neither by her individuality nor by her career.[12]

They were married in a Quaker ceremony in October 1875. Helen's marriage to William Jackson was very different from her marriage to Edward Hunt twenty-three years earlier. This time *she* rather than her husband was the more well known, though Jackson was widely respected in Colorado and in 1876 made a bid for Congress. Neither of the Jacksons wanted children, but Helen was pleased to have a real house of her own in Colorado Springs to remodel and decorate just as she chose. Although Will accepted her career, as Edward would not have, he certainly never gave her the literary companionship of a Calvin Stowe.[13] Instead, they shared a love of the beauties of nature and of traveling to new places in the Southwest.

Whether their marriage was satisfying to them is open to debate. They each maintained active careers and were frequently apart. One friend, commenting on the relationship after Helen's death, claimed their "cordial and admiring friendship . . . led to one of the happiest of marriages."[14] Yet other evidence suggests that as the years passed they slowly drifted apart, especially after Helen took up the Indian cause in the 1880s. Even then, however, they continued to respect each other: he did not interfere with her profession and she did not openly criticize him.

At the time of her second marriage, Helen Hunt Jackson was a successful and highly regarded writer. Samuel Bowles had recently claimed that she stood "on the threshold of the greatest literary triumphs ever won by an American woman."[15] Ralph Waldo Emerson, Thomas Wentworth Higginson, and thousands of readers across the country considered H. H. to be a major American poet. The Saxe Holm stories, which the public was not sure she had written, were also very popular. Thus, she had many requests for her work and in the mid-1870s felt daring enough to try novel writing, though she did so anonymously. Thomas Niles, editor at Roberts Brothers, was eager to publish her first effort in his "No Name Series," and she agreed to the proposition after Scribner, Armstrong and Company (soon to become Charles Scribner's Sons) refused to pay the price she wanted to publish her story as a Saxe Holm. Her first novel, *Mercy Philbrick's Choice* (1876), was the lead offering in Roberts Brothers' anonymous series, and *Hetty's Strange History* (1877) soon followed. Even though reviewers were more critical of these novels than Jackson's other works, the public response was favorable—8,000 copies of *Mercy Philbrick's Choice* sold in four months. In 1878 she published a children's novel, *Nelly's Silver Mine*, and submitted not only her own poems but also one of Dickinson's, "Success is counted sweetest," to the Roberts Brothers' "No Name" volume of poetry, *A Masque of Poets* (1878).

Although everyone knew Helen Hunt Jackson was the poet H. H., she worked hard to perpetuate the Saxe Holm mystery. Time and again she publicly denied writing the Saxe Holm stories and even privately admitted to only a few people beyond Scribner's that she was the author. To her friend Charles Dudley Warner, she wrote, "But of all things don't try to palm off the work of that Hydra Saxe Holm—i.e. Mrs. Harriet Prescott Spofford, on me." She also devised various ways to satisfy requests for Saxe Holm autographs while eluding detection, including, after her marriage, having Will Jackson sign the cards. When she became concerned that someone would recognize his handwriting, she asked that one of Scribner's clerks write the autograph seeker, "'Saxe Holm' being a fictitious signature, it is impossible to send you the autograph for which you ask." To further perpetuate the mystery, she insisted in 1882 that the *Atlantic* not describe her as a short story writer, since she had never publicly acknowledged being one.[16]

There was ample evidence for the sleuth that Helen Hunt Jackson was Saxe Holm. For instance, some poetry incorporated in the stories was similar to H. H.'s verses, the stories were set in New England or the West, and various situations they depicted could be tied to her personal biography. Despite the evidence, Jackson's denials led to speculations that other writers were involved and to false claims of authorship. For instance, the *Springfield Union* and the *Amherst Record* in July 1878 suggested that Emily Dickinson wrote the stories. Others attributed the stories to Mary Mapes Dodge, Marietta Holley, Harriet Preston, Sarah Woolsey (Susan Coolidge), and Lucia Runkle. Among several false claimants who came forward, one young man insisted he was the real author of one Saxe Holm story but had dropped the manuscript in the street. Not surprisingly, all of the mystery surrounding the works spurred their sales.[17]

On a trip to the East Coast in 1879, when she visited with Sarah Woolsey and attended the *Atlantic* birthday party for Oliver Wendell Holmes, Helen Hunt Jackson happened to hear a lecture about the government's mistreatment of the Ponca Indians. As a result, she found the cause—Indian rights—to which she would dedicate the rest of her life and literary career. Although known for her generosity to others, social activism was new to Jackson. When she lived in Washington with Edward, in fact, she had ridiculed everyone with a mission. She had not supported abolition and held conservative views about the equality of the sexes. Nevertheless, she had chosen Thomas Wentworth Higginson, the abolitionist and women's rights advocate, as her mentor, so she could hardly have avoided being somewhat influenced by his views; after attending a suffrage convention with Higginson, she had come away only slightly shaken in her opposition by the demeanor of Lucy Stone.[18]

Now, however, the plight of native Americans stirred Jackson so profoundly that she became, as she called it, "a woman with a hobby." She campaigned to raise money, helped organize the Boston Indian Citizenship Association, wrote editorials on the Indians' behalf, and solicited the support of her literary friends and acquaintances. To Charles Dudley Warner, she wrote (using a peculiarly racist metaphor for an Indian advocate), "I am going to try to get Gail Hamilton [Mary Abigail Dodge] on the track. I did not expect ever to desire to send her to unsling her vulgar tomahawk: but she can get at things nobody else can and if she could once be roused on the question, her 'dinging' would do good." As Dodge herself often did when berating public officials, Jackson aroused national attention and encountered censure when she publicly attacked Secretary of the Interior Carl Schurz on the Indians' behalf. She became so outspoken about the misdeeds of Colorado citizens that her husband as well as others in her adopted state expressed their displeasure to her.[19]

Determined to convince people with facts, not sentiment, as she was being accused of doing, Helen Jackson spent months in the Astor Library in New York City, researching broken treaties with seven Indian tribes and recording the details of them in what became her 457-page book, *A Century of Dishonor* (1881). At her own expense she had copies distributed to every member of Congress in hopes that new laws would be enacted for the protection of Indian rights. Some relief did go to the Poncas from her efforts, but little else. In 1882 she secured a commission with the Californian Abbot Kinney to investigate the needs of the Mission Indians in California and to submit a report to the government. Again, she did a thorough investigation but the response in Washington was minimal. Her recommendations were submitted to Congress, but they were allowed to die in the Senate.

Encouraged by J. B. Gilder of the *Critic* to do for native Americans what Harriet Beecher Stowe had done for blacks, Jackson wrote the now classic novel *Ramona* (1884), a tale of passionate love and of governmental injustice toward the Indians. As she began to write, the words poured out. "You know I have for three or four years longed to write a story that should 'tell' on the Indian question," she told Higginson. "Still I did not see my way clear; got no plot; till one morning late last October, before I was wide awake, the whole plot flashed into my mind. . . . I wrote the first word of it December 1. As soon as I began, it seemed impossible to write fast enough.... I *cannot* help it. It racks me like a struggle with an outside power." She felt as if she were inspired and signed her real name, Helen Jackson, along with her initials, H. H., on the title page of the work. Her hopes were high: "In my *Century of Dishonor* I tried to attack people's consciences directly, and they would not listen. Now I have sugared my pill, and it remains to be seen if it will go down."[20]

Ramona received mixed reviews, but the book was instantly popular and soon came to be considered a minor classic. Some favorably, some unfavorably compared her work to Stowe's. Although her friends—Higginson, Dickinson, Conway, Woolsey, and others—praised the work highly, Jackson was dismayed that so many reviewers focused their attention on the romance in the novel at the expense of its social message; it was the latter that she valued most highly and that made her consider *A Century of Dishonor* and *Ramona* her most important works.[21]

Within a year and a half after completing her novel, Helen Hunt Jackson was dead of cancer. A series of mishaps, beginning with a serious fall down a staircase, had incapacitated her for the last year of her life. Upon her death she was lauded as an important writer who had secured her place in American literature. The *New York Evening Post* claimed that her "literary execution" was "superior to Mrs. Stowe's" and the *Critic* asserted that her poetry was "profounder" than any woman's since the death of Elizabeth Barrett Browning. Though Charles Dudley Warner claimed "her genius ... [was] greater than her talent" and her personality more brilliant than her writing, most literary people asked, along with the *Independent*, "When such a bright light as 'H. H.' goes out, ... Who will take her place?" For family and friends, her death was a great loss; Emily Dickinson, deeply touched, wrote, "Helen of Troy will die, but Helen of Colorado, never. Dear friend, can you walk, were the last words that I wrote her. Dear friend, I can fly—her immortal (soaring) reply."[22]

How did this woman who had begun a literary career so late in life come to have so much public respect as a writer of poetry and prose and at the same time to mean so much to the private writer Emily Dickinson? Why only at the end of her career did she sign her real name to her work, and why did she refuse to claim the Saxe Holm stories as her own? What were the social, literary, and economic assumptions that shaped her career as a writer? Who was the Helen Hunt Jackson behind this career?

What is immediately apparent in Jackson's biography is that her choice of a literary career was much more arbitrary than Southworth's, Stowe's, or Dodge's but fit with her own life pattern. In many ways, she was simply carried along by circumstances: marriage, the need for self-support, her success, and, finally, the campaign for Indian rights. Like her heroine Mercy Philbrick, she had "a capacity for involuntary adaptation of herself to any surroundings" and could be a poet or a housewife with equal contentment, depending on "the hands she [fell] into."[23] To be carried along, however, did not mean Helen (or Mercy) was a passive participant. Rather, it seems to have been in her nature to adapt to each circumstance by striving to excel. Thus, with Edward she was the supportive wife; on becoming a widow, she followed her first instinct to write down her grief; after achieving some success as a writer, she worked hard for more; and when moved to support Indian rights, she used a variety of tactics—from activism to literature—to win converts to her cause. Throughout her life, she demonstrated a high level of energy, a strong work ethic, and a belief in herself as a capable woman.

It is also important to understand that Helen Hunt came to her literary career, not as a rebel against woman's sphere, as Dodge had been, but as a recent widow who had been deeply committed to it. Although she may have been awakening to women's legal disabilities at the end, in general throughout her life she seems to have ignored or to have been unconcerned with the negative implications of her status as a woman in nineteenth-century America.[24] In some ways her views of her sex were as traditional as E.D.E.N. Southworth's, yet, unlike Southworth, Helen Hunt Jackson seems not to have experienced the alienation, abuse, and despair that sometimes gave Southworth's views a critical edge. Having always lived in a relatively privileged environment and having often been able to get what she wanted with her own charismatic personality, Jackson never felt particularly confined by the concept of woman's sphere or by the social structures that enforced it. She was by temperament rebellious and individualistic, but until her fight for Indian rights she was not a rebel in the sense of wanting to change society. Consequently, she did not challenge, though she somewhat redefined, the popular conception of woman's sphere.

As revealed through the characters in her fiction, Jackson's views of womanhood fall much closer to True Womanhood than New Womanhood on the continuum of beliefs about women in the nineteenth century, although her characters appear in some ways to be New Women. However, though her heroines are teachers, preachers, and poets, as well as wives, they all demonstrate certain traditional characteristics. Like True Women, they are empathetic, sensitive, trusting, and nurturing; they raise the moral tone and improve the character of those around them. For example, when Margaret Warren, heroine in "A Four-Leaved Clover," was a teacher, "there was not a pupil in her school who was not more or less electrified by her enthusiasm and love. The standard of scholarship was rapidly raised; but this was a less[er] test of her power than the elevation and stimulus given to the whole moral tone of the school in which she taught." Jackson's heroines are by no means "feeble and clinging," but women who are "great and strong and serene" and let men care for them only because they love the men. Her ideal women have well-developed minds as well as hearts, yet sometimes choose, like the heroine Esther Wynn, to give their whole lives "to love and be loved." They never rebel against their lives as women but self-confidently express themselves within relatively traditional bounds.[25]

Jackson's views of womanhood would seem almost wholly conservative except for her insistence on the importance of what she called "individuality," one's uniqueness as a human being. Individuality, she thought, could be expressed through one's personality, behaviors, moral decisions, or interpersonal relations. This individuality apparently enabled, even justified, True Women doing things that might otherwise be deemed far outside woman's sphere, like being a serious artist or earning a living. Undoubtedly because she herself expressed a good deal of individuality while believing in True Womanhood, Helen Hunt Jackson concluded that True Womanhood could be compatible with any woman's desire to express herself. Her philosophy was similar to that of achieving women today who do not criticize traditional views of women.

To her, the creative drive of artists and writers was "the most inalienable and uncontrollable of individualities." Women with this "individuality" expressed it in various ways, though the women always remain womanly. Ally, the artist who creates exceptional painting and embroidery for her family's enjoyment in "My Tourmaline," and Mercy Philbrick, the popular poet portrayed in *Mercy Philbrick's Choice*, are empathetic, sensitive, trusting, and nurturing. Both raise the moral tone and improve those around them with art and literature. Jackson wrote of Mercy Philbrick, "Truth, truth, truth was . . . the war-cry of her soul. . . . Intensity in every word of her written or spoken pleadings on this subject . . . had sprung out of the depths of the profoundest experiences. Her influence as a writer was very great. . . . To do a little toward making people glad, towards making them kind to one another, towards opening their eyes to the omnipresent beauty,—these were her ambitions." The heroines' individuality both motivated and justified their unusual artistic achievements, but it did not move them very far beyond woman's sphere.[26]

Jackson's philosophy of individuality also explains her acceptance of the belief that working to earn a living is not necessarily inappropriate for women. Jackson's female characters who earn their own living or manage their own finances are happy doing so. Mercy Philbrick is overjoyed when she first earns money with her poems and insists that there is no difference between men and women taking money for what they can do. In *Nelly's Silver Mine*, Lucinda argues that selling can be as honorable a business for women and girls as for men. Nevertheless, the working women in Jackson's stories do not abandon woman's sphere but excel in domestic as well as career skills, in matters of the heart as well as of the head. Margaret Warren, the teacher, for example, "found as true a pleasure in contriving how to make a garment out of slender material as in demonstrating a problem in Euclid."[27] Such working women do not view themselves as "unnatural" women; their strength of character, individuality, and purpose bring them success without sacrificing their more conservative beliefs about womanhood.

In fact, in keeping with her philosophy of individuality, Jackson's heroines achieve success by finding individual, not social, solutions to the restrictions people try to impose on their lives. Mercy Philbrick's mother is appalled when Mercy mentions that she may be able to support herself someday. "Your father he'd never rest in his grave," her mother says, "ef he thought his little Mercy was a havin' to arn money for her livin'."[28] Rather than trying to change her mother's point of view, however, Mercy keeps her writing and financial success a secret. Without directly challenging the social custom of dependent female, Mercy finds her personal solution to the problem. This seems to have been Jackson's view of how women would succeed as well: by the application of their individual efforts, not by advocating social change.

It is interesting to see how Helen Hunt Jackson's childhood rebellion matured into both an acceptance of traditional views of womanhood and a philosophy of individuality that motivated and justified her own unconventional feminine behaviors. Though True Womanhood and individuality seem almost wholly contradictory to our contemporary thinking, for Jackson they were not. In fact, her paradoxical beliefs in True Womanhood and in the expression of individuality seem to have given her an effective approach to a marketplace in transition from the ideals of the Gentleman Publisher to those of the Businessman Publisher. Jackson pursued her career in the dress of a True Woman but with the drive of an individualistic worker. While maintaining strong beliefs in the traditional expectations of womanhood, she "rejoiced to call herself, and be called, a working-woman; there was no better title under heaven to her sense, and her life was a long enforcement of the belief, a fruitful illustration of how it could be practised with dignity and success."[29] The result was a career very different from that of earlier writers.

Jackson did, however, occasionally express the older ideals of a "genteel amateur," though her attraction to the ideal was more sentimental than real. In a letter to Moncure Conway in 1879, she lamented the lack of a respected literary class in America—the result, she thought, of the financial orientation of most people whose "only feeling about literature is that it is an uncommonly poor way of making a living. If they had to take their choice between being Mrs. Southworth and Hawthorne they would be Mrs. S.—unhesitatingly; she has written fifty-nine novels and made a fortune,—*that* is worth while." Similarly, in the story "My Tourmaline," Jackson defended artists who pursue their work without financial aims as being "dearer to the heart of the God of Art" than those who sell their work for money. But, while she occasionally idealized such genteel amateurs, she never really accepted some of their basic assumptions about literary work.[30]

The difference is most clear in her attitudes toward her literary work; she believed writing was not a matter of inspiration so much as a matter of developing one's talents. To that end, at the beginning of her career, Helen Hunt devoted much time and effort to study in order to become the best writer she could be. She listened to Higginson's advice and considered his examples. He taught her to write as he did: to use a clear, natural style, alive with detail and illustration, "neither too lax nor too precise" in word choice, neither too idiosyncratic nor too elegant and abstruse for a large public audience. He emphasized revision and care and conformity to rules of grammar and traditional rhyme schemes. Undoubtedly, he cautioned her to avoid the "uncontrolled" writing he saw in the poetry of Emily Dickinson. Jackson studied his *Outdoor Papers*, a book she described as one of the "most perfect specimens of literary composition in the English language," and spent hours examining his sentences to see if by transposing or changing words she could improve them. Together she and Higginson worked on her writing until she herself could critique it from his point of view. Jackson grew to trust Higginson's judgment so much that years later she even asked him to proofread *A Century of Dishonor* while she rested in Europe after completing the writing.[31]

Jackson took pride in her mastery of Higginson's literary techniques, held them up as the ideal style in her description of Mercy Philbrick's writing, and gave advice like his to other writers. She was proud of her controlled, concise, and careful writing and became indignant when someone suspected that Saxe Holm was Sarah Woolsey, whose style Jackson claimed was "careless, redundant, often inanimate and sometimes slang-y." By contrast, she praised the style of her heroine Mercy Philbrick, whose writing, like Higginson's, was concise, clear, well executed, and "went to people's hearts." Furthermore, as a mentor herself, Jackson told others to remember that simple, clear words and phrases were most effective. For instance, she wrote Emily Dickinson in 1876 that she liked her "simplest and most direct lines best," and she advised another writer that revisions necessitated artisanship more than art—the application of techniques that any writer could learn over time.[32]

Helen Hunt Jackson was a quick pupil and came to be admired by her contemporaries for the literary style she had learned from Thomas Wentworth Higginson.[33] But whether her style is as fine as some of her contemporaries claimed is of less importance here than noticing how hard and successfully she worked to perfect the most respected literary techniques of her time. While the other popular authors certainly paid attention both to what their contemporaries were writing and which works critics were praising in the press, none worked as hard as Jackson to perfect her literary technique. Although Dodge sought advice from other writers at the beginning of her career, even she did not search for a mentor with whom to study for an extended period. In order to develop her talents, Jackson adopted an approach to literary work that was more characteristic of literary professionals who would follow her than of those who preceded her; her method would increasingly distinguish literary careers in a more competitive, commercial environment at the end of the century. Ironically, she was not a rebel nor was she striving toward the more "masculine" ethic of the end-of-the-century marketplace; instead, she thought she was studying to develop her creative individuality—an individuality that gave her a more modern orientation to the literary marketplace than many of her predecessors.

In fact, conscientious attention to literary details became her trademark. Though she drafted her work quickly, she revised it carefully. Higginson admired her thoroughness, a quality he thought other women writers lacked. Other commentators recognized this attribute as well. After her death, a writer for the *Independent* commented that she erased and wrote above the lines of her original text more often than almost any other author who had ever written for that publication. Another obituary writer claimed that "in literature her work was conscientious and thorough beyond that of almost any American woman; she never slighted it, never willfully neglected details, never was weary of trying to perfect it. This applies especially to her prose." Helen Hunt Jackson seemed to thrive on the cares of "careers and exigencies" that Emily Dickinson so firmly rejected.[34]

In the delicate balance between inspiration and discipline that must characterize a literary career, then, Helen Hunt Jackson came to depend more on discipline than on creativity, on the application of literary techniques than on inspiration. It was to discipline, in fact, that she credited most of her success. In 1884, she wrote the business manager of the *Independent*, "I have the good fortune—or perhaps I ought not to call it fortune for it certainly has not come to me without very serious literary labor—, to find an increasing demand for my work, and a steady increasing market value to it as my audience widens."[35] It was an illuminating remark, one that neither Southworth, nor Stowe, nor Dodge would have made, though they, too, worked hard in pursuit of their literary careers. Jackson explicitly emphasized hard work, conscientiousness, and technical expertise, rather than inspiration or innate ability, as inherent in the process of the best literary creation. In this regard, her own individuality had given her a more work-oriented, rational approach to a literary career than the other writers discussed.

The paradox created by Jackson's conservative view of women and her expression of individuality also influenced her interactions with publishers. Throughout her career she aligned herself with highly respected firms that maintained the Gentleman Publisher's ideals while paying their authors well. Scribner's, which published her Saxe Holm stories, and Roberts Brothers, which published most of her other books, both emphasized trade courtesy, loyalty to authors, literary quality over quantity, and a sense of moral rectitude if not guardianship. These two publishing firms also pursued successful commercial practices. In 1871, the *American Literary Gazette* claimed that Roberts Brothers "are as fairly distinguished for their courteous and honorable business habits, as for their good taste and sound judgment, as displayed in the selection of books for the public. Their liberality to authors is proverbial and their reputation in England, among writers and publishers, is as high as that of any American publishing house." Jackson herself once remarked that Thomas Niles, editor at Roberts Brothers, was "the only Boston publisher who knew how to treat a lady," thereby applauding his courtesy to women as well as his fairness in compensating authors. Throughout her career, Jackson preferred to publish in magazines—*Scribner's Monthly*, *Atlantic*—and newspapers—*Christian Union*, *Independent*—that were known for embracing the Gentleman Publisher's ideals. Not coincidentally, they also provided opportunities, especially the newspapers, for a steadily increasing income.[36]

As a woman who espoused many of the values of True Womanhood, Jackson was definitely attracted to the Gentleman Publisher's views of the literary marketplace. She generally agreed with publishers and editors who encouraged authors' loyalty. As she informed the *Independent* editors, "I prefer, as you know, to confine myself to the three channels in which I have chiefly worked—the Ind[ependent], C[hristian] Union, & Scribners [*sic*]—I have a great dislike to [*sic*] the practice so many writers have, of having their names in *all* the papers and magazines—'infesting the magazines' as the cruel Nation said of Constance Woolson last month!"[37] While Jackson did send her work to some other publications, she did not seek to appear in very many different places. Unlike Southworth, however, she was never tempted to commit herself to "exclusive" arrangements, though she tried (unsuccessfully) in 1879 to talk William Hayes Ward of the *Independent* into guaranteeing her fifty dollars a month. Like Stowe, she was interested in author-publisher loyalty within certain limits.

Actually, she seems to have most frequently expressed agreement with the Gentleman Publisher's values when it was to her monetary advantage. In the midst of disputes with the *Independent* over general price cuts, Jackson expressed to William Hayes Ward the familylike loyalty that was idealized in author-publisher relationships: "I am sometimes asked, 'Why do you continue to write for the Independent' an[d] I always say—'for the same reason that I should cling to the house I was born in.'—'I gained my first hold on my audience as a writer there, and I feel always that when I say anything there I am saying it to friends.'" But her aim was not to reassure him of her loyalty; rather, she wanted to win an exclusion from the general price cuts. At another time, in her correspondence with Scribner's, she also appealed to the Gentleman Publisher's values to win her financial point. When the firm offered her what she considered far too little on the copyright of a proposed novel, she replied, "I have not entirely decided whether to bring this novel out, as a Saxe Holm, or not: but I felt, that in case it did appear as a Saxe Holm, I ought of course to offer it first, to you [as the original publishers of Saxe Holm]; and I am very sorry that your offer is one which I cannot accept." In this case, she alluded to the loyalty expected between author and publisher in order to reinforce her request to be paid what she wanted.[38]

Her desire for the prestige of association with Gentlemen Publishers was always balanced by her wish to receive the fair market value of her work. In December 1870 she told James T. Fields that she would rather write for the *Atlantic* at lower rates than she could earn elsewhere because it was an honor to appear in his publication; however, she admitted, perhaps with Mary Abigail Dodge's *Battle of the Books* in mind, that she was not being very businesslike in saying that. Ultimately, when Fields did not agree to her price, she asked him to return her manuscript so she could submit it elsewhere. Rarely did she give literary honor precedence over adequate compensation. Once, however, in 1882, she offered a paper to the *Atlantic* at a low price because Henry Houghton had complained about paying her the highest sum he had ever paid anyone on the two previous papers she had submitted. She said the low price on the third paper offset the *Atlantic*'s having met her high price on the others. But this was the exception, not the rule, in her attitude toward publishers' values and compensation. She summed up her view in 1883 in a letter to Thomas Bailey Aldrich, then editor of the *Atlantic*: "I consider part of the pay for an article in the Atlantic is always its being in the Atlantic—at the same time one must have some regard to one's 'market value.'"[39] She honestly felt, like Dodge and Higginson, that literary works could be sold at a high price without sacrificing their quality. Unlike many writers of the older marketplace, she openly asserted commercial aims.

Her belief in the appropriateness of arguing for the market value of literary works seems to have been strengthened by Mary Abigail Dodge's battle, though even before the Dodge-Fields dispute Jackson was an effective negotiator of high prices for her works. She may have learned the skill of negotiating as a child, watching her grandfather Vinal who "loved money" and often drove hard bargains. Perhaps she had learned it during the months of Edward Hunt's absences or when she was a widow and had to be responsible for the day-to-day business of making purchases and paying bills for her small household. In any case, she paid close attention to Dodge's suit against James Fields and discussed the outcome with her literary friend Elizabeth Stoddard. Her subsequent letters echo Dodge's views of the business of the literary marketplace: "I never 'write for money,'" she observed to Fields. "I write for love: then after it is written, I print for money.... 'Cash *is* a vile article'—but there is one thing viler; and that is a purse without any cash in it."[40] But while she agreed with

Dodge about the economic nature of the literary marketplace, she did not accept her view that she needed to adopt masculine behaviors in order to succeed.

Nevertheless, Helen Hunt Jackson seems to have taken to heart much of Dodge's advice in *A Battle of the Books*. Throughout her correspondence with editors and publishers, Jackson discusses her work in terms of its market value, an aspect of literary work Dodge had urged writers to recognize. In Jackson's opinion, market value was established most obviously by what she was earning elsewhere for similar pieces. Her letters are filled with such comparisons. One letter to William Hayes Ward in 1875 is typical: "I send you these $15 poems,—You have not yet told me, however, if you would prefer not to have any more of the longer and higher priced ones. . . . Scribners [sic] have just paid me $25 each for two poems—and $40 for a third:—So you see I am not in the least exaggerating the market value of my verses when I mark them $20 and $25—Scribners paid me $75 for the Singers Hills—not so long a poem as the Independent has had from me for $50 several times."[41] Occasionally, she also based her requests for compensation on what she knew others were earning. Market value was for her an acceptable measure of literary worth.

With a glance in the direction of her Gentlemen Publishers, Jackson asserted, however, that literary quality, not popularity, should establish market worth. Therefore, she argued that writing, like any other skilled job, deserved to be well paid: "Inferior pay means inferior work, in every department of labor, and literary work is no exception," she reminded the *Independent* editor. Furthermore, she believed that the amount of skill and labor involved in the creation of a particular literary piece, rather than its length, ought to determine its value. Though she sometimes argued for higher compensation on the basis of what other publications paid *per page*, she usually opposed payments according to length, saying they encouraged writers to be careless in their work; it is harder, she maintained, and demands more skill to write ten pages than twenty. Therefore, sonnets and other short verses should have the highest value: "anything requiring as much labor & finish as a carefully constructed sonnet," she asserted at the beginning of her career, "if it be at all worthy of the name, is not overpaid by $10."[42]

Although she sought high prices for her work, she often said she did not want to be "mercenary"; rather, she wanted to be fair to her publishers as well as to herself—as Dodge claimed the market ought to be. In one dispute over compensation with William Ward, Jackson summed up her position: "I am not setting a higher price on my work than I am justified in doing.—I fully recognize that this does not in the least touch the question as to the work's being worth to the Independent, what it is to me.—and nobody would be more unwilling than I should be to have an Editor pay for my work at my own valuations when his did not coincide with it."[43] She understood there were two sides in the negotiation for compensation, not just the author's or the publisher's.

When Helen Hunt Jackson's price was not met, she did not acquiesce to the publisher's or editor's view, but asked for her manuscripts back or returned the check sent to her. She was, as Dodge advised all writers must be, perfectly willing to send her work to other publishers. She was quite straightforward about this. For instance, she once assured William Ward that if he could not pay her the $50 she asked for a paper, she would submit it to William Dean Howells at the *Atlantic*; if *he* did not want it, she would send it back to Ward for his price. Similarly, when Scribner's would not meet her price for long Saxe Holm stories, she took them to Roberts Brothers. When the *Independent* turned down a series of six articles she offered at $300, she complained bitterly that, because they were "ignorant of true literary standards & values," she would take her articles where she could earn more.[44]

In spite of her insistence on fair market value and her success in financial negotiations, she did not want to leave all the Gentleman Publisher's values behind and completely accept a competitive, commercial marketplace. To the editors at the *Independent*, Helen Hunt wrote in 1875 that it was a "humiliation to a person of recognized and established position as a writer [to be] forced to 'dicker' like a peddler of his wares." Likewise, she was furious when Dr. Holland at *Scribner's* insisted on reading her latest Saxe Holm story before accepting it, because that seemed to be at odds with the ideals of author-publisher loyalty promoted by Gentlemen Publishers. She found the right balance between the Gentleman Publisher's values and the recognition of commercial aims in Thomas Niles at the small Boston firm of Roberts Brothers. Known for his adherence to trade courtesy, his appreciation of good literature, and his advertising skill, he was "said to be generous to a fault in dealing with authors. . . . [He was] a genial and entertaining gentleman."[45]

But Niles was not the only publisher who met her terms for compensation. During her career, Helen Hunt Jackson earned the reputation of being a good businesswoman who usually got the price she set on her literary works. It is estimated that she earned between $3,000 and $4,000 a year—less than E.D.E.N. Southworth and Harriet Beecher Stowe, but comparable to Mary Abigail Dodge and certainly respectable for a professional writer of her time. Some of her sales give a good indication of her negotiating success. In 1874 she was paid $400 for a Saxe Holm story. One of her anonymous novels brought over $1,000 for its copyright, and for a series of five articles in the *Century* she received $1,250. Henry Houghton once complained that he paid more for two of her articles than he had ever paid anyone, and Thomas Niles was so sure of the success of *Ramona* that he advanced her $1,000 on her 10 percent royalty contract. Yet after her death, her personal estate was appraised at only $12,643. Had she given her money away or spent it on herself or on behalf of Indian rights? The answer may always remain a mystery. What we do know is that in her lifetime she earned both respect and financial rewards from her writing.[46]

Given her literary skills and business acumen, and her belief that it was appropriate for her to express her individuality, why did she cling so firmly to anonymity and pseudonymity for most of her career? As mentioned earlier, when Helen Hunt sent off her first poems of grief, she signed them "Marah," while her earliest series of articles appeared (with one exception) under the name "Rip Van Winkle." Both those pseudonyms, however, were soon replaced by "H. H.," her most frequently used and least evasive pen name; it was the one she used to sign her poems and essays. Later, when she started writing short stories, she used the name "Saxe Holm." Her editorials in the *Independent* were published anonymously, as were her first novels in Roberts Brothers' "No Name Series." Only at the end of her career did she sign her work with her own name, "Helen Jackson," and even then she appended in parentheses "H. H."

There is evidence that, like some other women writers, Jackson originally chose to use disguises because she lacked confidence in her literary abilities. In an 1867 letter to the editor William Church, she wrote: "I shrink from any further publicity than attaches to the initials. If the things I say are good for anything, the initials are, I think sufficiently noticeable to be identified with them: if *not*, no added length of signature would help it, & the less identification, the better!" It appears that this concern may have persisted throughout her career, even after she had established a solid reputation. When critics attacked *Mercy Philbrick's Choice*, Jackson admitted to her friend Moncure Conway, "I have an unfortunate but unconquerable tendency always to doubt the praise—and believe the blame." Nevertheless, her self-doubts ought not to be exaggerated; after all, she never considered giving up her profession because of them. As

Higginson pointed out, she may have questioned her abilities with each new undertaking, "yet was eager to try everything and the moment each plunge was taken lost all fear." One wonders, then, if to some extent the expression of uncertainty was a cover for a very elevated self-esteem, such as was reflected in her assertiveness in negotiating high pay and in the enthusiasm with which she pursued her career.[47]

In any case, there are other reasons, even more compelling, to explain why Helen Hunt Jackson chose not to use her own name for most of her literary career. Those reasons reflect her beliefs both in True Womanhood and in the expression of her individuality. Her acceptance of True Womanhood seems to have inclined her to adopt the conservative demeanor of literary disguise and the equally conservative practice of separating public and private spheres. At the same time, the use of pseudonyms allowed her to express her personality and to increase her market value.

It was very much in character for the woman who adhered to conventional views of womanhood and of literary style to adopt and maintain the well-respected literary habits of anonymity and pseudonymity. Like all writers, Jackson was aware that many of her predecessors had used these devices to express their disdain of mere personal fame and popularity. By the 1860s and 1870s literary disguises were less common than they had been earlier in the century, but they were by no means passé. An article written in 1877 identifies no fewer than 239 pseudonyms, a large proportion in current use, of which approximately 60 percent were used by males and 40 percent by females.[48] Furthermore, many writers still maintained their anonymity for editorials and book reviews. So, by electing pseudonymity and anonymity for herself, Helen Hunt Jackson tried to place herself in the company of those who aspired to more than immediate fame.

Unfortunately, her choice may have had the opposite effect of limiting critical knowledge of her work. Thomas Wentworth Higginson and others pointed out that her disguises actually decreased public recognition of her varied talent. When she died, the *New York Evening Post* lamented: "Her [personal] fame was limited . . . by her preference for a somewhat veiled and disguised way of writing. It is hard for two initial letters to cross the Atlantic and she had therefore no European fame; and as she took apparently a real satisfaction in concealing her identity and mystifying her public, it is very likely that the authorship of some of her best prose work will never be absolutely known."[49] Being undervalued as a writer was probably an unintended result of her literary disguises.

A second, more important reason for choosing literary disguise was related to her belief in True Womanhood. As a True Woman, she valued privacy; she hated gossip about her personal life, even by her neighbors. Like Mary Abigail Dodge, Helen Hunt Jackson resisted requests to be part of biographical studies, even when her mentor Higginson made the request. She was as evasive as Dodge and even tried to mislead reporters by giving them an incorrect birth date. Indeed, at times she was almost paranoid about preserving her privacy. Laura Stedman told Kate Field in 1875 that Helen "nearly bit poor Louise Moulton's head off once for mentioning her name, *Mrs Hunt*, in a review of one of her books—She said, she did *not* belong to the public *personally* & must never be alluded to *save* as *H H*."[50]

Jackson's views about privacy definitely were related to her acceptance of certain proprieties of woman's sphere. In 1870 she became distressed when the *Atlantic* identified her work as written by Helen Hunt; she angrily told James Fields that, if he used her full name, he needed to add that she was the widow of Edward Hunt. After her second marriage, she bluntly asked a friend not to address her letters "Helen *Hunt* Jackson" because the use of "Hunt" seemed inappropriate to her new status. A few years later she requested that Bishop Whipple not mention her connection to the Hunt family in the introduction to *A Century of Dishonor* because the Hunts did not share her views. In each of these cases, she wanted to protect her private family life and conform to the traditional notion of feminine decorum. It seems reasonable to conclude, then, that literary disguise was one of the ways Jackson tried to maintain the privacy appropriate to her woman's sphere.[51]

But her sense of privacy certainly was not as extreme as that of her friend Emily Dickinson, though they probably felt some kinship in their beliefs. Dickinson may have trusted Jackson because Jackson understood that certain temperaments, especially artistic ones, needed isolation. On her side, Jackson was probably attracted to Dickinson's acceptance of a feminine life-style, out of the public limelight. Because she really did sympathize with Dickinson's public reticence, Jackson said she would hand copy Dickinson's poems herself before submitting them for the anonymous *A Masque of Poets*: "Surely, in the shelter of such *double* anonymousness as that will be, you need not shrink," she wrote.[52] But Jackson's motivation for maintaining her privacy had more to do with conforming to social standards of True Women than with protecting her creative energies, as Dickinson seems to have wished to do. Moreover, Jackson's belief in maintaining the modesty of womanhood was tempered by her belief in expressing her individuality. Thus, in contrast to Emily Dickinson, Jackson published her work, traveled widely in the United States and on two occasions in Europe, socialized freely with literary and personal friends, and, at the end of her career, took up the cause of native Americans.

While helping to maintain her privacy and the trappings of woman's sphere, anonymity and pseudonymity also facilitated Jackson's expression of her individuality, especially her mischievous side. In terms of her writing, she found that she could speak more pointedly and critically in anonymous editorials because she need not worry that the subjects of her essays could be identified through their connection to her. In addition, she discovered that anonymity and pseudonymity gave her the opportunity to trick people, a pleasure she had relished since childhood. For instance, in a letter to Moncure Conway about the speculations surrounding the authorship of *Mercy Philbrick's Choice*, she wrote: "I have had great fun in discussing it—having intimate friends say—'What utter trash!' Don't you think so?—.... The new Saxe Holm (a short one) which begins in next Scribner, will probably give rise to still more interesting discussions." Other correspondence confirms that she often laughed at the unknowing remarks of others about her work. In fact, it was this sort of private joke she offered Emily Dickinson as a reason to publish a poem or two in *A Masque of Poets*: "I think you would have much amusement in seeing to whom the critics, those shrewd guessers, would ascribe your verses."[53]

Although she generally enjoyed the Saxe Holm mystery, this trick sometimes backfired on her. So many people claimed to have written the stories that in 1878 she threatened to "come forward boldly, and cover these abominable liars with confusion." Still, she derived some satisfaction from knowing that such claims must mean that the stories were popular. "Even that does not wholly satisfy me," she wrote, laughing about the state of her soul. "If I have any share of responsibility for all these falsehoods on the part of people who say they did when they didn't, in addition to the responsibility of the true Saxe Holm who says she didn't when she did, shall I not have a big *account* to settle?" Yet, despite the frustration, she never broke her silence about these stories in public and their authorship was the best kept literary secret of the nineteenth century.[54]

But if her individuality thrived on the mystery of Saxe Holm and her True Woman's decorum was preserved by Saxe Holm and H. H., she also profited from the market value of her signatures. Just as she turned other expressions of the Gentleman Publisher's marketplace to her business advantage, she incorporated pseudonymity and anonymity into her marketing strategy. In 1867, early in her career, she wrote William Church of the *Galaxy*: "I hope my initials will not be omitted in the advertised index list, as they were last month. Of course that insertion is of advantage to me, in a business point of view, & I am by no means insensible to that."[55] Similarly, she told Horace Scudder that she wanted to make her initials "marketable." Because her initials had become so valuable at the time of her second marriage, she continued to use them and, even when she published *Ramona* under Helen Jackson, she attached H. H. in parentheses just to make sure the audience knew who the author was.

Market value was also a factor in the decision to maintain the Saxe Holm mystery and to publish her first novels anonymously. Even when annoyed by false claims to her work, she admitted to Charles Scribner that she concealed her identity as Saxe Holm because, among other reasons, "the market value of the work is much enhanced by the mystery and by the conflicting of claimants."[56] She herself stirred up the mystery by her denials and once even wrote "A History of the Claimants" to advertise a new Saxe Holm story. Her novels, *Mercy Philbrick's Choice* and *Hetty's Strange History*, planned as Saxe Holm publications, finally appeared anonymously because Roberts Brothers agreed to pay her asking price. She profited greatly from their highly rewarding publishing scheme.

Pseudonymity and anonymity offered additional advantages in the marketplace. Having two pen names, like having at least two publishers, was a good hedge against market failure of the one or the other. Two names also kept the public from becoming satiated with works by Helen Hunt Jackson, thereby preserving her market value. And the anonymity of editorials and book reviews made it possible to fail here and there without marring a long-term reputation.

Helen Hunt Jackson found several benefits in pseudonymity and anonymity that related to her views of herself. So, why did she finally abandon literary disguise by publishing under her own name, first her report on the Mission Indians in California (1883) and then, more importantly, her novel *Ramona* (1884)? And how do we reconcile her mature activism with her encouragement of the very quiet, private Emily Dickinson? Some might explain these apparently incongruous activities as the unpredictable reactions of, as Higginson called her, "the most brilliant, impetuous, and thoroughly individual woman of her time."[57] It is more probable, however, that her signature on *Ramona* and her support of Dickinson were the result of Jackson's mature sense of herself as a professional literary woman expressing her womanhood and her individuality.

Aspects of both sides of Jackson's personality were revealed in the creation of *Ramona*. Her vision of True Womanhood was embodied in the values and behaviors of her heroine, Ramona, while she herself asserted her True Womanhood by seeking to promote truth and love and to improve the moral behavior of whites toward native Americans. In addition, Jackson demonstrated her individual approach to literary work. With the same commitment and attention to detail she had shown in her extensive study with Higginson, she spent months in the Astor Library researching treaties for *A Century of Dishonor* and did not begin to write *Ramona* until she had absorbed a great deal of background history and local color. Indeed, *Ramona* represented the highest expression of Jackson's literary techniques, for, even though written "at lightening speed," it was, in her opinion and that of some critics, "the best [English] I ever wrote."[58]

What was somewhat new for Jackson with this novel was her aspiration to be a writer in the tradition of Harriet Beecher Stowe. That she might be of Stowe's stature undoubtedly occurred to her in December 1879, when she and Stowe were placed at the head table at Oliver Wendell Holmes's birthday party. She received further encouragement to think of herself as being like Stowe from the editor J. B. Gilder. The comparison clearly appealed to her and she mentioned it to several different people: "If I could write a story that would do for the Indian a thousandth part of what Uncle Tom's Cabin did for the Negro, I would be thankful." Though she felt she might be driven by a demon while she was in the midst of producing *Ramona*, in retrospect, she used a language more reminiscent of Stowe's sense of divine inspiration to describe the writing: "I did not write *Ramona*. It was written *through* me. My lifeblood went into it—all I had thought, felt, and suffered for five years on the Indian question." Given the implicit and explicit comparisons to Stowe, it is not surprising that she regarded this book, along with *A Century of Dishonor*, as her most important work. Her aspirations probably are one reason why she wanted her own name, rather than a pseudonym, on their title pages.[59]

Despite appearances, however, the signature did not signal a whole new sense of herself or her purpose as a writer. By the time *Ramona* appeared in print, her name was thoroughly identified with the cause of native Americans; disguise in the case of the novel would have been futile, even unnecessarily artificial, and certainly would have been less marketable than her own name in connection with Indian rights. But just to make sure she would not lose any sales, she added her initials in parentheses after her signature in order to attract those readers who were loyal to the work of H. H. What the use of her own name did *not* mean was that she was willing to abandon her privacy; after *Ramona*, she continued to resist journalists' probing of personal details of her life.[60]

In other words, Jackson's involvement with the Indian cause and the publication of *Ramona* under her own name was not a dramatically different phase of her life, but an extension of it. By publishing both with her name and with her initials, she asserted the connections between her previous work and *Ramona*. The respectable literary career she had built over almost twenty years, beginning by studying with Thomas Wentworth Higginson, came to fruition when she became a crusader like Higginson and like the other major woman writer of her time, Harriet Beecher Stowe. Though seemingly paradoxical, Helen Hunt Jackson's encouragement of the very private writer Emily Dickinson can also be understood as the logical expression of her mature literary career.

Certainly, Jackson led a more "wide-ranging and cosmopolitan" life than Dickinson, but, as indicated above, their lives were intertwined, though loosely, from beginning to end. They were never intimate friends, yet, having grown up in the small town of Amherst, they shared access to a network of people who kept them informed about each other. Thus, Austin Dickinson reported to his family and friends details about Edward Hunt after seeing him at a distance in Boston. And in March 1876, Helen reported to Emily one of the discussions she had had about her: "A Mr. Dudley of Milwaukee, spent a day with us last week, and we talked about you. So threads cross, even on the outermost edges of the web."[61] Furthermore, rumors often connected the two of them, such as when Emily was guessed to be the author of the Saxe Holm stories or was assumed to be the inspiration for one or another of Jackson's heroines. Probably more importantly, they shared interests and views of the world that made them appreciate each other. Both loved nature and wrote extensively about it. Both preferred to preserve their privacy, and both were committed to literary work.

Many biographers have concluded that Helen Hunt Jackson was the only contemporary who recognized the significance of Emily Dickinson's poetry and the only one to approach her as an equal. There is ample evidence that Jackson did hold Dickinson's work in high regard. In her letter of March 1876, Jackson told Dickinson, "You are a great poet," and urged her to publish her poems. Unlike Higginson, Jackson did not condescend to Dickinson and acknowledged to herself, and to Dickinson, the originality in Dickinson's work. In 1879, after receiving "Before you thought of spring," Jackson wrote her friend, "I know your 'Blue bird' by heart—and that is more than I do of any of my own verses. I also want your permission to send it to Col. Higginson to read. These two things are my testimonial to its merit. We have blue birds here—I might have had the sense to write something about one myself, but I never did: and now I never can." Despite her difficulties with understanding some of what Dickinson wrote, Jackson appreciated her creativity and understood that it was of a different sort than her own. Indeed, she so generously praised Dickinson's work to her publisher Thomas Niles that he made several requests to publish her poetry after Jackson had submitted "Success is counted sweetest" for *A Masque of Poets*.[62]

But we would exaggerate Jackson's understanding of Dickinson's greatness if we did not see that the support she gave Emily Dickinson was typical of her practice throughout her career of encouraging other writers, particularly women. Alice Wellington Rollins described Jackson's mentorship in her series "Authors at Home":

> It would be interesting to know how many of the younger writers for the magazines have owed their success, not to that instant recognition of genius by the editor which is popularly supposed to be the secret, but to the generous appreciation and recognition of Helen Jackson, who has approached many an editor with manuscript in hand, and insisted: "You don't want any more poetry, I know; but you shall listen to this!" and who will lend to [the reading of] the poem of the ox-eyed daisies, by one of the Goodale Sisters, or to the "Frost" of Edith Thomas, or a poem on an apple, by Amelia Barr, a depth of expression, a loveliness of meaning, and a grace of rendering, which she would never try to give to her own work; exclaiming, as she finishes, "I would give anything—anything—if I had written that myself!"[63]

Having been mentored so conscientiously by Thomas Wentworth Higginson, as well as believing in the importance of nurturing as a True Woman, Jackson always encouraged other writers. She also wanted to help them express their individuality. Thus, mentoring became an important part of her career.

A close look at some comments Jackson made to Emily Dickinson indicates that she (Jackson) often counseled the poet by offering advice that reflected her own vision of literary work. For instance, as mentioned earlier in this chapter, Jackson told Dickinson she appreciated her "simplest and most direct lines best." In the same letter, she encouraged Dickinson to publish as a way of pleasing others: "You say you find great pleasure in reading my verses. Let somebody somewhere whom you do not know have the same pleasure in reading yours." At another time, when attempting to persuade Dickinson to let her (Jackson) publish the portfolios of her poems, Jackson advanced conventional justifications—cheer and moral purpose—for literature of the time: "Surely, after you are what is called 'dead,' you will be willing that the poor ghosts you have left behind, should be cheered and pleased by your verses, will you not?—You ought to be.—I do not think we have a right to withhold from the world a word or a thought any more than a *deed*, which might help a single soul."[64] These comments suggest Jackson did not understand that Dickinson's originality lay in her ability to ignore such advice.

Whether or not Jackson fully realized Dickinson's literary genius, her importance to the poet (and to the other writers she mentored) cannot be denied. Dickinson clearly responded to Jackson's praise. She extravagantly complimented Jackson's poetry—"stronger than any written by women since Mrs. Browning," she told Higginson. Feeling Jackson's genuine respect for her, Dickinson wrote her without the coyness and game playing she used with Higginson. In addition, at a time in her life when she admitted few people to her presence, she warmly welcomed the Jacksons as visitors into her home. Furthermore, she never complained to Jackson about the publication of "Success" in *A Masque of Poets*, and, though she avoided the issue of literary executorship, she never stopped expressing friendship toward her friend. After Jackson's death, Emily Dickinson lovingly recalled, "The immortality she gave / we borrowed at her Grave— / For just one plaudit / famishing, / The Might of Human Love—." This was a sincere testament of Jackson's significance as a literary friend.[65]

In many ways, Helen Hunt Jackson, like Emily Dickinson, is an enigmatic figure and the paradoxes of her career may be open to various interpretations. One way they can be understood is by seeing her as a True Woman who also believed in the development and expression of her artistic individuality. Her individuality, in fact, led to her undertaking a career that was more businesslike and market oriented than the other writers examined in this study. Hers was one response (and a successful one at that!) to a literary marketplace that was struggling to balance the older Gentleman Publisher's values with more modern commercial goals. Emily Dickinson's rejection of the market was another kind of response to that increasingly impersonal marketplace, and Elizabeth Stuart Phelps's was a third.

7

Elizabeth Stuart
Phelps (Ward)
*Courtesy of the
Arthur and
Elizabeth Schlesinger
Library, Radcliffe
College, Cambridge,
Massachusetts*

*The Demise of
Feminine Strength*

The Career of Elizabeth
Stuart Phelps (Ward)

As the second half of the nineteenth century passed, the values of both publishers and authors underwent a transformation. No longer did publishers conform so readily to the Gentleman Publisher's values in dealing with their authors. No longer were authors so reluctant to be business people, too. Unlike Helen Hunt Jackson, whose personal drive fit with the emerging economic order, other authors, like Elizabeth Stuart Phelps (1844–1911), felt many anxieties. Letters from Phelps to her publishers at the end of her career make these anxieties clear. In 1894, for instance, she wrote angrily to her publishers Henry Houghton and George Mifflin in response to their letter informing her that they intended to review her latest book submission before accepting it. As their long-time contributor and friend, she expected them to publish anything she wrote without question. Thus, she argued that their review was unfair, that it put the publication of her work in question, and that, as a loyal contributor, she deserved better. In her letter, she appealed to the oldest values—loyalty, friendship, generosity, and trust—of the literary marketplace.[1]

Elizabeth Stuart Phelps claimed the privileges of the Gentleman Publisher's marketplace because she had been a successful, if not always popular, writer since the publication of her best-seller *The Gates Ajar* in 1868 by the predecessor of Houghton, Mifflin: Fields, Osgood and Company. Having begun her literary career in the era of Gentlemen Publishers, she continued to rely on many of its assumptions, even at the end of the century when the literary market, like modern society in general, was emphasizing the newer values of timeliness, profitability, efficiency, and objectivity. As we shall see, Phelps struggled to adapt to the new marketplace, but she never was as comfortable as she had been in the "old-fashioned" one. Indeed, many of the disappointments she expressed at the end of her career can be attributed to her continuing adherence to the personal and literary values that had facilitated her predecessors' success earlier in the century.

More than any other writer studied here, Elizabeth Stuart Phelps came naturally to her literary career: she was, as James T. Fields said, from a "family of large circulations." Her maternal grandfather, Moses Stuart (1780–1852), Professor of Sacred Literature at Andover Theological Seminary, was the author of many highly regarded scholarly publications. Her paternal grandfather, Eliakim Phelps (1790–1880), actually more of a reformer than a writer, wrote one religious tract that sold 200,000 copies. In addition, her own father, Austin Phelps (1820–90), the most well published of her family, produced devotional and pedagogical works, including a best-seller on prayer. And her mother, the first Elizabeth (Stuart) Phelps (1815–52), wrote several works of popular religious fiction for children and adults in the two years before she died; her book *The Sunny Side: Or, A Country Minister's Wife* (1851) sold over 100,000 copies in its first year. Even her favorite aunt, Sarah (Stuart) Robbins (1817–1910), was a prolific writer of Sunday school and juvenile literature.[2]

Into this religious and literary family a daughter was born on August 31, 1844. She was christened Mary Gray Phelps after one of her mother's friends.[3] At the time of her birth the family lived in Boston, where her father was pastor of the Park Street Congregational Church. In 1848 the Phelpses moved to Andover, Massachusetts, where Austin became Professor of Sacred Rhetoric and Homiletics and later president of Andover Theological Seminary, a conservative Congregational stronghold. Here, in an academic, religious community, "Lily," as she was called in her family, grew to adulthood. After her mother's death when Lily was eight, her father assumed a special importance in her life, both as a parent and as a role model of intellectual, literary life. In her autobiography, she claimed he was her "hero" and her "climate."[4]

Of him she wrote, "As soon as I began to think, I began to reverence thought and study and the hard work of a man devoted to the high ends of a scholar's life. . . . Day after day the watchful girl observed the life of a student—its scholarly tastes, its high ideals, its scorn of worldliness and paltry aims or petty indulgences, and forever its magnificent habits of *work*." While she learned to value the scholar's life, she also developed a passion for literature: "His department was that of rhetoric, and his appreciation of the uses and graces of language very early descended like a mantle upon me. I learned to read and to love reading, not because I was made to, but because I could not help it. It was the atmosphere I breathed."[5]

But if her father was the hero of her childhood, her mother was the tragic heroine. From her, Phelps first discovered both the possibilities and the burdens of an intellectual, literary life for a woman. At a young age, she observed that, because her mother was a writer, she was as important outside the home as within it. As a result, the daughter grew to believe that the elder Elizabeth was a better person for pursuing her career. Years later, she described her as an "unusual" woman who had "achieved the difficult reconciliation between genius and domestic life." Yet, when pressed to explain the reasons for her mother's untimely death in 1852, the daughter admitted that her mother had experienced many strains in trying to balance the obligations of career and home: "Her last book and her last [third] baby came together, and killed her," according to Phelps. "She lived one of those rich and piteous lives such as only gifted women know; torn by the civil war of the dual nature which can be given to women only. It was as natural for her daughter to write as to breathe." After her mother's death, Lily took her name, Elizabeth Stuart Phelps—an act that seemed to destine her to her own literary career as well as to her own struggles with a dual nature.[6]

By temperament Phelps was something of a rebel, like many other writers (including her mother) before her, but her rebellion was often suppressed. As a child she climbed trees, walked fences, and was "into every little mischief of snow or rainfall, flower, field, or woods or ice."[7] In fact, because of her poor health, her father advocated fresh air over lengthy piano lessons. But, on the whole, the Phelps family—unlike, for example, the family of Mary Abigail Dodge (Gail Hamilton)—did not encourage self-assertion. Instead, by their examples and teachings, they encouraged self-denial. Despite her career, her mother often was self-sacrificing and wrote stories in which the protagonists learned submission. Her father, both in his religious emphasis on unselfishness and unworldliness and in his traditional views of women as the helpers of men, also expected Lily to be compliant. Moreover, her stepmother, Mary Johnson Phelps (1829–1918), worked hard to teach Lily the traditional tasks—sewing, cleaning, and cooking—of self-denying women. As a result of all these messages, rebellion and self-denial warred in Lily as she was growing up, with self-denial often winning out. Thus, even though she resented having to dust the dining room and to cut "out underclothes in the March vacations," she never complained assertively or persuasively enough to be relieved of the tasks.[8]

Her education, while quite good, did not particularly foster self-assertion, either. As a young child, Lily attended Abbot Academy in Andover, though at this time in life she was as likely to be found in treetops as reading. Later, she became a day student at Mrs. Edwards' School for Young Ladies where she was "not at all a remarkable scholar," though she usually ranked near the head of her class. Actually, her intellectual opportunities were fairly broad. Like Abby Dodge, Lily studied mental philosophy, English literature, Latin, astronomy, physiology, mathematics, history, and chemistry—all the subjects of a male college education, except Greek and trigonometry. She not only had Bible lessons from the conservative theologian Edwards A. Park, but also heard lectures at the seminary by liberal speakers like Ralph Waldo Emerson. But, most significantly, her education, like her home life, stressed Christian witness and Christian values, especially those, she said, of unselfishness, integrity, honor, truthfulness, unworldliness, and work. Overall, her education was meant to prepare her to be a minister's wife—educated but submissive to his will.[9]

While growing up, Phelps alternately accepted and rebelled against the conservative expectations of the Andover community—an ambivalent response to her home and its values that she never outgrew. As an adult, she liked to recall the ways in which she and other women resisted the dictates of what she called this very "masculine" place, but her recollections suggest a very limited rebellion.[10] For example, she reported in her autobiography that her life, like other women's in the town, revolved around the lives and concerns of the university men, but, by way of resistance, she never attended an anniversary exercise at the seminary and always maintained her "abnormal objection to Trustees." Though usually she listened quietly to men's views, she occasionally challenged some, including Emerson's on one of his visits to Andover. Furthermore, even while caught up in an active social life with boys studying at Phillips Academy or the theological seminary, she says she most admired the single women who with "free will absolute . . . passed through life alone." Among them, she fondly described her teacher Mrs. Edwards, who "like other strong and gentle women . . . had her 'way' when nobody thought so." She also quietly observed the success of Harriet Beecher Stowe, her Andover neighbor from 1851 to 1864, whose fame "puzzled" the townsmen "too feudal in their views of women in those days, to understand a life like Mrs. Stowe's." But in those days, neither she nor the women whom she admired were outspoken rebels; their resistance, like Phelps's own, was more constrained. In fact, this was Phelps's approach throughout life. Despite some substantial disagreements with Andover's outlook, she never completely severed her ties with this home.

Phelps's ambivalence about her community is mirrored in her accounts of why she became a writer—explained at one time as following in her parents' footsteps and, at another, as trying to assert her independence and maturity. Both impulses certainly played a part. Two events in her sixteenth year, however, crystallized her commitment to a literary career. First, her father read to her works by Thomas De Quincey and William Wordsworth, giving her a greater appreciation of literature than ever before. Not long afterward, she read Elizabeth Barrett Browning's *Aurora Leigh*, the epic of a woman writer. Its impact on her was profound: "What Shakespeare or the Latin Fathers might have done for some other impressionable girl, Mrs. Browning—forever bless her strong and gentle name!—did for me. I owe to her, distinctly, the first visible aspiration (ambition is too low a word) to do some honest, hard work of my own in the World Beautiful, and for it."[11] A daughter, literally and figuratively, of the pioneering women writers, Phelps at sixteen had great hopes for her literary future and some foresight about the hard work it would entail.

Still, she was "shy and self-distrustful" and might never have pursued a career in writing if her first efforts had been unsuccessful. In the beginning, she lacked the self-confidence so characteristic of writers like Mary Abigail Dodge. In retrospect, Phelps readily admitted that "for the opinion of important editors, and for the sacredness of market value in literary wares, as well as in professorships or cotton cloth, I had a kind of respect at which I sometimes wonder."[12] Fortunately, her first efforts were well received. "A Sacrifice Consumed," a story inspired by her own loss of a young love at Antietam in 1862, was published in *Harper's New Monthly Magazine* in 1864 when she was twenty. Both her earnings of twenty-five dollars for the story and her father's "gentle word of approval" spurred her on. *Harper's* accepted several other stories from her in the 1860s and never sent one back. Encouraged by those successes, Phelps soon undertook commissions for Sunday school books, written to inspire young people to develop their Christian character, and created a series of "Trotty" stories, written for the magazine *Our Young Folks* while Mary Abigail Dodge (Gail Hamilton) was an editor. She began to think about unequal opportunities for young boys and girls and wrote her first two articles on women's work in 1867 and 1868.

Although most of Phelps's earliest stories were conventional, sentimental representations of love, increasingly she began addressing social issues. Her first novel, *Up Hill, or Life in a Factory* (1865), reflected her interest in the problems of the impoverished, as did her 1866 serial, "Jane Gurley's Story," published in a literary monthly *Hours at Home*. Ironically, while conforming to Andover's intellectual habits of work, Phelps found that her maturing social conscience put her at odds with Andover's scholasticism. Quietly, hesitatingly in her fiction, she began rebelling against Andover's rejection of social activism, its conservative theology, and its traditional views of women. To write "The Tenth of January" (1868), a love story set in the context of events surrounding the collapse of the

Pemberton textile mills in 1860, Phelps did the unheard of for an Andover woman: she conducted extensive research on the accident by interviewing workers, engineers, newspapermen, and others for information. Her work was rewarded outside Andover, if not within it. The story appeared in the prestigious *Atlantic Monthly*, and both John Greenleaf Whittier and Thomas Wentworth Higginson wrote her letters of praise.[13]

In the meantime, Phelps had been working on *The Gates Ajar* (1868), the book that would become the most popular work of her literary career. Since 1862, Phelps had been reading literature, philosophy, and theology, as she planned a book to speak to women grieving over their losses from the Civil War. She spent two years writing and rewriting the story of Mary Cabot, who lost her brother in the war, and of Aunt Winifred Forceythe, who challenges orthodox interpretations of the Bible, such as one might have heard in Andover, with her own views of heaven as the place for reunions with loved ones and of rewards for deprivations in this life, particularly for those suffered by women. Although he had published some of her early stories, James Fields was reluctant to accept this work. Finally he did so, two years after receiving the manuscript, at the urging of his wife Annie.[14]

Sales of *The Gates Ajar* moved rapidly and it soon became one of the most talked-about books of its time.[15] While presses and pulpits, including Andover's, debated its heretical religious views of an earthlike heaven, entrepreneurs made the most of the controversy by creating "Gates Ajar" collars, tippets, cigars, patent medicines, music, and funeral wreaths. So popular was the book that Phelps was deluged with mail for the next thirty years. By the end of the century, the American sales would approach 100,000, while British circulation would outrun that, and the book would be translated into French, German, Dutch, and Italian.

The success of this work radically changed Phelps's life. As she described it, she "whirled through readjustments of scene, of society, of purposes, of hopes, and now, at last, of ambitions."[16] Though she wrote the book shivering under her mother's old cape in the unheated attic of her home, after its publication her family gave her more time and space for her work. When she first began writing, she had dreamed of being able to escape Andover's summer heat; now she had enough money to get away to the Cape Ann shore. Prior to *The Gates Ajar* she was only an obscure writer from Andover; afterward she was considered to be an important part of the New England literary community.

Having successfully defied Andover's religious views and established herself as a well-respected author, Phelps confronted her conservative family with the declaration that she would henceforth work for women's rights. Though feeling more self-confident than she ever had in her life, it was still traumatic for Phelps to challenge so directly those whom she loved.[17] But in these years her confidence and assertiveness overcame her lessons in self-denial. Throughout the seventies, women's rights was the major focus of her novels and short stories as well as the articles she published in the *Independent* and the *Woman's Journal*, the official newspaper of the American Woman's Suffrage Association. In her articles, many of which she wrote in a debate with Mary Abigail Dodge (Gail Hamilton) for the *Independent*, Phelps argued in support of woman suffrage, coeducation, varied employment opportunities, equality in marriage, and dress reform. Her novel *The Silent Partner* (1871) challenged the view that women ought to marry and remain silent on social and economic issues, although in the end it hedged on the issue of women's complete autonomy. Her chapter in *Sex and Education* (1874), edited by Julia Ward Howe, argued against the prevalent notion that education made women sick, asserting instead that lack of intellectual stimulation was the cause of illness. Moreover, *The Story of Avis* (1877), the most powerful and searing of all of Phelps's work, poignantly illustrated the psychological conflicts between a woman's artistic longings and a family's demands on her time and energy. Its depressing vision of marriage was counterbalanced by *An Old Maid's Paradise* (1879), the humorous account of a single woman who set up housekeeping at the seashore, as Phelps herself did in 1876.[18] Despite the energy and self-affirmation of these works in the 1870s, other more conservative, somewhat contradictory, topics continued to crop up in Phelps's work. In her first poetry collection, about which she sought advice in Florida from Harriet Beecher Stowe, romantic love and Christian self-sacrifice were important themes.

The seventies were active, self-assertive years for Phelps in other ways as well. During this period, a reformer's and a writer's impulses seemed to war in her soul.[19] She circulated at least one women's rights petition in Andover in 1871 and urged Mary Livermore to speak there. She probably attended gatherings of local suffrage advocates, though she did not appear at national conventions, sending greetings instead to be read to participants. In 1873 she gave lectures to the New England Woman's Club on dress reform (republished as *What to Wear?*) and wore the beach dress she advocated. In 1876 she became the first woman to deliver a series of lectures at Boston University. Entitled "Representative Modern Fiction," the series centered on the work of George Eliot, with whom Phelps was then corresponding. She accepted requests to repeat the talks at Abbot Academy and in local Boston parlors, though she never enjoyed public speaking. She must have been effective, however, because Whittier said, "I have never heard a woman speak with such magnetic power."[20] In 1878, Phelps helped circulate a letter soliciting contributions to endow a woman's professorship at Boston University. In addition, she took up temperance work among her summer neighbors at Gloucester, Massachusetts, in 1875, leading a religious service in a rum shop and giving a public reading from her own writings.[21] For this cause, she also solicited funds, advised the tempted, and worked with a reform club. She ended the decade by writing poems to the graduating classes of Abbot Academy and Smith College. "Victurae Salutamus" (1879), a poem for the latter, charged the young women to live up to the ideals of "the Woman's Hour" that had now come.

By contrast, in these years Phelps presented herself less forcefully in her correspondence with editors and publishers than in her fiction and reform work. In general she seems to have assumed that the Gentleman Publisher's values would prevail. Having been paid quickly and fairly by James Fields for *The Gates Ajar*, she trusted that such treatment would continue. Consequently, only occasionally in this decade did she name a price for or make demands about her work. She did, however, urge her editors and publishers to take care with proofreading, illustrations, and the timing of the release of her work.[22]

At the end of this decade, Phelps's health, never good, collapsed, and she left her really active involvement in suffrage and temperance work forever.[23] In fact, a distinct phase of Phelps's career—symbolized by her many self-assertive activities—ended with her breakdown. Having inherited poor health from both sides of the family, she waged frequent battles during her life with insomnia, brain fever, sensitive nerves, partial blindness, sprains, laryngitis, and, finally, heart disease. What is notable, however, is that even though she was never healthy, Phelps seldom referred to her medical problems in her correspondence of the 1870s when she was feeling strong psychologically. But from 1879 until the late 1880s, her letters frequently mention her ailments. Her serious physical breakdown at the end of the 1870s and her subsequent complaints, especially about insomnia, seem to have been the result of many factors, including overwork, discouragement over what she felt were her own literary limitations, some critics' censure of *The Story of Avis*, and her father's disapproval of woman suffrage.

On a personal level, her father's criticism of her suffrage views must have been the most painful. The man who was her "hero" opposed women's rights, not simply in private conversations with her but also publicly in two antisuffrage articles: "Woman Suffrage as Judged by the Working of Negro-Suffrage" (1878) and "Reform in the Political Status of Women" (1881). Like many other antisuffragists, he supported concepts of separate but equal spheres of activity for men and women. He did not oppose higher education for women, expanding their employments to include those that would not lower their "caste," protecting their property rights, or extending their participation in charity. On those issues he and his daughter generally agreed. However, Austin Phelps felt women should not be given the vote because they had "no physical power to defend it," the Bible was against it, it flouted "the dignity of maternity," and agitation for it fostered antagonism between the sexes leading to divorce, "discontented" daughters, and "morbid individualism."[24] How much his articles hurt her, Phelps never publicly revealed, but her recurring bouts with insomnia may have been an indication of the anguish she felt. Instead of arguing back, she reverted to her earlier pattern of self-denial in response to her family: she repressed her criticism of her father, reiterated her public admiration of him, and muted (though never denied) her firm support of the movement to increase women's rights.

To be sure, there was a stubborn streak in Phelps that did not give way to criticism. In fact, throughout her career she showed a certain pride in always being "berated for something by somebody."[25] Though she wrote less prolifically in the eighties than in the seventies, she nevertheless continued regularly to publish short stories, novels, essays, and poetry. By the 1880s she was, in fact, in an enviable position for a writer. Her work was in demand by editors and publishers. She had a solid literary reputation and appeared in many biographical dictionaries of important writers. Critics compared her favorably to Nathaniel Hawthorne, Harriet Beecher Stowe, and George Eliot. Unlike Mary Abigail Dodge or Helen Hunt Jackson, she freely responded to requests for biographical information, even showing some fatigue because they were so frequent.[26]

Despite the acclaim and her determined pursuit of her career, signs of strain were apparent. In some respects, she seemed to be losing her self-confidence. Although she wrote a poem in honor of Harriet Beecher Stowe and brought it to the birthday party given by Houghton, Mifflin and Company for Stowe in 1882, Phelps did not read the poem herself, as she might have in the 1870s, but had Oliver Wendell Holmes read it for her instead.[27] Her thematic concerns in her writing also shifted. Although one of her novels, *Dr. Zay* (1882), portrayed a successful female doctor, and some short stories described self-supporting women, in this decade her concern for women's rights was subsumed by a greater interest in religious questions. Thus, Phelps promoted the cause of women only indirectly within her descriptions of heaven in *Beyond the Gates* (1883) and *The Gates Between* (1887), sequels to *The Gates Ajar*.

On the other hand, in the 1880s her business dealings became more assertive. In letters to publishers and editors, she more aggressively negotiated compensation; she more frequently advised them about illustrations, cover designs, and marketing strategies for her books; and, time and again, she self-righteously defended the quality of her work. In fact, defensiveness underlies much of her correspondence in these years. She was, at least in this arena of her life, speaking out on her own behalf.[28]

But, in the meantime, the literary and social world that had supported her in the past was beginning to fall apart. Important literary friends, including James T. Fields, Henry Wadsworth Longfellow, Edward R. Sill, George Eliot, Mary Clemmer, and Helen Hunt Jackson, all died. And no sooner had she rallied from the unexpected death of her brother Stuart in 1883, than her closest personal friend, Dr. Mary Briggs Harris, died in 1886. Late in that year she revealed to a biographer how much the strains of the decade, exacerbated by insomnia and ill health, had cost her: "I work when I can work at all, at the bayonet's point; often for months not a stroke; at best never more than two or three days out of a week, and, at most, not more than two hours a day."[29]

Perhaps in reaction against grief and loneliness, Phelps married Herbert D. Ward on October 20, 1888.[30] Herbert (1861–1932) was the son of William H. Ward, managing editor of the *Independent*, a newspaper to which Phelps frequently contributed. He had graduated from Andover's Phillips Academy in 1880, but Phelps did not meet or take any particular interest in him until 1884. He completed studies at Andover Theological Seminary in 1888, sometime before their marriage. When they married, she was forty-four and he was twenty-seven—an age difference that provided much sport for the press. Undoubtedly, she expected the union to bring what she thought was best in marriage: "mutual responsibility, mutual forebearance, and mutual comfort, to replace solitary labors and lonely failures, and unshared successes."[31]

Though their marriage did meet these expectations, at least in part, it also gave her more problems.[32] On the positive side, the partners seem to have inspired each others' literary work and commiserated together over their ill health. On the negative side, marriage for Phelps meant an increase in household responsibilities and financial worries. Since her husband was never very successful at writing or anything else, their income depended more on her work than on his. In 1893, for instance, she commented in a letter on the pressure she felt to write faster than usual in order to pay for their new home in Newton Centre. Furthermore, the confusions of house building and moving from the Gloucester shore to town each season fell principally on Elizabeth's shoulders. She was further distressed by her husband's yachting until he agreed to give it up after they had been together a few years. And he, like her father, did not support woman suffrage.

Yet, in the early years of her marriage, she experienced some happiness and her health improved. At middle age, a reporter described her as a woman of average height with hair

> brushed straight back on both sides, . . . of exquisite gray. Her face is full of healthy color and alert as a girl's. Her eyes, now blue, now gray, are full of sensitiveness. She has no crows' feet and her face is unwrinkled, with the exception of two deep horizontal lines on her forehead, which have been there since childhood. It is a young face, an ideal face, a madonna face, that inspires the reverence of all who see her. Here is the face of a philosopher, a seer, and a reformer; it is the face of a true woman who carries on her heart the sorrows and woes of many—a face of infinite tenderness and of delicate expression.[33]

Although this description probably reflects the reporter's perspective on women more than anything else, it also seems to mirror Phelps's view of herself in the last two decades of her life and career. While some of her youthful rebellion persisted in various reform efforts, increasingly hers was the way of self-sacrifice characteristic of the "feminine" woman.

Still, she was occasionally assertive. She continued to sign her works "Elizabeth Stuart Phelps," though she had privately added her husband's name to her signature. (Contemporary biographical dictionaries and libraries alphabetize her under "Ward," but she never used that name professionally.) Moreover, in her 1896 autobiography, *Chapters from a Life*, she described herself proudly as a professional woman with a strong belief in women's social advancement as well as Christian ideals. She helped somewhat to organize a suffrage meeting for authors and composers in 1890 and worked a little on a suffrage referendum committee in 1895. During these years, she also wrote outspoken articles criticizing the state's prosecution of Lizzie Borden, a short story hotly denouncing the Ku Klux Klan, an editorial against war with Chile, and another voicing opposition to the Spanish-American War.[34]

Nevertheless, the quality of her social criticism was much weaker than the sustained outspokenness apparent in her works of the 1870s. In contrast to her earlier writing, her themes in the 1890s emphasized religious self-sacrifice and self-denial. In her fiction, her characterizations of women were more conservative than they had been in the past. In fact, women's rights had essentially disappeared as a theme. Instead, her major books included an interpretation of Jesus' life, a laudatory memoir of her father, and *A Singular Life* (1895), the novel about her "favorite hero," Emanuel Bayard, a minister who tried to live like Christ in a fishing village plagued by intemperance.

At the turn of the century, Phelps's health again declined, and the last ten years of her life were plagued by degenerating illnesses and depression. Her only participation in the drive for women's rights was as an honorary vice-president of the Massachusetts State Suffrage Association and signing the "Million Name" petition sent to Congress in 1910. The subject of invalidism appeared frequently in her work, providing a forum for articulating her dissatisfactions and her belief in the unending struggles of life. Rather than women's advancement, marital disruption and reconciliation were now major themes in her fiction. Her *Confessions of a Wife* (1902), a first-person narrative of a wife's revenge for her husband's desertion, appeared pseudonymously in *Century Magazine* under the name "Mary Adams." Religious faith and self-sacrifice continued to pervade her writing, and she published a drama called *Within the Gates*, the fourth and final sequel to *The Gates Ajar*.[35]

The new theme of her fiction and her life in her last years was antivivisection, a cause that seems to have appealed to Phelps's dual nature of assertiveness and self-denial.[36] On the one hand, in her efforts to promote this reform some of her old vigor and rebelliousness returned. Between bouts with illness, she not only wrote short stories and novels about mistreated animals, but she also organized petition and letter-writing drives, convinced her publisher George Mifflin to print pamphlets on the subject, wrote several speeches and articles, and lobbied the Massachusetts legislature on behalf of the animals for six years. Yet, on the other hand, her support of this cause was but a shadow of her campaign for women's rights in the 1870s, first, because she lacked physical strength, but most importantly because she described her participation in terms of self-sacrifice and martyrdom, rather than in terms of enhancing opportunities for growth and development. That attitude kept her from being as empowered as she had been when working for women's rights. Furthermore, now she was a social critic for sentimental reasons—her love of dogs (perhaps her only faithful friends)—rather than because she thought the reform would improve her own life or the lives of those around her. While her antivivisection work may have been an indirect expression of her women's rights concerns, that is, as a challenge to the male medical community, it was just that: indirect. In this cause, as in her old age, self-denial had the upper hand.

Though there were continued demands for her work, her correspondence with publishers and editors reveals many difficulties in coping with the modern literary marketplace. She complained about not being paid what she deserved and about needing more money. She was constantly annoyed by mechanical restrictions on her writing. And she was particularly troubled by the increasing impersonality of the marketplace. These concerns were compounded by increasing ill health that made it difficult for her to meet deadlines.[37]

In fact, by the end of her life Phelps's literary career was no longer fulfilling, even though she still enjoyed a moderate degree of success. The contrast in tone and content between her letters before the late 1870s and after 1890 is striking. In the earlier period she had been modestly confident and trusting, saying little about publishing details. In the later period, however, she was increasingly questioning and argumentative with her publishers and editors, telling them how she thought her work should be presented and complaining about their treatment of her. The evolution in her attitude toward her career was the result both of circumstances in her personal life—the displeasure she felt from her father for her views on women's rights, her battles with ill health, the loss of supportive literary and personal friends, and a dissatisfying marriage—and of changes in the literary marketplace. Over the course of her career, that marketplace altered its expectations of authors as well as its mode of conducting business. As the years passed, Phelps felt increasing dissonance between her concept of herself as a woman writer and the aesthetic and business values of her publishers and editors.

Despite her apparently progressive views of womanhood, Phelps held some fairly conservative values that ultimately made her uncomfortable in the modern marketplace. The contradictory nature of her beliefs was expressed by her concept of "feminine strength": "I believe more solemnly than I know how to say, in feminine *strength*," she wrote Henry Wadsworth Longfellow in 1878. "Is the lily less sweet because it is the whitest and most self-reliant of flowers? I love women as, I think, all women do not love their own kind, and it seems to me that I understand them because I love them. Always I find the deepest tenderness in the strongest woman; there, too, the largest self-sacrifice and the most faithful friend. A woman of force without tenderness is not strong, but brittle."[38] In her vision, a woman could be both self-reliant and self-denying; though strong, she could be moral, tender, and faithful. While independent, she could still be self-sacrificing. This was the type of woman Phelps herself aspired to be.

In her many stories and articles on women's rights, she attacked the conservative stereotype of the True Woman, who was supposed to be pious, pure, domestic, and submissive. Nevertheless, her own views did not wholly escape its limits. Though she did not believe women needed to be more pious than men, she did think women had greater spiritual understanding. Even while she argued that morality was a matter of choice, not innate to women, she thought women ought to express the highest moral standards. Furthermore, despite her understanding that domestic cares could be lethal to women, she idealized romantic love and a family home. And, though she thought women should be assertive and personally fulfilled, she also wanted them to express the humility and submissiveness of a Christian life. Thus, Phelps's vision both challenged the messages of True Womanhood and perpetuated some of its conservative impulses. On the continuum of popular beliefs about women in the nineteenth century, her views fall on the conservative side of New Womanhood because, while she wished to expand women's rights and social opportunities, she only ambivalently rejected the ideals of the True Woman.[39]

Although it might be argued that her views of women were the most progressive of any writer considered in this study, her conservative leanings, which increased over the years, kept her from developing any more modern sensibilities than the other writers had. Though she believed more strongly than E.D.E.N. Southworth in the appropriateness of women's independence and was more conscious of the meaning of gender than Helen Hunt Jackson, Phelps shared their tendency to idealize the traditional feminine values of nurturance, love, and domesticity. Although she readily argued for women's participation in man's sphere, her vision was as tied to woman's sphere as was the domestic feminism of Harriet Beecher Stowe. And, though she advocated expanded opportunities for women, she did not want women to be as "masculine" as Mary Abigail Dodge had suggested might be necessary. In short, despite her support of women's rights, her concept had its conservative side. In fact, as Phelps gave increasing attention to the ideal of Christian self-sacrifice, her vision of womanhood came more and more to resemble that of the most conservative writer, E.D.E.N. Southworth.

Just as she expressed both conservative and progressive views of women, Phelps also had both conservative and more modern notions of literary life. On the one hand, she rejected any attachment to the ideals of the genteel amateur writer. "I read, with a kind of hopeless envy," she wrote in her autobiography, "histories and legends of people of our craft who 'do not write for money. . . .' Personally, I have yet to breathe the ether of such a transcendent sphere."[40] On the other hand, she insisted that artists and writers, like the ideal image of authors of old, had finer sensibilities than ordinary people, not, however, because they had aspirations beyond monetary reward, but because they had developed a fine-tuned sympathy with life brought about by deep suffering or delicate nerves. Accordingly, illnesses, like Phelps's own, were a manifestation of the sensitive nerves of artists, which could be injured by cold-hearted (healthy) editors and critics. Paradoxically, the same suffering that created great work could sometimes make it difficult to accomplish. But writers struggled on because they, like women of feminine strength, had spiritual insight and self-sacrificing strength.

While accepting to some degree the traditional idea of authorship as a higher calling, Phelps also insisted on the more progressive view that writing was as appropriate an undertaking for women as it was for men: "If you hem pillowcases," Phelps warned young women, "when heaven has qualified you to write a poem or paint a picture, you do so at your peril. . . . All energies and graces are Heaven's loan to the soul. . . . The *presumption* is always in favor of using them unless he indicate [sic] otherwise." This did not mean Phelps ignored the difficulties women like her mother faced in trying to reconcile authorship and domestic life: she knew a literary career demanded "the physical strength of an Amazon and talent of the highest order." Rather, Phelps thought that despite those difficulties, if a woman felt called, she should write and her family and society should make it possible for her to do so.[41]

Christian values were as deeply embedded in Phelps's concept of writer as they were in her concept of womanhood and, likewise, gave her work, especially at the end of the century, a conservative cast. For her, literary material came from God and led one to the mysteries of human life and to God: "Possibly the Creator did not make the world chiefly for the purpose of providing studies for gifted novelists," she asserted in her autobiography, "but if He had done so, we can scarcely imagine that He could have offered anything much better in the way of material.... The moral struggle, the creation of character, the moral ideal, failure and success in reaching it, anguish and ecstacy in missing or gaining it, the instinct to extend the appreciation of moral beauty, and to worship its Eternal Source,—these exist" everywhere as themes. God, in her opinion, inspired works like *The Gates Ajar*; when so motivated, art and music had the power to make "men clear and keen in brain, refined and pure in heart." Indeed, perfect art was, as she saw it, a form of worship. As a result of these views, much of her nonfiction as well as her fiction had religious themes and she herself rejoiced in being a writer from whom everyone expected "a more or less religious story."[42]

Because of her Christian values, Phelps stressed the moral intentions of her work, as did many other popular Victorian authors. Writing to Richard Watson Gilder about her short novel *Jack, the Fisherman* (1887), she claimed, "More than half of the success of 'Jack' is owing to its great *moral artery*; as with 'Uncle Tom' on the larger plan.... I never work 'for Art's sake.' I don't believe in it. I work for life's sake, and for truth's sake; for God's sake when I can." In Phelps's view, the exploration of moral issues in contemporary life was the "realistic" approach. Thus, William Dean Howells was wrong, she argued, to criticize the "Puritan" elements in such writers as Hawthorne, Longfellow, Whittier, Holmes, and Stowe because they were portraying life as they knew it, as it was. "The province of the artist," she wrote in her autobiography, "is to portray life as it is and life *is* moral responsibility.... An artist can no more fling off the moral sense from his work than he can oust it from his private life." Thus, in this regard she aligned herself with writers whose literary aims were popular at mid-century but became increasingly out of step with the emergence of modern realism and naturalism.[43]

In fact, many of the tributes to Phelps that appeared after her death in 1911 concentrated on her moral purposes rather than her literary strengths. An editorial in the *Independent* marked her passing by saying, "Mrs. Ward was remarkable for her earnestness and intensity, and whatever she wrote had a purpose somewhat beyond the mere desire to amuse or please. Indeed, her heart was more in her efforts for the benefit of sailors or the rights of women or the cause of antivivisection than for her own literary fame.... For pure ability as well as for literary power, she stood, notwithstanding her lifelong invalidism, at the head of our women writers." Another article, in the *Boston Evening Transcript*, assessed Phelps's life as "a 'dedicated life'—the epithet explains the fine quality of Elizabeth Stuart Phelps's work. Voluminous as it was—singularly so for one limited always by physical bars—it had in eminent degree the ethical fiber.... When all is said, it were easier to find a more restrained and faultless writer, than one of equal genius and far-reaching influence for good." While laudatory, these appraisals were actually the last hurrah for a fading literary reputation in a culture that no longer emphasized the ethical imperative in literature.[44]

But Phelps thought about her work not simply in terms of ethical goals, but also in terms of practical requirements. Like Helen Hunt Jackson, she knew that being a writer required discipline as well as inspiration: "Inspiration is all very well," she wrote, "but 'genius is the infinite capacity for taking pains.'" She claimed she took from four to six weeks to finish a magazine story, during which time she would "toil terribly" over it, often becoming ill with the strain. Always she seemed to be haunted by the worry that her stories could be done better. Thus, she revised and revised again, asserting about one piece in 1901 that "every word ... I had wrought over and over, I should say thirty times, so that each stroke was in its place like an ivory painting, and is just as I want it to be."[45]

As a professional writer, she also accepted the fact that economic forces were at work in the literary marketplace. As early as 1869, she pointed out to a younger author, as if she had been talking to Mary Abigail Dodge, that writing was "a question of demand and supply like any other trade." Expanding that observation in 1896, she advised prospective writers: "Respect the market laws. Lean on nobody. Trust the common sense of an experienced publisher to know whether your manuscript is worth something or nothing. Do not depend on influence. Editors do not care a drop of ink for influence. What they want is good material, and the fresher it is, the better. An editor will pass by an old writer any day for an unknown and gifted new one, with power to say a good thing in a fresh way." Contradicting the sentiments she sometimes expressed, she argued in 1908 that she herself did not "rely upon my 'spiritual value' to the disregard of my proved and accepted 'market value.'"[46]

Indeed, her financial success as a writer was crucial to her image of herself as an independent woman. "I am proud to say," she wrote, "that I have always been a working woman, and always had to be.... When the first little story appeared in 'Harper's Magazine,' it occurred to me, with a throb of pleasure greater than I supposed then that life could hold, that I could take care of myself, and from that day to this I have done so."[47] Like Helen Hunt Jackson, she openly admitted having some commercial aims. But she never thought that it was easy to earn a living as an author. In fact, the drawback to a literary career, she thought, was its poor pay.

But, though she accepted the economic underpinnings of literary business, Phelps's views of herself as a woman of feminine strength and as a writer of religious and moral literature made her prefer to work with publishers and editors who adhered to the Gentleman Publisher's view of author-publisher relations, rather than with those who seemed more commercially oriented. Early in her career, she began sending her work to some of the most prestigious Gentlemen Publishers and editors of her time, including James T. Fields of the *Atlantic* and Ticknor and Fields, Henry Mills Alden of *Harper's Monthly*, William Hayes Ward of the *Independent*, and, somewhat later, Richard Watson Gilder of *Scribner's* (later *Century*) *Monthly*. Although she never had "exclusive" arrangements with any of them, she maintained ongoing relationships with these people, their associates, and their successors for most of her career. From time to time she published in many other newspapers and magazines, but most, though less prominent, were run by the same type of middle-class Gentlemen Publishers.[48]

In her business connections, she shared the traditional expectations of a personal friendship as well as a professional relationship between author and publisher. Her association with James Fields in the 1860s and 1870s matched the ideal of the Gentleman Publisher's marketplace; they actually were good friends. They socialized frequently, and Annie Fields became one of Phelps's closest friends. In the Fields home, Phelps always found "a high range of thought, or feeling, or usefulness."[49] The Fieldses and Phelps also held many of the same social and moral values. In James Fields, Phelps found attitudes that complemented her own vision of herself as a woman of feminine strength. He not only supported the movement to broaden women's rights, but also was chivalrous to women simply because of their special qualities as women. Moreover, "he was incapable of that literary snobbishness which undervalues a woman's work because it is a woman's."[50] In her opinion, he was helpful, unselfish, loyal, and religious—a valuable friend, an ideal husband, and a "practical" Christian. He encouraged her when she was self-doubtful, stimulating her courage and her work. In short, their relationship fostered loyalty and trust. While most of her associations with other Gentlemen Publishers and editors were less close, with each of them she enjoyed some degree of personal rapport.

It is interesting to see how her relationships with the Gentlemen Publishers, and with Fields specifically, enabled her to express herself as a woman of feminine strength, a woman who was both assertive and deferential. For example, in 1869 she wrote Fields and his partner, James Osgood: "In regard to the Trotty Book, I said ten percent the other day without thinking much about the matter. It has since occurred to me to ask you whether the unusual sale of *The Gates Ajar* would make it worth your while to increase the percentage on my books. . . . I know very little about it, however, and am quite willing to trust to the business equity of the firm in helping me to make all the money I can!"[51] This combination of assertion and deference was particularly characteristic of Phelps's negotiating style and seems to have been a successful way for her to relate to the Gentlemen Publishers. In fact, although she must have been thoroughly familiar with the dispute between Mary Abigail Dodge and James Fields, since she knew both of them, Phelps never seems to have felt any mistreatment from Fields in her own case. When sales of *The Gates Ajar* rapidly mounted, Fields quickly forwarded to her a large check—an act for which she was ever grateful and by which she judged subsequent arrangements with publishers and editors. In contrast to Dodge, who found Fields's paternalism offensive, Phelps was comfortable with his chivalrous support.

Although Phelps preferred to work with Gentlemen Publishers, after the mid-1880s she also began publishing in *McClure's Magazine*, the *Ladies Home Journal*, and *Harper's Bazar*, which were run by a newer, more business-oriented generation of practitioners who dominated the literary marketplace by the turn of the century. The editors and publishers of these magazines expected more impersonal, commercial relationships with authors. They also had different ideals regarding the content and quality of literary work. About this time, Phelps also began encountering new attitudes toward writers and literature among the Gentlemen Publishers. She must have felt a turning point in author-publisher relations around 1889, when, having invited Fields's successor, Henry Houghton, to visit her to take care of some business, her husband rebuked her for mixing business and pleasure—a habit of the older marketplace but not of the new.[52] The reprimand was just a hint of the alienation yet to come.

Among the changes confronting Phelps during her career were two developments in literary criticism: (1) the increasing distinctions critics made between elite literature and popular writing, and (2) the decreasing interest overall in religious or ethical work. As early as 1874, she may have begun feeling the impact of the first development. In that year, when William Dean Howells claimed he could not understand the poem she had submitted to the *Atlantic*, she accused him of applying inappropriate literary standards, saying, "Perhaps *your* sense as a scholar of the deficiencies of the poem might be other than unscholarly heartaches will be likely to feel. I really do not *see* the obscurity, or know what to do for it." She rightfully sensed that he was encouraging a more intellectual, rather than popular, view of art. In 1881, implying that her work was less valuable than others, Howells asked her to shorten her piece to make additional room in the *Atlantic* for Henry James. In this case she defended herself by arguing, "The very fact that there is so much of Mr. James makes it more important to me that my story should have its fair artistic effect."[53] But to maintain her previous stature was a losing battle. By the end of the century, she had to concede that there were various literary audiences, though she would not rank them in importance or quality as the critics were doing. She staunchly maintained that she had an audience for her work, no matter what the newer literary dictates were.

Just as she felt the effects of changing aesthetic standards, she also experienced the impact of the decreasing popularity of literature with an ethical aim. In response to that change, she strove to make her work more appealing to a popular market that preferred entertainment to a moral lesson. Thus, Phelps assured Henry Houghton in 1893 that *Donald Marcy* had fun enough in it to sell, told Edward Bok of the *Ladies Home Journal* in 1899 he should not expect "a work of profound literary scope or moral width" on the topic of domestic service, and reassured Elizabeth Jordan of *Harper's Bazar* in 1900 that she (Phelps) could write a piece that was "strictly popular, not highly literary." In 1905 she offered the *Bazar* a story that "would have 'the happy ending' and could be as short as you like and would avoid all shocking details."[54] In each of these cases, Phelps attempted to adapt her writing to meet audience demands, but she never was very happy doing so. She preferred the older view of morally useful literature that had been so widely accepted in the Gentleman Publisher's marketplace.

In fact, despite these attempts to make her work more popular in the last two decades of her career, she continued to want to promote good, "to say something . . . needed," to help people to be better persons than they were.[55] Therefore, she usually tried to compromise between moral worth and entertainment. In defense of *A Singular Life* (1895), she argued with Horace Scudder that, though the story was religious, "Still I thought there was 'world' enough in it to carry the unsanctified reader." But she gave her deepest feeling away by observing, "I hope I am a better woman myself, for the year spent in his [the hero's] company; and I cannot but venture to hope that some of my readers may be able to say as much."[56] Phelps never gave up on the moral imperative in literature. When critics accused her of being too didactic or obvious in expressing her point of view, she retorted that she was not sacrificing aesthetics for ethics. Unfortunately for her, most critics did not agree.

Unable to slow the move away from moral fiction in the marketplace, Phelps complained bitterly about mechanical restrictions on her writing at the end of her career. Since the beginning of the 1870s, she, like other writers, had been coping with the requirements of serialization, but the increasing rigidity of editorial guidelines as the century drew to a close really annoyed her. In 1904 she complained to Edward Bok that the "mechanical peculiarities" of the *Ladies Home Journal* would make it difficult for her to use her work elsewhere if he ended up rejecting it. To Robert Underwood Johnson of the *Century*, she protested in 1910:

> If there is any trouble with that [recently submitted] paper it is owing to its mechanical limitations. As the thing has constructed itself in my mind (for many years) it was to be much longer. Your compulsion of four thousand words thwarted me at every step, and, at the last, put upon me the necessity of an abrupt ending, not in consonance with my own idea of the art of the paper at all. Sometime (if I live) I am going to make an onslaught on the whole modern magazine system of fitting an author to mechanics, instead of the mechanical spaces to the author. It was not so "befo' the war." Much good work is hurt by the modern editorial fashion.[57]

In the new marketplace, she had less autonomy in her work than she had experienced with the Gentlemen Publishers.

But what bothered her more than modern expectations about fitting literary works to particular magazine formats was the fading of other assumptions about author-publisher relations that had been prevalent "befo' the war"—in the Gentleman Publisher's marketplace. She experienced the results of that disappearance in several ways. For one thing, she was paid less for her work. To her, reductions in compensation represented a real breach in the etiquette of traditional author-publisher loyalty.

When in 1893 an official form letter arrived from the *Independent* stipulating that she would receive the standard rate of ten dollars a column for contributors, she complained bitterly to William Ward:

> For $10. a column I never wrote for any periodical since I was a novice in my calling. . . . Never since I first began to write for it have I received, in letters from strangers, the recognition which I have, this past year, for my work for your columns. . . . For twenty years, or over that, I have been a steady contributor to the 'Independent' and have been thoroughly and cordially associated with it. . . . No editor with whom I have ever dealt has ever, in any instance, sent me such a communication as comes to me from your office. . . . Perhaps, I might add, that the spirit which could propose such terms in such a way to so old a contributor seems to me one which can hardly extend to me such a welcome as is necessary to any self-respecting contributor of any periodical.[58]

When her book publisher, George Mifflin, wrote in 1905 to inquire about publishing a new book, she took the opportunity to question the loyalty of Houghton, Mifflin: "I may frankly say that you have considerably disheartened me. I have been so often *reminded* from the House when any particular book did not reach a large circulation, that I do not care to burden the Firm with another, just at present. I cannot help feeling that this is (when it happens) not altogether my fault. Your methods of pushing a book are conservative by the prevailing standards and it seems hopeless for you and me to discuss them."[59] The trust and acceptance that had earlier characterized her relationships with the Gentlemen Publishers and had been reflected in her compensation were no longer apparent. She had become distrustful and accusatory in response to their coolness toward her.

If Phelps was bothered by less personalized decision making in regard to compensation, she was equally disturbed by the more impersonal practice of reviewing an author's work, no matter who the author was. She was deeply hurt in 1894 when Houghton, Mifflin informed her that it would review her latest book submission before considering it for publication. Because she was a long-time contributor and friend, she wrote Henry Houghton, saying that she expected her work to be accepted without question. And she reinforced her argument by appealing to the Gentleman Publisher's values of loyalty, friendship, generosity, and trust. She concluded the letter with a plea stressing the familial ideal of the earlier marketplace: "I prefer to deal, as I have always done, directly with the

Firm which has published my work for a quarter of a century.... Dear Mr. Houghton, this is a personal letter, and as frankly written as if I were one of your family. I know you mean to do the always right and generous thing by me, and I think I can leave my interests in your hands, as long as you are there to care for them."[60]

Appeals to the personal concern, generosity, and honor of the Gentlemen Publishers increased dramatically in Phelps's correspondence around this period, as did the number of letters to publishers or editors that she marked "confidential" and "personal." The absence of such "personal" letters before the late 1880s is an indication that before then she assumed that her letters would be treated personally always. After the 1880s, apparently, her correspondence was sometimes relegated to relative strangers in the firms and not to the publisher or editor who was personally known to her. Often, the letters she marked "personal" contained requests for some special consideration for her own manuscripts or for those of Herbert Ward. In 1889, for instance, she wrote a "personal & confidential" letter to Henry Houghton asking him to make sure that the *Atlantic* accepted a story written by her husband. This request would not have been unusual twenty years earlier when publisher and editor were the same person and personal appeals were a matter of course; but in the newer market of more specialized divisions of labor and greater impersonality, Phelps had to plead unusual circumstances in making her request to the publisher. Likewise, when she sent her work for the *Atlantic* directly to Houghton, instead of to Horace Scudder, editor of the journal, she explained it was because she had always sent her work through the publisher, not because she felt any disrespect for Scudder. Some months later, however, she admitted that, in contrast to Houghton, Scudder was not her "friend."[61]

Phelps liked being treated as a friend by her publishers, but that expectation of author-publisher relations had lessened in the marketplace over time. In 1902 she expressed great annoyance when George Mifflin consulted a reader about one of her stories after she had asked him "to read the story yourself, as a friend, and give me your personal impression of it as a matter of individual taste.... [T]o have its publication *questioned* by you on the opinion of a reader—after I had done my best to be loyal to the House about it, and to meet your wishes in that respect—did disturb me, I grant.—I may as well say so much as just this, frankly, for I don't want reserves of 'feeling' between yourself and me." Time and again, she expressed her deep regret about the disappearance of "feeling" between author and publisher. In 1906 when Harper and Brothers insisted on issuing the book publication of a serial they had printed for her, she accused her own publisher—Houghton, Mifflin—of not paying her enough, thereby "forcing" her to accept the Harpers' offer, and claimed she felt more for her old publishers than they did for her; in self-defense, she reassured them that she wanted to maintain the old relations, even if they did not: "I am anxious to bring out all the books I can, as soon as I can, with *you* to make it quite clear to the trade, that I have, in no sense removed my work from you—. . . . I have dreaded writing this letter more than 'A Corporation which has no soul,' can believe. As my individual friends—whose friendship I value—I hope you will reassure me, and let me know that I have not wounded you. For, I think, *I* value our long and kindly relations more than you do." By the end of her career, Phelps was totally frustrated by the absence of the Gentleman Publisher's values.[62]

Nevertheless, she assumed that, as an author of established reputation, she deserved Gentleman's support, not just from her long-time publishers but also from the wider literary marketplace. Even with the newer magazine editors, she often adopted this line of defense. She wrote Elizabeth Jordan, editor of *Harper's Bazar*, in 1900 that she was "not used to sending out Mss. [manuscripts] 'for consideration.'" She explained her hesitation about sending her drama *Within the Gates* to the *Century* for review as the natural reaction of "a successful author who belongs to the era when successful authors' Mss. were not returned for any reason, unless the heavens fell." She reminded Edward Bok of the *Ladies Home Journal*, when he had forgotten the amount he agreed to pay her for a submission, that he had said "trust me" and she had. She expected him to honor that trust as a Gentleman Publisher would. A few years later she expressed her annoyance at editors like him who asked authors of "established position" for work they did not use and concluded with the request that he behave like a Gentleman Publisher and say "trust me" again.[63]

All of her frustrations with the new marketplace came out in a dispute in 1908 with Richard Watson Gilder—actually an editor from the Gentleman Publisher's era who had adopted some of the more modern business practices—when he indicated he might not accept her new story, "The Chief Operator." In a series of letters, she accused him of several breaches in the Gentleman's approach to publishing. First, she said he had betrayed her loyalty by treating her submission as if its author were unknown: "I like the Century—and its editor; and have always had reason to feel I was at least as warmly welcomed there as elsewhere, until of late. . . . I do not enjoy sending material which you seem to feel runs but 'a chance' of pleasing you." Second, she wondered why he was unwilling to pay a fair price, when she was willing to accept whatever he offered: "Why should I be supposed to bankrupt the magazine?!! Have you not welcomed this contributor for thirty years? I know my prices are not small, and are growing larger all the time, but I think I have always accepted what you offered me, in payments without comment—have I not?" Third, in response to his complaint that she relied on her spiritual rather than her market value, she continued to insist that there could be a "successful [profitable] union of art and ethics." Finally, by way of calling a truce with him and symbolically with all the new changes in the marketplace, she wrote, "I can readily understand your weariness of the editorial chair. So do we weary of the contributor's settee."[64]

Phelps's struggles at the end of her career were not simply those of a writer whose works were going out of style; rather, as we have seen, they represented the conflicts of a writer caught in the midst of a wholesale transformation in the literary marketplace. The marketplace of the 1860s and 1870s had been a comfortable one for Phelps as woman and as writer; in those years, editors and publishers espoused values compatible with her views of herself as a woman of feminine strength and as a writer of ethical literature. While in the early period neither the Gentlemen Publishers nor writers like Phelps ever ignored the economic underpinnings of the literary market, both authors and publishers tried to relate to one another in the context of personal relationships, noncommercial aims, and moral guardianship—"feminine" values that seem to have facilitated women's success in the mid-century. In contrast, by the early 1900s, the market had, in Christopher Wilson's words, become aggressively "masculine" in literary style and business approach, emphasizing instead competition, profits, and timeliness. For Phelps and writers who shared her perspective, those values were anathema.

8

Writer's Desk
From Women Authors of Our Day in Their Homes. *Edited by Francis Whiting Halsey. New York: James Pott and Company, 1903.*

A Final Word

Literary Professionalism and Women

In nineteenth-century America, authorship evolved from an avocation of the leisured to a profession in which it was possible to enjoy economic independence and cultural status. While early in the century writing was usually seen as an adjunct to other professional or cultural roles, by mid-century there were enough commercial outlets and full-time practitioners for authorship to be considered a viable career, at least for some. In fact, although the idealization of genteel amateurism persisted until mid-century or later, by that time many writers were successfully marketing their work and earning their living through their craft. It was in this context of genteel amateurism and economic opportunity that each of the five writers examined in this study got her start.[1]

After the Civil War, authorship began to shed the characteristics of genteel amateurism and increasingly assumed the appearance of modern professions. As Nelson Lichtenstein describes it, by the 1890s "American writers threw off the last vestiges of a pre-commercial, romantic view of their craft . . . [and] became conscious of their role as producers of a literary commodity, which in common with other fruits of a market economy might be bought and sold at the highest price."[2] Similarly, Christopher P. Wilson has shown in his work on (male) writers in the Progressive Era that the publishing industry and professional authorship at the end of the century adopted some of the trappings of modern businesses, among them market orientation and competitiveness, emphasis on skills rather than inspiration, accommodation to editors' and publishers' wishes, and "masculine" aggressiveness. It was to this new orientation that Elizabeth Stuart Phelps struggled to adapt at the end of her career.

Although studies of this evolution of attitudes toward literary careers in the nineteenth century have virtually ignored women, Lawrence Buell's work on *New England Literary Culture: From Revolution through Renaissance* (1986) provides some important information about their literary professionalism.[3] His evidence suggests that women as a group may have been the first to identify themselves as professional writers, since, unlike most male writers, women had no other professional role at the same time. Moreover, his findings indicate that women as a group may have understood the economic possibilities of a literary career earlier than men; as Buell points out, between 1820 and 1865 twice as many female as male authors in New England (34 percent versus 17 percent) depended mainly on their writing as a source of income. Even when women pursued a literary career because of financial need, most of them, Buell claims, had other motives, including an interest in their medium, a hope for acclaim, and a desire to say something important; writing for them was, in his words, "a passion as well as an enterprise." Those characteristics and others considered below made many women "literary professionals" in the fullest sense of the term.[4]

At the risk of overgeneralization, it may be helpful to draw a composite picture of women's literary professionalism as illustrated by the subjects of this book. Like the authors Buell described, the five women writers discussed here identified themselves as professionals, depended on writing for their income, and demonstrated a seriousness about their work that went beyond a simple desire to earn money. As a group, they adopted a style of literary professionalism that was characteristic of their time. It was expressed in their literary expertise and business skills, in their deep commitment to their career, in their expectation of self-determination as a writer, in their acceptance of moral and interpretive roles for their work, and in their understanding of the professional behaviors expected between authors and publishers.

As literary professionals, these five women took their literary expertise seriously, expressing their seriousness in various ways. At the beginning of their careers, most sought advice from more well-established authors in order to improve their literary style. For example, Mary Abigail Dodge (Gail Hamilton) consulted Sara Jane Lippincott (Grace Greenwood), while Helen Hunt Jackson actually went to study with Thomas Wentworth Higginson. Harriet Beecher Stowe had comments of members of the Semi-colon Club. More importantly, all five writers read widely in the literature and criticism of their contemporaries and could defend their own works by comparison. While none of them developed any more sophisticated theories of literary genre or style than most of their contemporaries, each learned to tell a story or write an essay or a poem in ways that were well respected by a large audience and/or a literary elite, and each fashioned her own distinctive literary style. Furthermore, each writer formed her own opinions about the merits of other writers and expressed those views to her peers and to editors and publishers. Finally, in varying degrees, each became confident enough of her own literary abilities to pass on advice to other authors, either through personal encouragement and mentoring like Helen Hunt Jackson or through articles, such as Harriet Beecher Stowe wrote, on pursuing a literary career.[5]

The five writers' sense of professionalism led them to develop not only an expertise in literary matters, but also the knowledge necessary to conduct successfully the business of their careers. As we have seen, some increased their knowledge to a greater degree than others, but each came to understand the workings of the literary marketplace well enough to negotiate compensation and to make judgments about their publishers' and editors' services. Among them they made use of a variety of negotiating techniques, from the straightforward requests of Harriet Beecher Stowe with James Fields to the manipulation of E.D.E.N. Southworth with Robert Bonner. They demonstrated their understanding of the market by voicing concerns to their publishers about such things as the timing of book announcements, copyright arrangements, and the physical appearance of books, as well as marketing and distribution. To some degree they all expressed their opinions in this regard, but Phelps was especially outspoken whereas Southworth was more guarded. Having developed her business expertise, each revealed her pride in her economic success and at least the younger ones described themselves as "working women."

Another measure of their professionalism was their deep commitment to their careers. None of them wanted to do slipshod or amateur work. They were willing to work hard and even, like Southworth, to exceed the expectations of their editors and publishers in completing their work. None of them was willing to give up her writing, even when she, like Jackson after her second marriage, had no pressing financial need; or when she, like Dodge, received negative criticism of her work; or when family responsibilities, like Southworth's, made the pursuit of her profession difficult. Perhaps the most dramatic evidence of commitment to career is seen in the physical breakdowns of writers like Southworth, Stowe, and Phelps after completing some article or book; they worked with such intensity or were under so much pressure that they sometimes literally collapsed in exhaustion, yet they never gave up their careers.

E.D.E.N. Southworth, Harriet Beecher Stowe, Mary Abigail Dodge, Helen Hunt Jackson, and Elizabeth Stuart Phelps (Ward) all enjoyed a considerable degree of autonomy in their careers, particularly at midcentury. Although they had to conform to certain magazine requirements, such as the length of a serial installment, on the whole these women planned and wrote what they wished, not what publishers and editors told them to write. Southworth, for instance, really appreciated Bonner's free rein and Dodge always demanded it from her publishers. It bothered Phelps greatly when this autonomy was disappearing at the end of the century. As a result of their freedom and their general confidence in their work, most of them were angered by editorial changes when they occurred. Furthermore, having made their own choices about what and how to write, they were not hesitant to express pride in their achievements, either directly like Phelps in naming her favorite books or indirectly like Southworth in mentioning other people's praise of her work.

Another characteristic of these mid-century women was their acceptance of the view that literature needed to have a moral or cultural significance, even when intended for entertainment, as Southworth's was. They shared this perspective with their male peers. As Buell has observed, "Before 1865 no New England writer of any consequence argued for the position that the moral dimension of art was unimportant."[6] If women were at all different than men in this regard, it may have been in the degree to which they saw themselves as moral guides for their society because they were Victorian women. That, however, is difficult to measure. For the most part, they, like their male counterparts, wanted to say something worthwhile to their culture that would elevate their work above the commercial, material realm.

Finally, each writer's professionalism was apparent in her understanding of the tenor of the Gentleman Publisher's marketplace. As we have seen, each writer understood, even if like Dodge she did not accept, the ideal of a personal relationship with her editors and publishers. In contrast to most twentieth-century assumptions about professional behavior as formal, impersonal, and separate from private life, this nineteenth-century style did not discourage self-disclosure or trusting ways of relating to each other. To a greater degree than today, this approach integrated the public and private realms. This is not to say that business letters were filled with information about private lives—they were not; but when they did contain some such commentary, the authors were not being unprofessional in the context of their own times. Business lives and personal lives were often intertwined. According to this professional style, then, writers were not lax when they failed to demand a contract; they assumed they need not be distrustful of friends. It is no wonder that Dodge's views of a marketplace of supply and demand were so alien to her contemporaries.

Given these characteristics, it is clear that E.D.E.N. Southworth, Harriet Beecher Stowe, Mary Abigail Dodge, Helen Hunt Jackson, Elizabeth Stuart Phelps (Ward), and many other women writers were literary professionals in the fullest sense, although that status was not always granted them by their contemporaries. The women in this study each had well-developed literary and business skills, was deeply committed to her career, and took pride in her literary self-determination. Furthermore, each accepted her role as moral interpreter and each understood the expectations of author-publisher relationships in the Gentleman Publisher's marketplace. They behaved with as much professionalism as the men of their time. Nevertheless, their professionalism did not guarantee women equal acceptance in the literary marketplace. The writers examined here still had to contend with limiting stereotypes of women. They still could be ignored on occasions such as Henry Houghton's celebration in honor of John Greenleaf Whittier or when critics listed the most important writers of the time. They still could be pushed aside, like Phelps, at the end of their careers. Despite that devaluation, however, they pursued their craft with dignity, a marked degree of self-confidence, and style.

By the end of the nineteenth century literary professionalism had to evolve in response to a more complex, commercial publishing industry and to new cultural ideals. What had previously been a relatively autonomous career was now more closely directed by editors and publishers who increasingly commissioned the articles they wanted written. Thus, one's professionalism was measured more than ever by one's ability to produce what the market demanded. While performing an interpretive role remained an aim of literary professionals at the end of the century, playing an explicitly moral role faded in importance.[7] Finally, relationships between authors and publishers at the end of the century were more likely to be measured in terms of economic success, rather than in terms of their conformity to the norms of friendship. Overall in literary business, there was a growing separation between public and private lives.

The kind of professionalism called for by the mid-century literary marketplace, as argued previously, was not antithetical to many "feminine" values. But, as the century drew to a close, the publishing marketplace increasingly emphasized "masculine" values and called for a literary professionalism that was more aggressive, competitive, and self-aggrandizing than before. Such masculinization was occurring in other professions, which also chose to institutionalize values of rationality, objectivity, specialization, and authority.[8] In other professions, the net result was often to place additional limitations on women's participation. It may be that in literary circles, too, masculine values were being propounded in order to bring control of the literary marketplace to men. Phelps's experience would fit that hypothesis. Christopher Wilson's study of literary professionalism in the Progressive Era also leads one to that conclusion. Studies of British writers at the end of the century also show a pattern of "edging women out."[9] This hypothesis needs to be tested further, but at the very least one can argue that most women like Phelps with "feminine"

Literary Professionalism and Women 199

values would have had to struggle to adapt to the more modern professional ethos. Only those women with personalities like Jackson's might fit.

But if the writers discussed here, with their roots in the mid-century, shared some common assumptions about literary professionalism, individually, as we have seen, each had her own distinct variation on the common professional style. In fact, with their various temperaments they appear, though in a different historical context with different professional demands, very much like people we all know today: Southworth is the one always eager to please, while Stowe is the grande dame who remembers from whence she came. Dodge, the disgruntled colleague with an acerbic wit, is quick to spot injustice, while Jackson pushes on, a conscientious, enthusiastic worker. Finally, Phelps, who expects workplace ideals to be reality, is disillusioned and sometimes thinks of herself as a martyr. In their similarities as well as in their individuality, they each can teach us a good deal about the complexity of human lives and the pursuit of a career.

Abbreviations

AAS	American Antiquarian Society, Worcester, Mass.
AHS	Andover Historical Society, Andover, Mass.
BC	Bowdoin College Library, Brunswick, Maine
BPL	Boston Public Library, Boston, Mass.
BYU	Brigham Young University Library, Provo, Utah
CC	Colorado College: Tutt Library, Colorado Springs, Colo.
CHS	Chicago Historical Society, Chicago, Ill.
CrU	Cornell University: John M. Olin Library, Ithaca, N.Y.
CU	Columbia University: Rare Book and Manuscript Library, New York, N.Y.
DU	Duke University: William R. Perkins Library, Durham, N.C.
EI	Essex Institute: James Duncan Phillips Library, Salem, Mass.
HC	Haverford College Library, Haverford, Pa.
HL	Huntington Library, San Marino, Calif.
HSP	Historical Society of Pennsylvania, Philadelphia, Pa.
HU	Harvard University: Houghton Library, Cambridge, Mass.
JL	Jones Library, Amherst, Mass.
LC	Library of Congress, Washington, D.C.
LSU	Louisiana State University Libraries, Baton Rouge, La.
MHS	Massachusetts Historical Society, Boston, Mass.
MNH	Minnesota Historical Society, St. Paul, Minn.
NPL	New York Public Library: Rare Books and Manuscripts Division, Astor, Lenox, and Tilden Foundations, New York, N.Y.
PSU	Pennsylvania State University: Fred Lewis Pattee Library, University Park, Pa.
PU	Princeton University Library, Princeton, N.J.
RH	Rutherford B. Hayes Presidential Center, Fremont, Ohio
RS	Radcliffe College: Arthur and Elizabeth Schlesinger Library,

	Cambridge, Mass.
SC	Smith College Library: Sophia Smith Collection, Northampton, Mass.
S-D	Stowe-Day Foundation, Hartford, Conn.
SU	Stanford University Libraries: Department of Special Collections and University Archives, Stanford, Calif.
TC	Trinity College: Watkinson Library, Hartford, Conn.
VC	Vassar College Library, Poughkeepsie, N.Y.
UV	University of Virginia: Special Collections Department, Manuscripts Division, Clifton Waller Barrett Library, Charlottesville, Va.
YU	Yale University: Collection of American Literature, Beinecke Rare Book and Manuscript Library, New Haven, Conn.

Notes

Chapter 1. Why Try a Writing Career?

1. This event is usually remembered for Clemens's speech about Emerson, Longfellow, and Holmes. See Ballou, *The Building of the House*, 218–19.

2. Statistics in this paragraph can be found in Dexter, *Career Women of America*, 97; Baym, *Novels, Readers, and Reviewers*, 100; Hart, *The Popular Book*, 306–7; Tebbel, *History of Book Publishing*, 2:170; Garrison, "Immoral Fiction," 81; Reynolds, *The Fiction Factory*, 38.

3. Reprinted in Derby, *Fifty Years among Authors*, 283–85. The final joke was that Mary Abigail Dodge (Gail Hamilton) was only fifty-five years old at the time.

4. Scudder, *Henry Oscar Houghton*, 136, 150; Ballou, 268.

5. For an example of continued discrimination, see "Our 'Forty Immortals.'" Houghton, however, had been somewhat sensitized. He defended himself in his opening remarks at the Holmes breakfast, claiming he had been too shy to ask the "ladies" to attend before. Others in attendance also commented on the presence of women. See "The Holmes Breakfast."

6. Bartlett, *The American Mind*, 32–72; Sara M. Evans, *Born for Liberty*, 67–92.

7. Baym, for example, finds that, in the reviews of literary works, individualism was applauded only when expressed on behalf of social stability. Baym, *Novels, Readers, and Reviewers*, 193. On sentimentalism in Victorian culture, see Douglas, *The Feminization of American Culture*.

8. Said by a character in the work of Catharine Sedgwick quoted in Kelley, *Private Woman, Public Stage*, 67. For a fuller discussion of Victorianism, see Howe, "American Victorianism as a Culture," and the special issue of *American Quarterly* in which it appears.

9. See Ryan, "The Empire of the Mother."

10. This phenomenon persisted through the Gilded Age. See Tomsich, *Genteel Endeavor*.

11. See Sara M. Evans, esp. 70–76; Woloch, *Women and the American Experience*, 116; Epstein, *The Politics of Domesticity*.

12. See Kessler-Harris, *Out to Work*.

13. An excellent discussion of the connections between True Womanhood and New Womanhood is found in Hersh, "The 'True Woman.'"

14. Welter, "Cult of True Womanhood."

15. Quotes in this paragraph are from a passage quoted in Derby, 574; from Spofford, Introduction, xviii–xix; and from a passage quoted in Wood, "'Scribbling Women,'" 5.

16. Quotes in this paragraph are from Kirk, "Women Fiction Writers of America," 203, and "Literary Women," 610. See also Jeffrey, "The Family as Utopian Retreat."

17. Baym, *Novels, Readers, and Reviewers*, 97–107. The quotes that follow in this paragraph are from reviews quoted in Baym, 102, and from Baym, 249. *The Sunny Side* was written by the mother of Elizabeth Stuart Phelps (Ward), who is discussed in Chapter 7. It should be pointed out, as Baym does (p. 104), that reviewers did not understand the subversive implications of some of the nineteenth-century heroines any more than those describing True Women saw the real women behind the expected image. See also Baym, 172.

18. Hersh, 273–74; Sklar, *Catharine Beecher*.

19. Hamilton, "Men and Women," in *Country Living*, 123. Hersh (p. 276) also makes this point.

20. Charvat, *The Profession of Authorship*, 6–7. The quotes that follow in this paragraph are from passages quoted in Ferguson, "Literature and Vocation," 142, and Kelley, *Private Woman, Public Stage*, 203.

21. Buell, *New England Literary Culture*, 58–69.

22. Buell (pp. 61–62) describes this attitude in relation to Emerson.

23. Page, *A Publisher's Confession*, 53. For a fuller discussion of authors' responses to deviance, see Bell, "Casting Off," in *Development of American Romance*, 25–36.

24. Quotes in this paragraph are from Griswold, *Female Poets*, 7, and W. A. Jones, "Female Novelists," 488–89; cf. Wayne, "The Male Artist as Stereotypically Female."

25. Buell, 40, 388; Baym, *Novels, Readers, and Reviewers*, 131.

26. Ames, *Outlines of Men, Women, and Things*, 109–10.

27. Quotes in this paragraph are from Lyman, "Grace Greenwood—Mrs. Lippincott," 153; Arthur Franklin Johnson, "Poetry of Louise Chandler Moulton," 473–74; and a passage quoted in Elizabeth Evans, "Mrs. Sigourney's Friend," 77.

28. Arthur Franklin Johnson, 474. See also Baym, *Novels, Readers, and Reviewers*, 143–46, 250; Geary, "Scribbling Women," 137–43.

29. Greenwood, "Fanny Fern—Mrs. Parton," 84.

30. Showalter, "Women Writers and the Double Standard," 460. The quotes that follow in this paragraph are from passages quoted in Geary, "Scribbling Women," 118, and Wood, 3. See also Huf, *Portrait of the Artist as a Young Woman*, 18.

31. Baym, *Novels, Readers, and Reviewers*, 257. The quote that follows is from Stephens, "Women of Genius," 243.

32. Quotes in this paragraph are from a passage quoted in Elizabeth Evans, 86; "Azarian: An Episode" [Baym (*Novels, Readers, and Reviewers*, 110) points out that males were also criticized for diffuseness]; and Griswold, 7.

33. "Literary Women," 609–10; also cited in Geary, "Scribbling Women," 143–44. See also Geary, 145.

34. Quotes in this paragraph are from a passage quoted in Hart, 91; "Woman in the Domain of Letters," 84; and passages quoted in Baym, *Novels, Readers, and Reviewers*, 255, and Geary, "Scribbling Women," 132.

35. Quotes in this paragraph are from "American Women of Letters," 127; Thorpe, "Grace Greenwood," in *Female Persuasion*, 147; and Griswold, 7.

36. Fern, *Ruth Hall: A Domestic Tale*, 307. Nina Baym (*Novels, Readers, and Reviewers*, 258) claims that, although reviewers made rigid theoretical pronouncements about women writers and their works, when it came to actually reviewing those works, critics could evaluate them as individuals.

37. Fetterley, *Provisions*, 5. See also pp. 2–7.

38. Baym, *Woman's Fiction*, 11, 19–20.

39. Cooke, "The Memorial of A. B." (excerpt on p. 81 of reprint in *Legacy*); see also Fern, "Fresh Leaves."

40. Cf. Tompkins, *Sensational Designs*, esp. 122–85; Buell, 382.

41. Scholars who have found examples of women's ambivalence include Mary Kelley in *Private Woman, Public Stage*, Sandra M. Gilbert and Susan Gubar in *Madwoman in the Attic*, and Mary Poovey in *Proper Lady*.

42. Buell, 387; Buell's description parallels Kelley's in many ways. Kelley, *Private Woman, Public Stage*, 31–36.

43. Statistics in this paragraph come from Woloch, 125–26, and Elbert, "Changing Education of American Women," 222; see also Kelley, *Private Woman, Public Stage*, 35, 59–62, and Buell, 379, 40.

44. Davidson, *Revolution and the Word*, 73.

45. See O'Brien, "Tomboyism and Adolescent Conflict."

46. Sara M. Evans, 67–92; Riley, *Inventing the American Woman*, 90.

47. Brumberg and Tomes, "Women in the Professions," 279, 281.

48. Buell, 378, 381–82.

49. Kessler-Harris, 46–48, 90.

50. Buell (pp. 378–79) claims that 22 percent of women writers in the second era of the antebellum period were single, but only one-quarter of those seem to have remained single in order to pursue a literary career. This, however, is a higher percentage of single women than the 7–8 percent of never-married women in the United States from 1835 to 1855 (Woloch, 274). Birthrate statistics are from Woloch, 118.

51. Chambers-Schiller, "The Single Woman."

52. Kessler-Harris, 111–12.

53. Geary discusses many examples of family support in "Scribbling Women," 121–24.

Chapter 2. Gentlemen and Ladies

1. French, "'Honor to Genius.'"
2. Tebbel, *History of Book Publishing*, 1:56.

3. This quote and the quote in the preceding paragraph are from Tebbel, 1:115–16; a discussion of Carey's career is found in Tebbel, 1:106–16.
4. Tebbel, 1:145n, 145; Tassin, "American Authors," pt. 1, 181. Many others published the book as well.
5. Tebbel, 1:207. See also Charvat, *Literary Publishing*, 35.
6. Tebbel, 1:274–75, 214, 229; Sheehan, *This Was Publishing*, 15, 66.
7. Tebbel, 1:217, 227–28; Charvat, *Literary Publishing*, 55.
8. Charvat, *Literary Publishing*, 45; see also 55.
9. French, 361–62; "Authors among Fruits."
10. Quotes in this paragraph are from Rev. Julius H. Ward quoted in [George Haven Putnam], *Authors and Publishers*, 7, and Browne, "American Publishing," 341.
11. On the growth, see Tebbel, 2:12.
12. At one time G. P. Putnam attempted to invoke trade courtesy with the Harpers, who refused to recognize Putnam's claim, saying, "Courtesy is courtesy and business is business." Quoted in Madison, *Book Publishing*, 19; see also Bracher, "Harper & Brothers." Ann Douglas describes them as "a case study in the commercialization of northeastern culture." See Douglas, *The Feminization of American Culture*, 96–98.
13. For a discussion of women publishers, see Tebbel, 2:174–77.
14. Sheehan, 15. John Tomsich (*Genteel Endeavor*, 1–26) sees these three ideals as part of the genteel tradition.
15. Tebbel, 2:11. There were many instances of such friendships; see also Tomsich, 9–12.
16. On the size of firms, see Kilgour, *Messrs. Roberts Brothers*, 258; Tebbel, 1:279, 2:189–90; and Coser, Kadushin, and Powell, *Books*, 36.
17. Quotes in this paragraph are from Christopher P. Wilson, *Labor of Words*, 68, and Tryon and Charvat, *Cost Books*, xxi. See also Christopher P. Wilson, 44; Francis, "The Atlantic's Pleasant Days."
18. Christopher P. Wilson, 45; William Dean Howells, *Literary Friends*, 118–20; Cochran, *American Business*, 56; Sheehan, 23–24.
19. Tebbel, 2:4: "No other businesses in America could match such continuity of [family] control"; Tebbel, 1:264. The involvement of the women in the family was quite helpful. Today, the same role may be filled by women editors. Judith Rossner, for example, believes her first novel was accepted only because a female editor was moved by the heroine and story (Coser, Kadushin, and Powell, 167).
20. Quotes in this paragraph are from Christopher P. Wilson, 68, 44.
21. George Princhard to Miss Cummins, Boston, August 13, 1857, Maria Cummins Collection (#7076), UV.
22. Quotes in this paragraph are from Austin, *Fields of the Atlantic Monthly*, 69, and Holt, *Garrulities of an Octogenarian Editor*, 119. A similar idea was expressed by Page in Gerald Gross, *Publishers on Publishing*, 48. A study of British author-publisher friendships can be found in Sutherland, *Victorian Novelists and Publishers*, esp. 78–98.
23. Scudder, *Henry Oscar Houghton*, 116–17.
24. Christopher P. Wilson, 42; on Appleton, see Tebbel, 2:278.

25. Tassin, pt. 5, 645; on Graham, see Charvat, *The Profession of Authorship*, 166.

26. Tassin, pt. 4, 535–38; Susan Warner to G. P. Putnam, The Island, December 29, 1870, Susan Bogert Warner Collection (#7313), UV; Austin, 208–43.

27. Quoted in Austin, 101. A description of the Christian Gentleman can be found in Rosenberg, "Sexuality, Class, and Role."

28. Tassin, pt. 4, 531: see also Tomsich, 13–14; Exman, *The Brothers Harper*, 90; Derby, *Fifty Years among Authors*, 283–85; Gilman, "Atlantic Dinners"; Tompkins, "Masterpiece Theatre"; Howard Mumford Jones, *Age of Energy*, 61.

29. Author's risk means the author will assume the expenses of publishing. On unequal wages, see "New York Herald on Women's Work and Wages" and Josiah G. Holland, "Sex and Wages." Compensation rates are discussed in Charvat, *The Profession of Authorship*, 311; on periodicals, see J. Albert Robbins, "Fees Paid to Authors," 2:95–104. I base my conclusion on readings of author-publisher correspondence between twenty nineteenth-century women writers and their publishers. It is difficult, however, to compare figures mentioned in letters, which may or may not accurately reflect the price received. Other sorts of publishing arrangements between authors and publishers—author's purchase of stereotype plates and the half-profits system, for instance—are even more difficult to compare. I did not have enough information to evaluate the compensation of unsuccessful women writers.

30. Examples mentioned are from Stronks, "Author Rejects Publisher," 550; Rose Terry Cooke to Editor, *Literary World* [Edward Abbott], Winstead, May 25, 1880, BC; Harriet Prescott Spofford to Mr. [William Conant] Church, Washington, April 25, 1868, William Conant Church Papers, NPL.

31. Quoted in Austin, 24.

32. Quotes in this paragraph are from Tassin, pt. 2, 274, and Kilgour, *Lee and Shepard*, 115–16. The *American Publisher's Circular* of 1855 asserted "the wisdom and necessity of a perfect understanding and friendly business intercourse" in order "to constitute so mighty and beautiful a commercial system" as publishing was (T. W. M., "Publishers," 165).

33. Quotes and examples in this paragraph are from Tebbel, 2:4; Sheehan, 4–6; an excerpt quoted in Gerald Gross, *Publishers on Publishing*, 76; and a passage quoted in Tebbel, 2:10.

34. Quotes in this paragraph are from Scudder quoted in Tebbel, 2:132, and *Publishers' Weekly* quoted in Tebbel, 2:135. See also George Palmer Putnam, "'Freestone'-Authors-Publishers," 395. On Henry Holt, see Tebbel, 2:137.

35. Tebbel, 2:12–13, 135; Sheehan, 4, 23–25. George H. Putnam estimated that half of the books published failed. See [George Haven Putnam], *Authors and Publishers*, 1888, 14.

36. Quoted in Tebbel, 2:146.

37. Quoted in Christopher P. Wilson, 75; see also Tebbel, 2:10. Information in the paragraph is from Wilson, 43, 54; Page, *A Publisher's Confession*, 115–18; Sheehan, 244; Tebbel, 2:11; Tomsich, 19–22; Austin, 24.

38. Sheehan, 244.

39. Charvat, "James T. Fields and the Beginnings of Book Promotion, 1840–1855," in *The Profession of Authorship*, 168–87; Tassin, pt. 5, 642; Liedel, "The Puffing

of *Ida May*." Susan Geary points out that publishers successfully tried many techniques of advertising ("The Domestic Novel as a Commercial Commodity").

40. Sheehan, 15.

41. Tassin, pt. 1, 181. See also Sheehan, 107.

42. Derby, 27; see also Austin, 27.

43. W. P. H., "The Centennial Exhibition"; Christopher P. Wilson, 42; Sheehan, 108: Writers could describe "sexual irregularities" later in the century if they did not condone them.

44. Quoted in Reynolds, *The Fiction Factory*, 12. On Fields, see Exman, 30.

45. Quotes in this paragraph are from passages quoted in Reynolds, 74–75, and Tebbel, 1:292; see also Sheehan, 104–18.

46. Hart, *The Popular Book*, 306–7; Douglas, 114. Donald E. Liedel (p. 287) reports that women wrote over half of the antislavery novels in the 1850s; according to Fred Lewis Pattee, nearly half of the short stories in the *Atlantic* under Lowell's editorship were by women (*The Feminine Fifties*, 328); Tebbel, 2:170.

47. For an overview of the changes, see Christopher P. Wilson, 17–91; generalizations about the late century are drawn from his work. See also Knopf, "Random Recollections," 99–100; Tebbel, 2:15–16, 144–46; Coser, Kadushin, and Powell, 36. Many small presses, even today, have such lofty aims.

48. Christopher P. Wilson, 142–43. Wilson (p. 142) speculates that "the popularity of this masculine style put constraints upon many female novelists and journalists."

Chapter 3. E.D.E.N. Southworth

1. E.D.E.N. Southworth (hereafter cited as EDENS) to Robert Bonner (hereafter cited as RB), Prospect Cottage, December 26, 1869, DU.

2. On her success, see Noel, *Villains Galore*, 116; H. C. B., "A Noted Novel Writer." Southworth claims in this article to have written seventy-three books, but that number probably included some issued under multiple titles. See also Boyle, *Mrs. E.D.E.N. Southworth*, 74; Huddleson, "Mrs. E.D.E.N. Southworth," 74; Habegger, "A Well Hidden Hand," 199. On her income, see Hofstadter, "Southworth," 3:327. Until someone writes a very careful biography of Southworth, we can only piece together the evidence on her income. In T. B. Peterson's obituary ("Theophilus B. Peterson"), her book royalties were said to be $6,000 a year. When those are added to the $7,800 she could have earned from her $150-a-week contracts with Bonner after 1878, the total is well over $10,000.

3. EDENS to RB, Yonkers, N.Y., March 24, 1887, DU; H. C. B., 1. On her popularity, see Mott, *History of American Magazines*, 2 (1850–65):359; "Some 'Lady Novelists,'" 185; Papashvily, *All the Happy Endings*, 180; The Lounger, "Mrs. E.D.E.N. Southworth," 31.

4. Hart, *The Popular Book*, 306–8; Stoddard, "Mrs. Emma D. E. N. Southworth," 190; Noel, 164; Habegger, 200; Mott, *Golden Multitudes*, 142.

5. Quoted in several places, including Huddleson, 54. On the house where she was born, see p. 56.

6. Southworth, *The Deserted Wife*, 156; for other comparisons between South-

worth and Hagar, see Harris, "The House that Hagar Built." For the comparison with her sister, see Forrest, "Emma D. E. N. Southworth," 218.

7. T. H. Y., "Biographical Sketch of the Author," 31; Forrest, 218–19.

8. Quoted in several places, including Huddleson, 55.

9. Dobson, Introduction to *The Hidden Hand*, xv.

10. Huddleson (p. 79) says she joined the Swedenborgs at the end of her life. On her visits to Maryland, see T. H. Y., 34–36.

11. Information on her separation can be found in Kelley, *Private Woman, Public Stage*, 159, and Gallup, "More Letters of American Writers," 32. Others who comment on her heroines include Papashvily, 115, and Kelley, *Private Woman, Public Stage*, 324. Her comments on cruelty are quoted in Huddleson, 76. On her inquiries about divorce, see EDENS to Hon. Henry A. Wise, Washington, March 1850, HC, and Kelley, 238. For social views of divorce at the time, see Hindus and Withey, "The Law of Husband and Wife."

12. Quoted in several places, including Huddleson, 58.

13. T. H. Y., 36; Dobson, Introduction to *The Hidden Hand*, xvi–xvii. Poverty was, she said, her "*bete noire*" (Huddleson, 76).

14. Information in this paragraph is drawn from Kelley, *Private Woman, Public Stage*, 20; Huddleson, 62; Boyle, 8–9; Huddleson, 63–64; EDENS to A. Hart, Prospect Hill, October 12, 1852, HSP.

15. Ellen Knight Bradford, "A Remarkable Life." Huddleson (p. 68) says she received only fifteen dollars for "Retribution."

16. Quoted in several places, including Forrest, 220–21.

17. The first review quoted here is included in Henry Peterson to EDENS, n.p., October 15, 1849, DU; the second is quoted in Boyle, 51. On favorable reactions, see Cady and Clark, *Whittier on Writers*, 153; Mott, *Golden Multitudes*, 137. Sarah J. Hale, *Woman's Record*, 794, credits Bailey with recognizing her "genius" and encouraging her to pursue a literary career.

18. Boyle, 36, 51–56, 59; Mott, *History of American Magazines*, 4 (1885–1905):679. With Abraham Hart she began the practice of selling the copyrights to her books, rather than arranging royalty payments. See EDENS to A. Hart, Prospect Hill, November 17, 1852, HSP.

19. T. B. Peterson to EDENS, Philadelphia, April 12, 1854, DU. This letter contradicts the popular story, repeated in T. B. Peterson's obituary in *Publishers' Weekly*, that she initiated their association. In 1855, Robert Bonner pirated a Southworth story running anonymously in the *London Journal*, which had pirated it from the *Post*. Bonner discontinued the serial after one installment when he received an irate letter, Mary Noel (pp. 62–63) says, from T. B. Peterson claiming copyright. Bonner, by way of apology, inserted a note in the *Ledger* saying, "Mrs. Southworth is, beyond a doubt, the BEST FICTION WRITER in the United States." I suspect the irate letter actually was from Henry Peterson of the *Post*, although T. B. Peterson would also have had reason to be annoyed.

20. Gallup, 30. On her early years as a writer, see Huddleson, 69.

21. One of many instances of telling others about her trials is reported in Stoddard, 189. Other examples are from many of her letters. See also Kelley, *Private Woman, Public Stage*, 163.

22. Quotes in this paragraph are from Huddleson, 77, and "Southworth, Em-

ma," *National Cyclopedia of American Biography*, 1:432. See also EDENS to RB, Prospect Cottage, Monday morning [ca. October–November 1862], DU, and Stoddard, 186.

23. Dobson, Introduction to *The Hidden Hand*, xxvii–xxxv; Harris.

24. All quotes in this paragraph are found in Huddleson, 75–77.

25. Huddleson, 61–62. On authors in general wanting to please readers, see Baym, *Novels, Readers, and Reviewers*, 44.

26. Quotes in this paragraph are from "A Christian Novelist," and EDENS to RB, Prospect Cottage, Monday morning [ca. 1863], DU.

27. *The Hidden Hand*, edited by Dobson, 7, 14.

28. Quotes in this paragraph are from EDENS to RB, Yonkers, N.Y., April 7, 1887, and Monday [ca. 1878], DU.

29. Quotes in this paragraph are from "Mrs. E.D.E.N. Southworth," *Book News*, 66–67; EDENS to RB, Prospect Cottage, Thursday noon [December 1863], DU; and Baym, *Novels, Readers, and Reviewers*, 135.

30. EDENS to RB, Yonkers, N.Y., Monday evening [ca. 1878], DU. See also Boyle, 54; Savoyard, "Mrs. Southworth, Mr. Bonner and the Ledger"; Carrier, *Fiction in Public Libraries*, 286.

31. Quotes in this paragraph are from Gallup, 32, and EDENS to RB, Prospect Cottage, October 25, 1890, DU. Other writers even tried to use close variations of her name on their works (Mott, *Golden Multitudes*, 142).

32. EDENS to RB, Prospect Cottage, Friday [1863–64], DU. See also EDENS to RB, Yonkers, N.Y., March 29, 1887, DU.

33. *Saturday Evening Post* quoted in Boyle, 51. More information on the *Post* can be found in Mott, *History of American Magazines*, 4:678–79.

34. November 30, 1850, quoted in Boyle, 55; other examples of Peterson's praise are found on pp. 53, 57. Though she was an exclusive contributor, she did publish three more serials in *Era* (in 1850, 1853, and 1856) (Boyle, 47).

35. Henry Peterson (hereafter cited as HP) to EDENS, Philadelphia, September 10, 1849, DU.

36. HP to EDENS, Philadelphia, December 24, 1854, DU.

37. HP to EDENS, Philadelphia, September 10, 1849, DU.

38. HP to EDENS, Philadelphia, December 24, 1854, DU.

39. Quoted in Boyle, 63.

40. Quotes in this paragraph are from HP to EDENS, Philadelphia, October 20, 1854, and December 24, 1854, DU.

41. EDENS to All Interested, Prospect Cottage, April 10, 1857, DU. Peterson's editorial (April 11, 1857) is reprinted in Boyle, 63–64.

42. RB to EDENS, New York, October 10, 1856, DU.

43. Unless otherwise noted, details about Bonner's career are taken from Admari, "Bonner and the Ledger."

44. Both quotes in this paragraph are from Admari, 191.

45. Noel, 63, 74–75; Papashvily, 125.

46. Quotes in this paragraph are from passages quoted in Carrier, 286, and Boyle, 74.

47. EDENS to RB, Prospect Cottage, March 8, 1876, DU; details on other

aspects of their personal relationship are from her many letters to him.

48. EDENS to RB, Yonkers, May 18, 1883, DU. Sometimes she made up for lost time by writing forty to sixty pages a week to count for two to three weeks' obligations. See EDENS to RB, London, February 18, 1861, DU. As noted in the text, Bonner typically gave writers five-year contracts. Sylvanus Cobb's first agreement made about the same time as Southworth's was for fifty dollars a week (Noel, 88).

49. EDENS to RB, Prospect Cottage, Tuesday morning, DU. See also EDENS to RB, Prospect Cottage, Friday morning [ca. 1862] and Monday morning [June 1867], DU.

50. EDENS to RB, Prospect Cottage, Monday morning, DU.

51. This series of quotes are found in EDENS to RB, Prospect Cottage, Sunday afternoon [ca. 1869], January 5, 1869, and January 12, 1869, DU.

52. EDENS to RB, Prospect Cottage, January 21, 1869, DU.

53. Quotes in this paragraph are from passages quoted in Pattee, *The Feminine Fifties*, 196, and Mott, *History of American Magazines*, 2:359.

54. "Some 'Lady Novelists,'" 185.

55. RB to EDENS, New York, October 22, 1856, DU.

56. Quotes in this paragraph are from EDENS to RB, Prospect Cottage, Monday [ca. 1862], and EDENS to RB, Yonkers, May 18, 1883, DU.

57. Noel, 90, 64–65; EDENS to RB, Yonkers, January 30, 1878, DU.

58. Papashvily, 131. See Receipt with letter, EDENS to RB, Prospect Cottage, September 25, 1867, DU. In a similar situation, Bonner did not release Sylvanus Cobb's *Gunmaker of Moscow* as a book until after Cobb's death (Noel, 187).

59. EDENS to RB, Prospect Cottage, Monday morning [June 1867], DU.

60. EDENS to RB, Norwood, July 20, 1860, and EDENS to RB, Prospect Cottage, Monday morning [ca. 1866], DU; "Theophilus B. Peterson." Unless otherwise noted, information about him comes from this obituary. See also EDENS to RB, Yonkers, October 23, 1876, and Prospect Cottage, October 25, 1890, DU.

61. Reportedly, she earned royalties of $6,000 a year from Peterson, although I have only seen evidence that he purchased the copyright on books and, thus, did not pay her royalties; see "Theophilus B. Peterson."

Chapter 4. Harriet Beecher Stowe

1. The best biography of Harriet Beecher Stowe is still Forrest Wilson, *Crusader in Crinoline*. Unless otherwise noted, biographical details about Stowe's life are taken from this or other readily available biographical sources. Lyman Beecher Stowe, *Saints, Sinners, and Beechers* (p. 154), makes specific reference to her father's wish.

2. Erskine, *Leading American Novelists*, 277. See also Kelley, *Private Woman, Public Stage*, 123; Wagenknecht, *Harriet Beecher Stowe*, 133.

3. On aspects of her education, see Cooke, "Harriet Beecher Stowe," 588: Sarah Pierce claimed that Harriet was always bowed down "to the idol, 'scribble.'" See

also Sklar, *Catharine Beecher*, 75–77; Cross, "Harriet Beecher Stowe," 3:394; Gamaliel Bradford, *Portraits of American Women*, 119–20.

4. Forrest Wilson, 112–14; Pringle, *When They Were Girls*, 82, says 100,000 copies of the geography book were sold in the first two years. In contrast to her later self-confidence, she told her brother Edward she was very dependent on the good opinions of others as a young woman. See Charles Edward Stowe, *Life of Harriet Beecher Stowe*, 46.

5. Adams, *Harriet Beecher Stowe*, 36. On the Semi-colon Club, see Parker, "Harriet Beecher Stowe," 306–7. On her increased writing, see Charles Edward Stowe, 68. On the encouragement she received, see Forrest Wilson, 127.

6. All quotes in this paragraph are from Harriet Beecher Stowe (hereafter cited as HBS) to Mrs. Follen, Andover, December 16, [1852], VC. See also Cross, 3:395. Kelley (*Private Woman, Public Stage*, 170) says she took charge of the family finances in 1853.

7. Quoted in Lyman Beecher Stowe, 164–65.

8. Reprinted in Boydston, Kelley, and Margolis, *Limits of Sisterhood*, 69.

9. The first letter is reprinted in Boydston, Kelley, and Margolis, 69; the second is quoted in Forrest Wilson, 214.

10. Kelley, "At War with Herself."

11. HBS to Madam [Sarah Josepha Hale], Brunswick, November 10, HM 24166, HL. In contrast to my interpretation, Forrest Wilson (p. 234) asserts that when she left Cincinnati she had gained "courage and self-reliance, humility and wisdom."

12. These motives are discussed in many works on Stowe, including Gamaliel Bradford, 119–20, and Forrest Wilson, 230–31, 251–58. See also Pattee, *The Feminine Fifties*, 136.

13. Mott, *Golden Multitudes*, 117–19.

14. Mott, *Golden Multitudes*, 116; Forman, "Uncle Tom's Cabin," 29–30. The contract was signed on March 13, 1852 (Forrest Wilson, 279). Southworth, incidentally, signed her own contracts, but she did have trouble with her husband's claims on her money while he was still alive (Gallup, "More Letters of American Writers," 32).

15. HBS to James Derby, Mandarin, March 11, 1884, HM 24163, HL. See Geary, "Harriet Beecher Stowe," for a complete analysis of the ins and outs of the contract dispute; see also the interview with Jewett in Forman.

16. Details in this paragraph are from Gerson, *Harriet Beecher Stowe*, 107; Wagenknecht, 168; and Forrest Wilson, 133. See, for instance, the letter on income and expenses in Charles Edward Stowe, 148. In Forman (p. 30), Jewett asserted that the Stowes knew nothing about checks and depositing money in the bank.

17. HBS to Jewett, n.p. [1854], RS.

18. HBS to Jewett, n.p. [1854], RS.

19. HBS to Richard Bentley, Andover, November 13, 1852, and December 1, 1852, Harriet Beecher Stowe Collection (#6318), UV.

20. Quotes in this paragraph are from HBS to Edward [Beecher], n.p. [1854], RS; HBS to Clark, Beeton & Co., Andover, February 19, 1854, Harriet Beecher Stowe Collection (#6318), UV.

21. HBS to Gaskell, Andover, July 10, 1860, S-D. Other details in this paragraph are from HBS to Gamaliel Bailey, Brunswick, Maine, April 18, HU; HBS to Sir, n.p. [1852], MHS; HBS to Mr. Johnson, Andover, October 7, CrU [the first laws to grant dramatic copyrights were passed in 1856, according to Pattee, 136]; Forrest Wilson, 416.

22. Details in this paragraph are found in Forrest Wilson, 289, 436–37; Adams, 114; McCray, *Life-Work of the Author*, 252–54.

23. HBS to Gamaliel Bailey, Brunswick, Maine, April 18, HU. Other details in this paragraph are from HBS to Jewett, n.p. [1854], RS; Forrest Wilson, 442. She usually avoided seeking criticism, however.

24. Forrest Wilson (p. 215) thought she learned humility from the poverty and sorrow of the 1840s.

25. Ammons, "Heroines in *Uncle Tom's Cabin*," 153.

26. Tompkins, "Sentimental Power," 98; republished in *Sensational Designs*, 145.

27. See Boydston, Kelley, and Margolis for a comparison of the sisters' views. See also Sklar, "Victorian Women," 35; Berkson, "Millennial Politics," 252.

28. Quotes in this paragraph are from HBS to Gamaliel Bailey, Brunswick, March 9, [1851], BPL, and Wagenknecht, 161.

29. Quotes in this paragraph are from HBS to Fields, n.p. [1868], FI 3962, and October 27, [1863], FI 4002, HL. (Some punctuation added.)

30. Quoted in Forrest Wilson, 271. She avoided reading someone like Oliver Wendell Holmes so his style would not influence her writing; see HBS to James Fields, Hartford, February 19, [1867], FI 3978, HL. On her views of style, see Wagenknecht, 162–63.

31. Quoted in Forrest Wilson, 204.

32. Both statements are quoted in Fields, *Life and Letters of Harriet Beecher Stowe*, 313, 316.

33. HBS to Major, n.p., October 21, 1875, S-D. See also Forrest Wilson, 416: She said writing a story was as exhausting as bearing a child.

34. For an account of the meeting, see Fields, 254–57. See also Tryon, *Parnassus Corner*, still the standard biography of Fields.

35. Quotes are from HBS to Sarah Willis [Parton], n.p., Saturday evening, February 15, [1868], SC, and HBS to Friend [Annie Fields], Mandarin, November 30, 1881, FI 3994, HL. See Adams, 109–22, for a full treatment of Stowe's friendships in magazine and newspaper publishing.

36. Quotes in this paragraph are from HBS to Fields, New York, November 29, [1865], FI 4007, HL; HBS to [James Osgood], fragment [1871], CrU.

37. Details in this paragraph are from Fields, 326. On Lowell and Hawthorne, see Austin, *Fields of the Atlantic Monthly*, 30, 53–54. Forrest Wilson (p. 531) says *Oldtown Folks* was her greatest success since *Dred*.

38. Quotes in this paragraph are from HBS to Fields, n.p., October 27, [1863], FI 4002, and [August, 1866], FI 3940, HL. On negotiations for her husband's obituary, see Wagenknecht, 175.

39. Examples of her strategies can be found in HBS to Fields, n.p. [November 9, 1864], FI 4005, [November 29, 1864], FI 3995, May 18, [1865], FI 3986, and September 6, [1865], FI 3996, HL.

40. Quoted in Forrest Wilson, 531. See also Wilson, 395, 464, 518: she held out for $1,000 for a biography of her brother, Henry Ward Beecher, from a Hartford publishing company.

41. HBS to Parton, Hartford, February 6, 1868, SC. There is an exception to my generalization about her assertiveness in a letter to Smith and Elder, n.p., May 18, 1861, S-D. On her expenses, see Forrest Wilson, 371–72.

42. William Dean Howells, *Literary Friends*, 119; see also, for example, HBS to Fields, n.p., June 3, 1864, FI 4017, HL.

43. Cf. Wagenknecht, 171–75; Andrews, *Nook Farm*, 158; Warner, "Story of *Uncle Tom's Cabin*," 315.

44. Quoted in Fields, 314.

45. Fields, 312. See also Lentricchia, "Harriet Beecher Stowe," 221.

46. Quotes in this paragraph are from M. Howells, *The Life in Letters of William Dean Howells*, 148, and Hamilton, *Woman's Worth and Worthlessness*, 242–43. Contemporary critics are not any more sympathetic, even though incest is now a discussable topic. Douglas, *The Feminization of American Culture*, 297; Forrest Wilson, 550–51; Austin, 292; Lentricchia. There are more sympathetic treatments in Edmund Wilson, *Patriotic Gore*, 50–52, and Ashton, "Harriet Stowe's Filthy Story." Mark Twain defended her in the Buffalo *Express* but did so anonymously (Lentricchia, 227). Elizabeth Cady Stanton and Susan B. Anthony both claimed the story was an example of woman's plight (Ashton, 381–82); Austin, 67.

47. Quotes in this paragraph are from Forrest Wilson, 541, and from an excerpt quoted in Donovan, "Harriet Beecher Stowe," 50.

48. Quotes in this paragraph are from letters quoted in M. Howells, 149, and Forrest Wilson, 537.

49. Quotes in this paragraph are from Harriet Beecher Stowe, *Lady Byron Vindicated*, 194, 196. See also Lentricchia, 222.

50. Johnston, *Runaway to Heaven*, 410. Stowe, however, was soon corresponding with him. See letters in LC and HL; Forrest Wilson, 547–48.

51. HBS to Fields, n.p., n.d., AC 7033, LC.

52. M. Howells, 150.

53. Quotes are from HBS to Mr. [Lyman] Abbot, n.p., June 1, 1883, BC, and Forrest Wilson, 545 (letter sent to James Osgood); Wagenknecht, 170.

54. Forrest Wilson, 565.

Chapter 5. Mary Abigail Dodge versus James T. Fields

1. Descriptions come from "Gail Hamilton," *Independent*, 2713; Fern, "Gail Hamilton—Miss Dodge," 206; Harriet Beecher Stowe to Sarah Willis [Parton], n.p., February 15, [1868], SC; Rebecca Harding Davis to Annie Fields, fragment, n.p. [September 1863], Richard Harding Davis Collection (#6109), UV.

2. Pulsifer, "Gail Hamilton," 166.

3. Quoted in Beasley, "Mary Abigail Dodge," 84–85; on her parents' encouragement, see Pulsifer, 171.

4. Fern, "Gail Hamilton—Miss Dodge," 1:215–16; see also Hamilton, *Country Living*, 125, 142.

5. On her education, see Pulsifer, 191; G. G., "Mary Abigail Dodge," 5:350; Beasley, 85; June 18, 1847, in Dodge, *Gail Hamilton's Life in Letters* (hereafter cited as *Life in Letters*), 1:18. Helen Hunt Jackson also attended Ipswich Female Seminary.

6. Quotes in this paragraph are from passages quoted in Beasley, 85 [Beasley explains Dodge's love of elaborate evening dresses as her armor, 88]; Hamilton, *Gala Days* (Boston: Ticknor and Fields, 1863), 64; and "Gail Hamilton," *Woman's Journal*.

7. October 6, [1854], in *Life in Letters*, 1:74.

8. *Life in Letters*, 1:129; April 10, 1854, in *Life in Letters*, 1:57.

9. 747 [signature used by Mary Abigail Dodge; hereafter cited as MAD] to Gamaliel Bailey, Hartford, Conn., January 17, 1856, in *Life in Letters*, 1:107. On Bailey's response, see February 15, 1856, in *Life in Letters*, 1:118.

10. On wanting time to write, see MAD to My Dear, June 9, 1857, in *Life in Letters*, 1:140–41.

11. Quotes from letters dated December 13, 1858, in *Life in Letters*, 1:200–201; November 6, [1858], in *Life in Letters*, 1:185.

12. February 27, [1860], in *Life in Letters*, 1:266; Beasley, 90–91; March 5, [1860], in *Life in Letters*, 1:270. She always refused to provide personal information for her biographies. On the money from George Wood, see *Life in Letters*, 1:229.

13. Quotes in this paragraph are from Hamilton, *Country Living*, 193; MAD to Grace Greenwood, Hartford, April 15, 1857, in *Life in Letters*, 1:140; and MAD to Sir Mentor [Curtis], January 10, 1859, in *Life in Letters*, 1:206–7.

14. Quotes and examples in this paragraph are from Hamilton, *Gala Days*, 64; Hamilton, *A New Atmosphere*, 28; and *Country Living*, 185.

15. Quotes in this paragraph are from MAD to Grace Greenwood, April 15, 1857, in *Life in Letters*, 1:139; MAD to Mr. Wood, May 18, 1864, in *Life in Letters*, 1:411; March 12, [1860], in *Life in Letters*, 1:275.

16. Quotes in this paragraph are from March 12, [1860], in *Life in Letters*, 1:276–77, and a passage quoted in Pulsifer, 176. Reportedly, she received a number of marriage proposals in her life, none of which she accepted. It is also said that she herself proposed to John Greenleaf Whittier; he declined the offer but they always remained friends. On the Bailey's child, see February 27, [1860], in *Life in Letters*, 1:266.

17. Ipswich, October 3, 1850, in *Life in Letters*, 1:30.

18. Quotes in this paragraph are from Spofford, "Gail Hamilton," in *A Little Book of Friends*, 99, and "Gail Hamilton," *Woman's Journal*. See many of Dodge's own letters as well. Dodge reportedly helped to prepare Blaine's diplomatic dispatches when he was in the Garfield cabinet. She was working on Blaine's biography at the time of her first stroke in 1895.

19. Quotes in this paragraph are from Spofford, *A Little Book of Friends*, 102, and the poem quoted in Thrasher, "The Last Year of Gail Hamilton's Life," 117.

20. Quotes in this paragraph are from "Gail Hamilton," *Woman's Journal*; "Gail Hamilton," *Independent*, 2713; Rice, "Leaves from a Busy Life," 180; and Whipple quoted in Pulsifer, 172.

21. Hamilton, *A New Atmosphere*, 284.

22. Quotes in this paragraph are from Hamilton, *A New Atmosphere*, 7, and

MAD to Irene Hardy, n.p. [1865–67], Anne Hadden Collection (M103), SU.

23. The quote in this paragraph is from Hamilton, *Woman's Wrongs*, 174. Explanations and examples of character development come from Hamilton, *Country Living*, 114, 118–19, 122–24, 154, 202; "Gala Days," 298, 295; and *Worth and Worthlessness*, 176–77.

24. Quotes in this paragraph are from Hamilton, *Country Living*, 111, and a passage quoted in Beasley, 92. See also Hamilton, *Woman's Wrongs*, 96–97, 106–15; *Worth and Worthlessness*, 206–45, 267–71; *Country Living*, 98.

25. *Skirmishes and Sketches*, 432–33, 444.

26. Quotes in this paragraph are from Hamilton, *Country Living*, 188, 177, 191–92, 189, and Vedder, 196.

27. Quotes in this paragraph are from Hamilton, *Country Living*, 191, and *Worth and Worthlessness*, 94–95.

28. Both quotes in this paragraph are from Hamilton, *Country Living*, 95, 40–41.

29. Quotes in this paragraph are from Hamilton, *A New Atmosphere*, 33, and from a letter dated 1885 in *Life in Letters*, 2:859.

30. MAD to Wood, Hamilton, March 21, 1862, Mary Abigail Dodge Collection (#7557), UV.

31. Hamilton, *Country Living*, 38–40.

32. Quotes in this paragraph are from MAD to Dear Sir, n.p., February 22, 1887, in *Life in Letters*, 2:889; Fern, "Gail Hamilton," 1:204–5. See also MAD to My Dear Judge, June 3, 1867, in *Life in Letters*, 1:592; MAD to Editor, "Library," Newburyport, January 8, 1889, YU; MAD to Sir, Hamilton, November 15, 1894, BYU.

33. Edel, *Literary Biography*, 29.

34. MAD to Wood, Hamilton, May 29, 1862, Mary Abigail Dodge Collection (#7557), UV.

35. Quotes in this paragraph are from a letter dated December 13, 1858, in *Life in Letters*, 1:201; Harriet Beecher Stowe to Sarah Willis [Parton—Fanny Fern], February 15, [1868], SC. Other details are drawn from MAD to My Dear Friend [Wood], April 24, 1862, Mary Abigail Dodge Collection (#7557), UV; May 1863, in *Life in Letters*, 1:351; and Hamilton, *Battle of the Books*, 132, 54.

36. MAD to [Wood], March 23, 1868, in *Life in Letters*, 2:611–12.

37. Quotes are from April 18, [1864], in *Life in Letters*, 1:393, and May 11, [1869], in *Life in Letters*, 2:630–31. Details of the dispute, unless otherwise noted, come from *A Battle of the Books* (hereafter cited as *Battle*); Tryon, *Parnassus Corner*, 334–49; and Stewart, "'Pestiferous Gail Hamilton.'"

38. Quotes are from *Battle of the Books*, 64–65, 81; see also MAD to Higginson, Hamilton, February 12, 1869, HU.

39. Tryon, *Parnassus Corner*, 343–46; Stewart; MAD to Mrs. Hawthorne, Hamilton, August 24, 1868, and September 2, 1868, Sophia Peabody Hawthorne Pers.-Misc., NPL.

40. Tryon, 339.

41. MAD to Wood, Cambridgeport, December 16, 1868, in *Life in Letters*, 2:620. See also Tryon, 341.

42. Quotes in this paragraph are from James T. Fields Memoranda and Account Book, n.d., n.pp., Fields addenda box 10 (2), HL [referees included James G. Blaine]; MAD to Madam, [March 1891], in *Life in Letters*, 2:1020; and *Battle*, 267.
43. All information except on Stowe from Tryon and Charvat, *Cost Books*, xviii–xix. For Stowe, see Chapter 4.
44. Quoted in Tryon, 290; see also MAD to Ticknor, n.p., n.d. [July 18, 1865], Mary Abigail Dodge Collection, EI.
45. Quotes in this paragraph are from *Battle*, 3, 42, 117.
46. MAD to Mrs. Hawthorne, Hamilton, September 2, 1868, Sophia Peabody Hawthorne Pers.-Misc., NPL.
47. *Battle*, 286–87.
48. Quotes in this paragraph are from *Battle*, 285, 256, 266, 286.
49. *Battle*, 132.
50. Quotes in this paragraph are from *Battle*, 172, 21.
51. Quotes in this paragraph are from *Battle*, 286–87, 266.
52. Quotes in this paragraph are from *Battle*, 269, 278.
53. *Battle*, 287–88.
54. Hamilton, *Worth and Worthlessness*, 151; see also 105–6.
55. *Battle*, 280.
56. MAD to Parton, Hamilton, Mass., September 27, 1869, HU.
57. March 29, 1870, in *Life in Letters*, 2:650.
58. On other authors' interest, see letters HBS to Sarah Willis [Parton] from 1868, SC. Lydia Maria Child was one writer who became wary of Fields after Dodge's charges. See Patricia G. Holland, "Lydia Maria Child," 162. On the Hawthornes, see Stewart, 421. On Fields, see Tryon, 358–62.
59. Stewart, 422–23, passim; Austin, *Fields of the Atlantic Monthly*, 312–13.
60. MAD to Pettingill, Brooklyn, N.Y., November 9, 1868, YU.
61. April 24, 1876, in *Life in Letters*, 2:771. See Harper's contract, Mary Abigail Dodge Collection, EI.
62. MAD to Redpath, Hamilton, Mass., November 24, 1886, Louisiana and Lower Mississippi Valley Collections, LSU. See also MAD to [William Hayes] Ward, Hamilton, October 28, 1878, Mary Abigail Dodge Collection (#7557), UV.
63. Quotes in this paragraph are from *Life in Letters*, 2:1065; MAD to H. L. Ensign, Hamilton, Mass., September 7, 1877, in *Life in Letters*, 2:789–90; and MAD to Sirs, Hamilton, January 14, 1887, in *Life in Letters*, 2:885. See one exception in MAD to [William Hayes] Ward, Philadelphia, April 15, 1873, Mary Abigail Dodge Collection, EI.
64. Quotes in this paragraph are from MAD to Booth, Hamilton, September 5, 1874, Mary Abigail Dodge Collection (#7557), UV; and January 21, 1885, in *Life in Letters*, 2:826.
65. MAD to [William Hayes] Ward, Hamilton, July 30, 1879, Mary Abigail Dodge Collection (#7557), UV.
66. MAD to William C. Church, Washington, D.C., April 4, 1876, William Conant Church Papers, NPL.
67. Clipping, March 1891, in *Life in Letters*, 2:1020–21.
68. MAD to Sir [Henry James, Sr.], March 23, 1864, in *Life in Letters*, 2:384.

Chapter 6. Helen Hunt Jackson

1. Coolidge, "H. H.," *Independent*. Details in this paragraph are from Banning, *Helen Hunt Jackson*, 226; Wilkins, "Helen Maria Fiske Hunt Jackson," 2:259; Leyda, *The Years and Hours of Emily Dickinson*, 1:xlvi; and Washburn, "The Mother of 'H. H.'" Most biographical details, unless otherwise noted, are from the biography by Banning cited above.

2. Quotes in this paragraph are from Banning, 3; Leyda, 1:xlvi. See also Banning, 11–12; Odell, *Helen Hunt Jackson*, 20.

3. Quoted in Leyda, 1:36. An alternate rendition of this comment is in Banning, 11. Other brief quotes in this paragraph are from Banning, 11, 13. In regard to her relationship with Dickinson, Banning (p. 19) believes they did exchange some letters.

4. Information in this paragraph is from Banning, 20, 26, 29; Odell, 35; Sewall, *Life of Emily Dickinson*, 2:577; Carr, "Helen Hunt Jackson"; and Whitaker, "Helen Hunt Jackson," 56.

5. Information in this paragraph is from Banning, 29; "'H. H.': A Reminiscence from an Old Letter of 1873"; and Higginson, *Contemporaries*, 148. Marsden, "Helen Hunt Jackson," 16, implies that her first marriage was not particularly happy, but I have not seen evidence and Banning does not mention any.

6. All quotes in this paragraph are from Conway, *Autobiography*, 1:202. On her attitude toward Stowe, see Odell, 51; Banning, 42.

7. Sewall, 2:578; Thomas H. Johnson, *Emily Dickinson*, 159. See also Banning, 48, 58–59, 69–70.

8. Quoted in Banning, 65. See also Banning, 66–68.

9. Quoted in Sewall, 2:578. Many details of their relationship are found in Banning, esp. 71–75, 82, 154. See Higginson's praise in his essay, "Helen Jackson"; see also Leyda, 2:130. Higginson encouraged Dickinson, among others, to read H. H.'s *Verses*; see Leyda, 2:214.

10. Quoted in Sewall, 2:580. See also Thomas H. Johnson, 159–60.

11. Higginson, *Contemporaries*, 150. Details on the growth of her career can be found in Banning, passim; Odell, 74; Helen Hunt (hereafter cited as HH) to James T. Fields, Bethlehem, September 18, 1870, HC; "Helen Jackson," *Independent*.

12. Quotes in this paragraph are from Thomas H. Johnson, 155; Apponyi, "Last Days of Mrs. Helen Hunt Jackson," 310; Coolidge, "H. H.," *Christian Union*. See also Higginson, *Contemporaries*, 157. A typical comment in her obituaries was, "Her likes and dislikes were spontaneous, ardent, sometimes unjust; yet even the injustice was sometimes an inaccurately aimed impulse of justice in disguise." *New York Evening Post*, August 13, 1885.

13. See, for instance, Will's comment, "I'm not qualified to give any suggestions. You're the literary one in this house." Quoted in Banning, 135.

14. Carr, 288. For indications of some problems in their relationship, see Banning, 126, 142, 161, 163, 181, 219.

15. Quoted in Leyda, 2:215. Assessments of her reputation can be found in Higginson, "Helen Jackson," 41; Armstrong, "Helen Hunt Jackson," 448; Dorr,

"Emerson's Admiration"; Conway, "Mrs. Jackson." On her anonymous novels, see Banning, 136; Odell, 27; Kilgour, *Messrs. Roberts Brothers*, 143. It is not clear whether she had Dickinson's permission to submit her poem. See Sewall, 2:582–83; Thomas H. Johnson, 164–69.

16. Quotes in this paragraph are from Helen Hunt Jackson (hereafter cited as HHJ) to Charles Dudley Warner, Colorado Springs, August 12, 1877, TC; HHJ to Charles Scribner, Boston, October 18, 1879, Author Files 1, box 82, Charles Scribner's Sons Archive, PU. See also HH to William Hayes Ward, Colorado Springs, February 4, 1874, HM 13939, HL; "Saxe Holm's Stories"; Leyda, 2:215–16; HHJ to Thomas Bailey Aldrich, Colorado Springs, October 16, 1882, HU.

17. See "Helen Jackson," *Independent* (August 20, 1885): 16; "Who Saxe Holm Is"; Odell, 138–40; Leyda, 2:295–97. For examples of guesses about Saxe Holm, see "'H.H.' Did Not Write the 'Saxe Holm' Stories"; Higginson, "Helen Jackson," 46–47; Conway, *Autobiography*, 2:428–31; "Literary News—Saxe Holm"; "Celia Burleigh and Saxe Holm"; and Coolidge, "The 'Saxe Holm' Stories." On sales, see "Recent Fiction—Saxe Holm's Second Series."

18. Details in this paragraph are from Apponyi, 313–14; Higginson, *Contemporaries*, 157–58, 164–65; Swinburne, "Reminiscences of Helen Jackson," 78; Conway, *Autobiography*, 1:203; Banning, 99–100.

19. Quotes in this paragraph are from a passage quoted in Higginson, *Contemporaries*, 155; and HHJ to Charles Dudley Warner, Brevoort House, N.Y., November 18, 1879, TC. See also Mathes, "Helen Hunt Jackson"; Banning, 147–57; Nevins, "Helen Hunt Jackson," 271–74, but Nevins has some errors in chronology.

20. Quotes in this paragraph are from Higginson, "How Ramona Was Written," 713; Gould, "The Author of Ramona," 184.

21. Samples of reviews and comments can be found in Tourgée, "Study In Civilization," 246; Scudder, "Recent American Fiction—*Ramona*," 127. For a summary of reviews, see Martin, "Helen Hunt Jackson," 162–63. See also Armstrong, 445; "Ramona," *Overland Monthly*, 331; Martin, 163–64; Higginson quoted in Banning, 215–16, 224. Dickinson's favorable remarks are quoted in Sewall, 2:589. Jackson's own views are recorded in "Helen Jackson," *New York Evening Post*. By the end of 1885 *Ramona* had sold 24,000 copies and by 1893, 100,000; see Kilgour, *Messrs. Roberts Brothers*, 206.

22. Quotes in this paragraph are from "Helen Jackson," *New York Evening Post*; "Helen Jackson," *Critic*, 85; Hollands, "Helen Hunt Jackson," 481; "Helen Jackson," *Independent*; and Sewall, 2:591.

23. [Jackson], *Mercy Philbrick's Choice*, 90.

24. Carr, 288.

25. Quotes in this paragraph are from [Jackson], "A Four-Leaved Clover" (p. 13) and "My Tourmaline" (p. 155), in *Saxe Holm's Stories*, 2d ser.; and "Esther Wynn's Love Letters," in *Saxe Holm's Stories*, 1st ser., 327.

26. Both quotes in this paragraph are from [Jackson], *Mercy Philbrick's Choice*, 88, 284.

27. [Jackson], "A Four-Leaved Clover," 11. See also [Jackson], *Mercy Philbrick's Choice*, 96; Odell, 66.

28. [Jackson], *Mercy Philbrick's Choice*, 80.

29. Swinburne, 79.

30. Quotes in this paragraph are from HHJ to Moncure D. Conway, in Conway, *Autobiography*, 2:427–28; [Jackson], "My Tourmaline," 248.

31. Quotes and examples in this paragraph are from Thomas H. Johnson, 113; Apponyi, 312; and Sewall, 2:579. The most well-known summary of Higginson's views is found in his "Letter to a Young Contributor."

32. Quotes and examples in this paragraph are from HH to William Hayes Ward, Colorado Springs, February 28, 1874, JL; [Jackson], *Mercy Philbrick's Choice*, 185, 238; Apponyi, 312–13; Sewall, 2:582.

33. Examples of reviews of her work praising her style include a review of *Verses* in "Recent Literature"; "Bits of Travel," 118; Shinn, "Verse and Prose of 'H.H.,'" 318–19; "*Mercy Philbrick's Choice*," 80; "Recent Literature—*Mercy Philbrick's Choice*"; Tourgée, 246.

34. Quote of obituary writer is from "Helen Jackson," *New York Evening Post*. See also Apponyi, 313; Leyda, 2:153; "Helen Jackson," *Independent*. Dickinson's words "careers and exigencies" are from "How happy is the little stone," quoted in Thomas H. Johnson, 174.

35. HHJ to Mr. Bowen, The Berkeley [Hotel, New York], April 16, 1884, Helen Hunt Jackson Collection (#7080), UV.

36. Quotes in this paragraph are from *American Literary Gazette* quoted in Kilgour, *Messrs. Roberts Brothers*, 98, and HHJ quoted in Kilgour, 243. See also Tebbel, *History of Book Publishing*, 2:222–26.

37. HH to William Hayes Ward, Colorado Springs, January 19, 1875, HM 13942, HL. Scribner's had once proposed to fill an entire issue of *Scribner's Monthly* with her work. Whether she or they finally vetoed the idea is unknown but the issue never appeared. See Ellsworth, *Golden Age of Authors*, 36. See also HHJ to William Hayes Ward, Colorado Springs, April 10, 1879, HM 13972, HL.

38. Letters quoted in this paragraph include HHJ to William Hayes Ward, Parker House, November 1, 1876, HM 13957, HL; HHJ to Messrs. Charles Scribner's Sons, Colorado Springs, n.d. [March 1, 1879], Author Files 1, box 82, Charles Scribner's Sons Archive, PU.

39. HHJ to Aldrich, Kansas, February 22, 1883, HU. See also HH to James T. Fields, New York, December 21, 1870, FI 2683, HL; HH to James T. Fields, Newport, December 26, 1870, FI 2670, HL; HHJ to Thomas Bailey Aldrich, Colorado Springs, October 16, 1882, and November 23, 1882, HU; Higginson, "Letter to a Young Contributor," 408.

40. HH to Fields, Newport, December 26, 1870, FI 2670, HL. See also HH to William C. Church, Newport, February 20, 1867, William Conant Church Papers, NPL; Odell, 20; E. D. B. Stoddard to Mrs. Hunt, New York, November 11, 1870, CC.

41. HH to Ward, Colorado Springs, February 25, 1875, HM 13943, HL. See also HH to James T. Fields, Newport, December 26, 1870, FI 2670, HL.

42. Letters quoted in this paragraph include HHJ to William Hayes Ward, Parker House, November 1, 1876, HM 13957, HL; and HH to William C. Church, Newport, April 24, 1867, William Conant Church Papers, NPL. See also HH to James T. Fields, New York, December 21, 1870, FI 2683, HL; HHJ to Thomas Bailey Aldrich, Kansas, February 22, 1883, HU.

43. HH to Ward, Colorado Springs, February 4, 1874, HM 13939, HL. In [Jackson], *Mercy Philbrick's Choice*, 92–93, a character states that editors do not pay more than poetry is worth.

44. HHJ to William Hayes Ward, The Berkeley [Hotel, New York], April 16, [1884], HM 14193, HL. Examples of strategies mentioned in this paragraph are found in HH to Mr. Clarke, Bethlehem, October 21, 1870, JL; HHJ to William Hayes Ward, Ashfield, Mass., October 5, 1876, HM 13951, HL; Banning, 124, 137.

45. Quotes in this paragraph are from HH to William Hayes Ward, Princeton, August 22, 1875, HM 13945, HL, and Tebbel, 2:280. See also HHJ to Richard Watson Gilder, draft letter, 1877, CC.

46. Details on her earnings are from Higginson, *Contemporaries*, 151; Marsden, 16; Wylkom, "Our Native Authors"; Banning, 115; HHJ to Charles Scribner's Sons, Colorado Springs, n.d., CC; HHJ to Mr. [John Eliot?] Bowen, Colorado Springs, November 6, 1882, HM 13999, HL; HHJ to Thomas Bailey Aldrich, Colorado Springs, October 16, 1882, HU; Kilgour, *Messrs. Roberts Brothers*, 206. On her personal estate, see "News and Notes—Helen Hunt Jackson."

47. Quotes in this paragraph are from HH to William C. Church, Newport, February 20, 1867, William Conant Church Papers, NPL; HHJ to Moncure D. Conway, fragment, n.p., n.d. [1876], CU; Higginson, *Contemporaries*, 150. See also other early examples in HH to William C. Church, Newport, May 16, 1867, William Conant Church Papers, NPL; HH to James T. Fields, Bethlehem, October 16, 1870, FI 2678, HL.

48. "Pseudonyms—Old and New."

49. "Helen Jackson," *New York Evening Post*. See also [Gilder?], "Mrs. Jackson's Last Book"; Higginson, "Helen Jackson," 40.

50. Quoted in Leyda, 2:236. See also Banning, 113–14; Jackson, "Glass Houses" and "The Old-Clothes Monger in Journalism," in *Bits of Talk about Home Matters*, 212–19; Odell, 85; Banning, 78; Higginson, *Contemporaries*, 143; Leyda, 2:216.

51. Details in this paragraph are from HH to James T. Fields, Bethlehem, July 29, 1870 (FI 2677), and October 30, 1870 (FI 2679), HL; HHJ to Moncure D. Conway, Colorado Springs, November 16, 1875, CU; HHJ to Bishop [Henry B.] Whipple, The Berkeley [Hotel, New York], October 29, 1880, Henry B. Whipple Papers, MNH.

52. Quoted in Sewall, 2:581. See also [Jackson], *Mercy Philbrick's Choice*, 87; Dobson, "Emily Dickinson," esp. 72–75. Dobson (p. 81) argues that Dickinson was conforming to social mores even more than most women writers of the time. I share Adrienne Rich's view that she was protecting her creative energies; see "Vesuvius at Home," esp. 171.

53. Quotes in this paragraph are from HHJ to Moncure Conway, fragment, n.p., n.d. [1876], CU, and a passage quoted in Leyda, 2:292. Niles of Roberts Brothers also thought about the fun to be had with the "No Name Series"; see Kilgour, *Messrs. Roberts Brothers*, 140. See also HH to William Hayes Ward, Colorado Springs, January 10, 1873, HM 13929, HL. Elizabeth Stuart Phelps (hereafter cited as ESP) also considered writing anonymously to protect others' privacy; see ESP to Sir [Lyman Abbott], Andover, Mass., March 22, 1880, BC.

54. All quotes in this paragraph are from HHJ to Charles Scribner, Colorado Springs, June 25, 1878, Author Files 1, box 82, Charles Scribner's Sons Archive, PU.

55. HH to Church, Bethlehem, August 26, 1867, William Conant Church Papers, NPL. See also Banning, 73.

56. HH to Scribner, Colorado Springs, July 11, 1878, Author Files 1, box 82, Charles Scribner's Sons Archive, PU. Note, however, Leyda, 2:216. She said she would maintain the pseudonym even if she did not make money. Given other evidence, I am not sure she would have. See also Ellsworth, 37. She discussed the preparation of "A History of the Claimants" in HHJ to Scribner, Armstrong & Co., Colorado Springs, May 13, 1878, and June 5, 1878, CC. On the "No Name Series," see Kilgour, *Messrs. Roberts Brothers*, 140–51.

57. Higginson, *Contemporaries*, 142.

58. HHJ to Higginson, Berkeley [Hotel, New York], February 5, 1884, quoted in *Writer* 14 (January 1901): 12.

59. Quotes in this paragraph are from a passage quoted in Marsden, 17, and from one quoted in Nevins, 276. In a letter to William Ward, she said she wanted to do "one-hundredth part." Banning, 201–2. See also "The Holmes Breakfast," 2.

60. See Banning, 219. Her annoyance at one intrusion into her privacy is expressed in HHJ to Thomas Bailey Aldrich, Los Angeles, March 8, 1885, HU.

61. Sewall, 2:580. It is Sewall who describes Jackson's life as "wide-ranging and cosmopolitan," 578. See also Banning, 35–36, 86; Leyda, 2:295–97, 265.

62. Quotes in this paragraph are from passages quoted in Sewall, 2:580, and Thomas H. Johnson, 171. See also Sewall, 2:592; Johnson, 179; Banning, xx. Jackson compared herself to an ox and Dickinson to a moth. See Sewall, 2:582. On her praise, see also Sewall, 2:584–88; Johnson, 174–76; Leyda, 2:394–97.

63. Rollins, "Authors at Home," 194. Mabie, "Helen Jackson," also mentions other people she was mentoring. She began mentoring writers as early as 1870 when she sent some of Sarah Woolsey's work to James T. Fields; see HH to Fields, Bethlehem, September 12, 1870, FI 2674, HL. Extant letters at Colorado College from Richard Watson Gilder, who called her "Poet and Applauder and Sympathizer & friend & Crony" (October 4, 1873), suggest she advised and encouraged him; see R. W. Gilder to HHJ, New York, October 4, 1873, CC. See also Banning, 89, 185.

64. Quotes in this paragraph are from Sewall, 2:582, 588.

65. Quotes in this paragraph are from passages quoted in Leyda, 2:181, and Sewall, 2:592. See also Sewall, 2:582–83, 588.

Chapter 7. Elizabeth Stuart Phelps (Ward)

1. Elizabeth Stuart Phelps (hereafter cited as ESP) to Henry Houghton, Newton Centre, Mass., May 4, 1894, HU.

2. An extensive treatment of her ancestry is found in Kessler, "'The Woman's Hour,'" 21–57. See also Elizabeth Stuart Phelps, *Chapters from a Life* (hereafter cited as *Chapters*), 1–17. Unless otherwise noted, details about Phelps's life are from this autobiography. Other valuable information about her life can be found in Coultrap-McQuin, "Elizabeth Stuart Phelps"; Bennett, *Elizabeth Stuart Phelps*; and Kelly, "'Oh the Poor Women.'" See also Starr, "Austin Phelps"; Kessler, "A

Literary Legacy"; Kessler, *Elizabeth Stuart Phelps*, 14; "Sarah Stuart Robbins," obituary.

3. Bennett, 8.

4. Kessler argues that one of Phelps's problems in life was that she was always seeking the approval of her very patriarchal father ("'The Woman's Hour,'" 59); *Chapters*, 16–17.

5. Both quotes are from *Chapters*, 17.

6. Quotes in this paragraph are from *Chapters*, 12. See also Kessler, "'The Woman's Hour,'" 48. Her mother's death also encouraged her life-long interest in death and dying, as Kelly (pp. 35–36) points out.

7. *Chapters*, 60; see also 61. On her mother, see Kessler, "'The Woman's Hour,'" 48; Kessler, *Elizabeth Stuart Phelps*, 13. On her father's attitudes, see Elizabeth Stuart Phelps, *Austin Phelps*; *Chapters*, 52–58. On her stepmother, see *Chapters*, 103–4.

8. *Chapters*, 104.

9. On her education, see *Chapters*, 44–63, 67–71 passim.

10. *Chapters*, 133. Examples and quotes in the rest of this paragraph are from *Chapters*, 32–33, 39–40, 44–47, 27–29, 60, 133–34. Phelps was a schoolmate of Stowe's youngest daughter.

11. *Chapters*, 65–66; see also 15, 18–19, 64.

12. *Chapters*, 77; see also 76–79 passim; Bennett, 24. Bennett has an excellent bibliography of Phelps's published works. Most are also cited and discussed in Coultrap-McQuin, 1–44.

13. *Chapters*, 91–93; ESP to John G. Whittier, Andover, Mass., March 13, 1868, HU.

14. Bennett, 46–50; *Chapters*, 99–100, 108.

15. *Chapters*, 110–30; Hart, *The Popular Book*, 120–21. An advertisement in the front of *Chapters* (1896) says *The Gates Ajar* was in its 81st thousand printing. See also ESP to Madam, Andover, Mass., February 14, 1880, Elizabeth Stuart Phelps Ward Collection (#6997), UV.

16. *Chapters*, 110; see also 103, 84, 192–94.

17. *Chapters*, 250.

18. A complete treatment of her views on women's issues is found in Coultrap-McQuin, "The Female Reconstruction of Society," in "Elizabeth Stuart Phelps," 275–343. Other treatments are in Kessler, "'The Woman's Hour,'" esp. 260–61 (n. 12), 160–62, 187, 218; Kelly; and Fetterley, "'Checkmate.'"

19. *Chapters*, 249. On her reform activities, see ESP to John G. Whittier, Andover, Mass., April 5, 1878, HU, and ESP to Mary Livermore, Andover, Mass., September 6, 1871, both in Elizabeth Stuart Phelps Ward Collection (#6997), UV; ESP to Abby May, Andover, Mass., May 29, 1876, RS; ESP to Lucy Stone, Andover, Mass., September 29, 1873, in Anthony, *History of Woman Suffrage* (Anthony, 1881), 2:831; ESP to John G. Whittier, East Gloucester, Mass., July 7, 1873, Whittier Collection, EI; ESP to George Eliot, Andover, Mass., December 1, 1876, YU; Spring, "Elizabeth Stuart Phelps," 569–70; ESP to George Eliot, Andover, Mass., May 27, 1877, YU; Kessler, "'The Woman's Hour,'" 210–12; *Chapters*, 254–55.

20. Spring, 570.

21. ESP to Abby May, East Gloucester, Mass., August 10, 1875, RS; ESP to Col. Etting, East Gloucester, August 14, 1875, case 7, box 8, Gratz Collection, HSP; *Chapters*, 201–20.

22. For examples, see ESP to William Hayes Ward, Andover, Mass., June 9, 1871, Elizabeth Stuart Phelps Ward Collection, EI; ESP to James R. Osgood, Andover, Mass., May 17, 1869, and June 8, 1874, HU.

23. *Chapters*, 226–27; ESP to Lucy Larcom, November 6, 1867, in Bennett, 63; Coultrap-McQuin, 14, 103–8; Kessler, "'The Woman's Hour,'" 340–43; ESP to Henry Wadsworth Longfellow, Andover, Mass., February 27, 1879, HU.

24. Austin Phelps, "Woman Suffrage" and "Reform in the Political Status of Women." See also Kessler, "'The Woman's Hour,'" 218–21; Kraditor, "The Rationale of Antisuffrage," in *Ideas of the Woman Suffrage Movement*, 12–37.

25. ESP to Richard Watson Gilder, Newton Highlands, Mass., February 8, 1891, Richard Watson Gilder Papers, NPL.

26. ESP to Sir [W. W. Griswold], Andover, Mass., November 22, 1884, YU; ESP to Sir (F. A. Cox), Andover, Mass., May 18, 1885, PSU. Some examples of entries in dictionaries include Spring, 560–80, and Hays, *Women of the Day*, 158. Phelps was asked to write a revised Bible in 1881; see ESP to William Hayes Ward, Andover, Mass., May 23, 1881, CHS. Comparisons to other important writers are found in Kessler, "'The Woman's Hour,'" 132, and "Recent Novels."

27. *Chapters*, 137–38; Gilman, "Atlantic Dinners," 656.

28. For examples, see ESP to My dear Sir [Lyman Abbott], Andover, Mass., March 22, 1880, BC; ESP to Francis Garrison, East Gloucester, Mass., July 26, 1883, YU; ESP to William Dean Howells, Andover, Mass., February 9, 1881, HU.

29. ESP to Mrs. Bolton, Andover, Mass., December 17, 1886, Octavo vol. #30, AAS. See also ESP to John G. Whittier, Andover, Mass., February 24, 1884, HU; Kessler, "'The Woman's Hour,'" 203–5.

30. Kessler agrees and points to other evidence of her lack of a support group to maintain a single state. "'The Woman's Hour,'" 301. See also 303–5, for people whom Phelps believed had happy marriages. The first letter I have seen that mentions Herbert Ward is ESP to William Ward, East Gloucester, Mass., August 22, 1884, Elizabeth Stuart Phelps Ward Collection, EI. On their relationship, see Kessler, "'The Woman's Hour,'" 305–19, and Bennett, 88–89.

31. Elizabeth Stuart Phelps, "A Dream within a Dream"; reprinted in Kessler, *Daring to Dream*, 107–11.

32. Among letters that reveal aspects of her marriage discussed in this paragraph, see ESP to the Claflins, Newton Highlands, Mass., Good Friday 1893, William Claflin Papers, RH; ESP to William Ward, Andover, Mass., May 15, 1888, Elizabeth Stuart Phelps Ward Collection (#6997), UV; ESP to Richard Watson Gilder, Andover, Mass., April 20, 1888, Richard Watson Gilder Papers, NPL; *Chapters*, 243; ESP to William Ward, Newton Highlands, May 21, [1893], Elizabeth Stuart Phelps Ward Collection, EI; ESP to Oliver Wendell Holmes, Sr., Newton Highlands, January 3, 1893, LC; ESP to Miss Hetta [Ward], Eastern Point, July 28, 1888, and Gloucester, Mass., August 30[?], 1888, Elizabeth Stuart Phelps Ward Collection, EI; ESP to George Mifflin, East Gloucester, Mass., July 30, 1902, HU. Her

husband did attend one suffrage affair in 1890; see ESP to W. D. Howells, Newton Highlands, March 31, 1890, HU.

33. "Elizabeth S. Phelps," clipping, UV.
34. ESP to William Dean Howells, Newton Highlands, Mass., March 31, 1890, HU; Anthony, *History of Woman Suffrage*, 4:707, 735; Coultrap-McQuin, 19.
35. Information in this paragraph is drawn from "Many Grieve over Mrs. E. S. P. Ward"; Anthony, 4:720; Coultrap-McQuin, 22–23; Kessler, "'The Woman's Hour,'" 129. Phelps herself was not deserted, though her husband was frequently absent from home.
36. Actually she had mentioned vivisection in Kessler, ed., *The Story of Avis*, 83. On her vivisection work, see ESP to William Claflin, Gloucester, Mass., August 10, 1902, William Claflin Papers, RH; ESP to George Mifflin, Newton Highlands, Mass., March 19, 1902, HU; Elizabeth Stuart Phelps, "Spirits in Prison" and "A Plea for the Helpless"; ESP to Richard Watson Gilder, Newton Centre, Mass., January 30, 1907, Richard Watson Gilder Papers, NPL.
37. All of these difficulties are reflected in ESP to Edward Bok, Newton Centre, Mass., December 31, 1904, Elizabeth Stuart Phelps Ward Collection (#6997), UV.
38. ESP to Longfellow, East Gloucester, Mass., August 22, 1878, HU.
39. A fuller discussion of Phelps's views of women can be found in Coultrap-McQuin, 275–343. Her critique of "The True Woman" was reissued with *The Story of Avis*, edited by Kessler, 269–72.
40. *Chapters*, 79. On the other hand, see also *Chapters*, 165, 171, 180, 225, 230–33. For example, she wrote, "George Eliot's will fought its way through suffering to create great novels," in Elizabeth Stuart Phelps, "George Eliot."
41. Quotes in this paragraph are from Elizabeth Stuart Phelps, "Too Much Conscience," 3, and "What Shall They Do?" 520. See also Coultrap-McQuin, 306–8.
42. Quotes in this paragraph are from *Chapters*, 261–62; Elizabeth Stuart Phelps, *The Struggle for Immortality*, 20; ESP to Horace Scudder, East Gloucester, Mass., September 20, 1894, HU; also ESP to Elizabeth Jordan, Newton Centre, Mass., March 3, 1900, Elizabeth Stuart Phelps Papers, NPL. Like Harriet Beecher Stowe in regard to *Uncle Tom's Cabin*, Phelps claimed that an angel told her to write *The Gates Ajar*. She wrote Richard Watson Gilder that writing her *Story of Jesus* was more difficult work than the Apostle John's. See ESP to Gilder, East Gloucester, Mass., August 26, 1897, CM 353, HL; ESP to Mrs. Lewes [George Eliot], Andover, Mass., December 1, 1876, YU.
43. Quotes in this paragraph are from ESP to Gilder, Eastern Point, Gloucester, Mass., June 22, 1887, Richard Watson Gilder Papers, NPL; *Chapters*, 260, 263.
44. Quotes in this paragraph are from "Elizabeth Stuart Phelps Ward," *Independent*, 269, and Ives, "Elizabeth Stuart P. Ward," 5.
45. Quotes in this paragraph are from *Chapters*, 87, 267; ESP to Edward Bok, Newton Centre, Mass., January 22, 1901, Elizabeth Stuart Phelps Ward Collection (#6997), UV. See also ESP to William Ward, Andover, Mass., December 6, 1885, Elizabeth Stuart Phelps Ward Collection, EI; *Chapters*, 267–68.
46. Quotes in this paragraph are from ESP to Miss Thompson, Andover, Mass., February 5, 1869, CU; *Chapters*, 86; ESP to Richard Watson Gilder, Newton Cen-

tre, Mass., November 10, 1908, Richard Watson Gilder Papers, NPL.

47. *Chapters*, 79. See also ESP to Miss Thompson, Andover, Mass., February 5, 1869, CU; Elizabeth Stuart Phelps, "What Shall They Do?" 519–23.

48. For a close study of her relationships with individual publishers, see Coultrap-McQuin, 168–236.

49. Elizabeth Stuart Phelps, "Whittier," 363. See also *Chapters*, 146–48.

50. *Chapters*, 147; see also ESP to Henry Houghton, Andover, Mass., May 20, 1882, HU. See also Elizabeth Stuart Phelps, "In Memoriam"; *Chapters*, 142–52; ESP to John G. Whittier, Andover, Mass., May 2, [1881], Elizabeth Stuart Phelps Ward Collection (#6997), UV.

51. ESP to James R. Osgood, Andover, Mass., May 17, 1869, HU. It is possible that she and Dodge discussed the Hamilton-Fields dispute, but their correspondence has been destroyed; see ESP to Harriet Prescott Spofford, Newton Centre, Mass., February 2, 1903, Miscellaneous Manuscripts "W," AAS. See also *Chapters*, 108–9.

52. ESP to Houghton, East Gloucester, Mass., August 30, 1889, HU.

53. Quotes in this passage are from ESP to Howells, East Gloucester, Mass., August 11, 1874, and Andover, Mass., February 9, 1881, HU. See also ESP to Richard Watson Gilder, Newton Centre, Mass., November 1, 1904, Richard Watson Gilder Papers, NPL.

54. Examples and quotes in this paragraph are from ESP to Henry Houghton, Newton Highlands, Mass., January 23, 1891, HU; ESP to Edward Bok, Newton Centre, Mass., October 9, 1899, Elizabeth Stuart Phelps Ward Collection (#6997), UV; ESP to Elizabeth Jordan, Newton Centre, Mass., April 11, 1900, and East Gloucester, Mass., July 10, 1905, Elizabeth Jordan Papers, NPL.

55. ESP to Madam, Andover, Mass., February 14, 1880, Elizabeth Stuart Phelps Ward Collection (#6997), UV.

56. ESP to Scudder, East Gloucester, Mass., September 20, 1894, HU. See also *Chapters*, 256; ESP to Richard Watson Gilder, Newton Centre, Mass., November 1, 1904, and November 10, 1908, Richard Watson Gilder Papers, NPL.

57. ESP to Johnson, Newton Centre, Mass., July 1, 1910, CM 369, HL. See also ESP to Edward Bok, Newton Centre, December 31, 1904, Elizabeth Stuart Phelps Ward Collection (#6997), UV.

58. ESP to Ward, East Gloucester, Mass., August 5, 1893, Elizabeth Stuart Phelps Ward Collection, EI.

59. ESP to George Mifflin, Newton Centre, Mass., October 11, 1905, HU.

60. ESP to Henry Houghton, Newton Centre, Mass., May 4, 1894, HU.

61. Details in this paragraph are drawn from ESP to Henry Houghton, East Gloucester, Mass., September 10, 1889, HU; ESP to Henry Houghton, Newton Centre, Mass., November 20, 1893, and May 4, 1894, HU. Unfortunately for Phelps, it was Horace Scudder who created the Riverside Literature Series and the Cambridge Poet Series that immortalized such writers as Emerson, Thoreau, Whittier, Longfellow, and Holmes as the core of American literature. See Howard Mumford Jones, *Age of Energy*, 61.

62. Quotes in this paragraph are from ESP to George Mifflin, East Gloucester, Mass., July 30, 1902, HU, and ESP to Publishers, Newton Centre, Mass., May 25, 1906, HU.

63. Quotes and examples in this paragraph are from ESP to Elizabeth Jordan, Newton Centre, Mass., April 11, 1900, Elizabeth Jordan Papers, NPL; ESP to R. U. Johnson, East Gloucester, Mass., July 3, 1900, Century Company Records, NPL; ESP to Edward Bok, Newton Centre, Mass., December 17, 1899, and December 31, 1904, Elizabeth Stuart Phelps Ward Collection (#6997), UV.

64. Quotes in this paragraph are from ESP to Gilder, Newton Centre, Mass., November 10, 1908, and November 13, 1908, Richard Watson Gilder Papers, NPL; ESP to Gilder, Newton Centre, November 19, 1908, Century Company Records, NPL.

Chapter 8. Literary Professionalism and Women

1. For an early history of literary professionalism, see Charvat, *The Profession of Authorship*, 1–28; Buell, *New England Literary Culture*, 57–64. Ultimately, genteel amateurism evolved into the attitude of the so-called serious writers today who disdain commercial success as the antithesis of literary merit.

2. Lichtenstein, "Authorial Professionalism," 35. See also Christopher P. Wilson, *Labor of Words*.

3. Buell, 375–92.

4. The term "professional" has been used in a variety of ways. At a minimum, it means earning an income for one's work. Usually, however, the term is applied to work that calls for commitments beyond that—for instance, to public service, advanced education, skill development, and so forth. I am using the word professional in this second, fuller sense. It should be noted that the status of professional often excludes fields dominated by women.

5. Stowe's articles included "Can I Write?"; "How Shall I Learn to Write?"; "Faults of Inexperienced Writers"; "How May I Know that I Can Make a Writer?"; and "Writing—Commercially."

6. Buell, 68.

7. Lichtenstein, 46–47.

8. See Brumberg and Tomes, "Women in the Professions," 288; Scott, "The Profession that Vanished," 26–28; Bledstein, *The Culture of Professionalism*, 118–20.

9. Christopher P. Wilson, esp. 142–43; Tuchman, *Edging Women Out*.

Bibliography

Adams, John R. *Harriet Beecher Stowe*. New York: Twayne, 1963.
Admari, Ralph. "Bonner and the Ledger," *American Book Collector* 6 (May–June 1935): 176–93.
"American Women of Letters." *Literary World* 14 (April 21, 1883): 127.
Ames, Mary Clemmer. *Outlines of Men, Women, and Things*. New York: Hurd and Houghton, 1873.
Ammons, Elizabeth. "Heroines in *Uncle Tom's Cabin*." In *Critical Essays on Harriet Beecher Stowe*, edited by Elizabeth Ammons, 152–65. Boston: G. K. Hall and Company, 1980.
Andrews, Kenneth R. *Nook Farm: Mark Twain's Hartford Circle*. Cambridge: Harvard University Press, 1950.
Anthony, Susan B. *History of Woman Suffrage*. Anthony, 1881.
Apponyi, Flora Haines. "Last Days of Mrs. Helen Hunt Jackson." *Overland Monthly* 2, no. 6 (September 1885): 310–15.
Armstrong, Augustine W. "Helen Hunt Jackson." *Methodist Review* 74 (May 1897): 440–50.
Ashton, Jean Willoughby. "Harriet Stowe's Filthy Story: Lord Byron Set Afloat." *Prospects: An Annual Journal of American Culture Studies* 2 (1976): 373–84.
Austin, James C. *Fields of the Atlantic Monthly: Letters to an Editor, 1861–1870*. San Marino, Cal.: Huntington Library, 1953.
"Authors among Fruits: The Banquet of the Publishers." *New York Daily Times* 5 (September 28, 1855): 1.
"Azarian: An Episode." Review article. Source unknown (1865): 275.
Ballou, Ellen B. *The Building of the House: Houghton Mifflin's Formative Years*. Boston: Houghton Mifflin, 1970.
Banning, Evelyn I. *Helen Hunt Jackson*. New York: Vanguard Press, 1973.
Bartlett, Irving H. *The American Mind in the Mid-Nineteenth Century*. New York: Thomas V. Crowell Company, 1967.
Baym, Nina. *Novels, Readers, and Reviewers: Responses to Fiction in Antebellum America*. Ithaca, N.Y.: Cornell University Press, 1984.

———. *Woman's Fiction: A Guide to Novels by and about Women in America, 1820–1870*. Ithaca, N.Y.: Cornell University Press, 1978.
Beasley, Maurine. "Mary Abigail Dodge: 'Gail Hamilton' and the Process of Social Change." *Essex Institute Historical Collections* 116, no. 2 (1980): 82–100.
Bell, Michael Davitt. *The Development of American Romance: The Sacrifice of Relation*. Chicago: University of Chicago Press, 1980.
Bennett, Mary Angela. *Elizabeth Stuart Phelps*. Philadelphia: University of Pennsylvania Press, 1939.
Berkson, Dorothy. "Millennial Politics and the Feminine Fiction of Harriet Beecher Stowe." In *Critical Essays on Harriet Beecher Stowe*, edited by Elizabeth Ammons, 244–58. Boston: G. K. Hall and Company, 1980.
"Bits of Travel." *Literary World* 5, no. 2 (January 1, 1872): 118–19.
Bledstein, Burton J. *The Culture of Professionalism: The Middle Class and the Development of Higher Education in America*. New York: W. W. Norton and Company, 1976.
Boydston, Jeanne, Mary Kelley, and Anne Margolis. *The Limits of Sisterhood: The Beecher Sisters on Women's Rights and Woman's Sphere*. Chapel Hill and London: University of North Carolina Press, 1988.
Boyle, Regis Louise. *Mrs. E.D.E.N. Southworth, Novelist*. Washington, D.C.: Catholic University Press, 1939.
Bracher, Peter S. "Harper & Brothers: Publishers of Dickens." *New York Public Library Bulletin* 79 (Spring 1976): 315–35.
Bradford, Ellen Knight. "A Remarkable Life." Newspaper article, n.d. DU.
Bradford, Gamaliel. *Portraits of American Women*. New York: Houghton Mifflin, 1919.
Browne, Francis F. "American Publishing and Publishers." *Dial* (May 1, 1900): 340–43.
Brumberg, Joan Jacobs, and Nancy Tomes. "Women in the Professions: A Research Agenda for American Historians." *Reviews in American History* 10, no. 2 (1982): 275–96.
Buell, Lawrence. *New England Literary Culture: From Revolution through Renaissance*. Cambridge, England: Cambridge University Press, 1986.
Cady, Edwin Harrison, and Harry Hayden Clark, eds. *Whittier on Writers and Writing*. [Salem, Mass.]: Essex Index Reprinting Series, 1950.
Carr, Jeanne C. "Helen Hunt Jackson." *Woman's Journal* 16 (September 5, 1885): 288.
Carrier, Esther Jane. *Fiction in Public Libraries, 1876–1900*. New York: Scarecrow Press, 1965.
"Celia Burleigh and Saxe Holm." *Boston Globe*, February 9, 1874.
Chambers-Schiller, Lee. "The Single Woman: Family and Vocation among Nineteenth-Century Reformers." In *Woman's Being, Woman's Place: Female Identity and Vocation in American History*, edited by Mary Kelley, 334–50. Boston: G. K. Hall and Company, 1979.
Charvat, William. *Literary Publishing in America, 1790–1850*. Philadelphia: University of Pennsylvania Press, 1959.
———. *The Profession of Authorship in America, 1800–1870*, edited by Matthew Bruccoli. Columbus: Ohio State University, 1968.

"A Christian Novelist." Newspaper article, n.d. DU.
Cochran, Thomas C. *American Business in the Twentieth Century*. Cambridge: Harvard University Press, 1972.
Conway, Moncure Daniel. *Autobiography: Memories and Experiences*. 2 vols. Boston and New York: Houghton Mifflin, 1904.
———. "Mrs. Jackson." *Athenaeum: A Journal of Literature, Science, the Fine Arts, Music, and the Drama* (August 29, 1885): 271.
Cooke, Rose Terry. "Harriet Beecher Stowe." In *Our Famous Women: An Authorized Record of the Lives and Deeds of Distinguished American Women of Our Times*, 581–601. Hartford, Conn.: A. D. Worthington and Co., 1884.
———. "The Memorial of A. B., or Matilda Muffin." *Atlantic Monthly* 5 (1860): 186–91. Reprinted in *Legacy: A Journal of Nineteenth-Century Women Writers* 2, no. 2 (Fall 1985): 80–82.
Coolidge, Susan. "'H. H.'" *Christian Union* (September 17, 1885): 6.
———. "H. H." *Independent* 37 (September 3, 1885): 1.
———. "The 'Saxe Holm' Stories." *Literary World* 16 (October 3, 1885): 355.
Coser, Louis A., Charles Kadushin, and Walter P. Powell. *Books: The Culture and Commerce of Publishing*. New York: Basic Books, 1982.
Coultrap-McQuin, Susan. "Elizabeth Stuart Phelps: The Cultural Context of a Nineteenth-Century Professional Writer." Ph.D. dissertation, University of Iowa, Iowa City, 1979.
Cross, Barbara M. "Stowe, Harriet Beecher." In *Notable American Women, 1607–1950: A Biographical Dictionary*, edited by Edward T. James, Janet Wilson James, and Paul S. Boyer, 3:393–402. Cambridge: Harvard University Press, 1974.
Davidson, Cathy N. *Revolution and the Word: The Rise of the Novel in America*. New York: Oxford University Press, 1986.
Derby, James C. *Fifty Years among Authors, Books, and Publishers*. New York: G. W. Carleton and Co., 1884.
Dexter, Elisabeth Anthony. *Career Women of America, 1776–1840*. Francestown, N.H.: Marshall Jones Company, 1950.
Dobson, Joanne A. "Emily Dickinson and Mid-Nineteenth Century American Women Writers: A Community of Expression." Ph.D. dissertation, University of Massachusetts, Amherst, 1985.
———. Introduction to *The Hidden Hand or Capitola the Madcap*, by E.D.E.N. Southworth, edited by Joanne Dobson, xi–xli. New Brunswick, N.J.: Rutgers University Press, 1988.
Dodge, H. Augusta, ed. *Gail Hamilton's Life in Letters*. 2 vols. Boston: Lee and Shepard, 1901.
Donovan, Josephine. "Harriet Beecher Stowe and the Emergence of a Female Arcadia." In *New England Local Color Literature: A Women's Tradition*, 50–67. New York: Frederick Ungar Publishing Company, 1983.
Dorr, Julia C. R. "Emerson's Admiration of 'H. H.'" *Critic: An Illustrated Review of Literature, Art, and Life* 7 (August 29, 1885): 102.
Douglas, Ann. *The Feminization of American Culture*. New York: Avon, 1977.
Edel, Leon. *Literary Biography*. London: Rupert Hart-Davis, 1957.
Elbert, Sarah. "The Changing Education of American Women." *Current History* 70, no. 416 (May 1976): 220–23, 233–34.

Ellsworth, William Webster. *A Golden Age of Authors: A Publisher's Recollection*. Boston: Houghton Mifflin, 1919.
Epstein, Barbara Leslie. *The Politics of Domesticity: Women, Evangelism, and Temperance in Nineteenth-Century America*. Middletown, Conn.: Wesleyan University Press, 1981.
Erskine, John. *Leading American Novelists*. New York: Henry Holt and Company, 1910.
Evans, Elizabeth. "Mrs. Sigourney's Friend and Mentor." *Bulletin of the Connecticut Historical Society* 36, no. 3 (1971): 77–91.
Evans, Sara M. *Born for Liberty: A History of Women in America*. New York: The Free Press, 1989.
Exman, Eugene. *The Brothers Harper: A Unique Publishing Partnership and Its Impact upon the Cultural Life of America from 1817 to 1853*. New York: Harper and Row, 1965.
Farmer, Lydia Hoyt, ed. *What America Owes to Women*. Buffalo, N.Y.: C. W. Moulton, 1893.
Ferguson, Robert A. "Literature and Vocation in the Early Republic: The Example of Charles Brockden Brown." *Modern Philology* 78, no. 2 (November 1980): 139–52.
Fern, Fanny [Sara Payson Parton]. "Fresh Leaves." *New York Ledger*, October 10, 1857. Reprinted in *Legacy: A Journal of Nineteenth-Century Women Writers* 2, no. 2 (Fall 1985): 59.
———. "Gail Hamilton—Miss Dodge." In *Eminent Women of the Age; Being Narratives of the Lives and Deeds of the Most Prominent Women of the Present Generation*, edited by James Parton, 2 vols., 1:202–20. Hartford, Conn.: S. M. Betts and Company, 1869.
———. *Ruth Hall: A Domestic Tale of the Present Time*. New York: Mason Brothers, 1855.
———. *Ruth Hall and Other Writings*, edited by Joyce W. Warren. New Brunswick, N.J.: Rutgers University Press, 1986.
Fetterley, Judith. "'Checkmate': Elizabeth Stuart Phelps's *The Silent Partner*." *Legacy: A Journal of Nineteenth-Century American Women Writers* 3, no. 2 (Fall 1986): 17–29.
———. *Provisions: A Reader from 19th-Century American Women*. Bloomington: Indiana University Press, 1985.
Fields, Annie. *Life and Letters of Harriet Beecher Stowe*. 1897. Reprint. Detroit: Gale Research Company, 1970.
Forman, W. H. "Uncle Tom's Cabin." *Manhattan* 1 (January 1883): 28–31.
Forrest, Mary. "Emma D. E. N. Southworth." In *Women of the South Distinguished in Literature*, 216–44. New York: Derby and Jackson, 1861.
Francis, Susan. "The Atlantic's Pleasant Days in Tremont Street." *Atlantic Monthly* 100 (November 1907): 716–20.
French, Warren G. "'Honor to Genius': The Complimentary Festival to Authors, 1855." *New York Historical Society Quarterly* 39, no. 4 (October 1955): 357–67.
"Gail Hamilton." *Independent* 53 (November 14, 1901): 2712–13.
"Gail Hamilton." *Woman's Journal* (August 22, 1896).

Gallup, Donald. "More Letters of American Writers." *Yale University Library Gazette* (July 1962): 30–35.
Garrison, Dee. "Immoral Fiction in the Late Victorian Library." *American Quarterly* 28 (September 1976): 71–89.
Geary, Susan Elizabeth. "The Domestic Novel as a Commercial Commodity: Making a Best Seller in the 1850s." *Papers of the Bibliographical Society of America* 70, no. 3 (1976): 365–94.
———. "Harriet Beecher Stowe, John P. Jewett, and Author-Publisher Relations in 1853." *Studies in the American Renaissance* (1977): 345–67.
———. "Scribbling Women: Essays on Literary History and Popular Literature in the 1850s." Ph.D. dissertation, Brown University, Providence, R.I., 1976.
Geison, Gerald L. *Professions and Professional Ideologies in America*. Chapel Hill: University of North Carolina Press, 1983.
Gerson, Noel B. *Harriet Beecher Stowe*. New York: Praeger Publishers, 1976.
G. G. "Mary Abigail Dodge." In *Dictionary of American Biography*, edited by Allen Johnson and Dumas Malone, 5:350–51. New York: Charles Scribner's Sons, 1930.
Gilbert, Sandra M., and Susan Gubar. *The Madwoman in the Attic: The Woman Writer and the Nineteenth-Century Literary Imagination*. New Haven: Yale University Press, 1979.
[Gilder, J. B.?] "Mrs. Jackson's Last Book—*Zeph*." *Critic: An Illustrated Monthly Review of Literature, Art, and Life* (February 6, 1886): 67.
Gilman, Arthur. "Atlantic Dinners and Diners." *Atlantic Monthly* 100, no. 5 (November 1907): 646–57.
Gould, Elizabeth Porter. "The Author of Ramona." *Education* (November 1900): 182–84.
Greenwood, Grace. "Fanny Fern—Mrs. Parton." In *Eminent Women of the Age; Being Narratives of the Lives and Deeds of the Most Prominent Women of the Present Generation*, edited by James Parton, 66–84. Hartford, Conn.: S. M. Betts and Company, 1869.
Griswold, Rufus Wilmot. *The Female Poets of America*. Philadelphia: Carey and Hart, 1849.
Gross, Gerald. *Publishers on Publishing*. New York: R. R. Bowker Company, 1961.
Gross, Robert A. "A Response." *Massachusetts Review* 20, no. 3 (1979): 461–67.
Habegger, Alfred. "A Well Hidden Hand." *Novel: A Forum on Fiction* 14, no. 3 (1981): 197–212.
Hale, Sarah J. *Woman's Record: Or Sketches of Distinguished Women from the Creation to A.D. 1854*. New York: Harper and Brothers, 1855.
Hamilton, Gail [Mary Abigail Dodge]. *A Battle of the Books*. Cambridge, Mass.: Riverside Press, 1870.
———. *Country Living and Country Thinking*. Boston: Ticknor and Fields, 1865.
———. "Gala Days." *Atlantic Monthly* 11 (May 1863): 629–42.
———. *Gala Days*. Boston: Ticknor and Fields, 1863.
———. *A New Atmosphere*. Boston: Ticknor and Fields, 1865.
———. *Skirmishes and Sketches*. Boston: Ticknor and Fields, 1865.
———. *Woman's Worth and Worthlessness*. New York: Harper and Brothers, 1872.

———. *Woman's Wrongs: A Counter-Irritant*. Boston: Ticknor and Fields, 1868.
Harris, Susan K. "The House that Hagar Built: Houses and Heroines in E.D.E.N. Southworth's *The Deserted Wife*." *Legacy: A Journal of Nineteenth-Century American Women Writers* 4, no. 2 (Fall 1987): 17–29.
Hart, James D. *The Popular Book: A History of America's Literary Taste*. Berkeley: University of California Press, 1963.
Hays, Frances. *Women of the Day: A Biographical Dictionary of Notable Contemporaries*. Philadelphia: Lippincott and Company, 1885.
H. C. B. "A Noted Novel Writer." *Washington Post*, December 2, 1894, 1.
"Helen Jackson." *Critic: An Illustrated Monthly Review of Literature, Art, and Life* (August 22, 1885): 85–86.
"Helen Jackson." *Independent* (August 20, 1885): 16.
"Helen Jackson." *New York Evening Post*, August 13, 1885.
Hersh, Blanche Glassman. "The 'True Woman' and the 'New Woman' in Nineteenth-Century America: Feminist Abolitionists and a New Concept of True Womanhood." In *Woman's Being, Woman's Place: Female Identity and Vocation in American History*, edited by Mary Kelley, 271–82. Boston: G. K. Hall and Company, 1979.
"'H. H.' Did Not Write the 'Saxe Holm' Stories." *Daily Graphic*, January 27, 1874.
"'H. H.': A Reminiscence from an Old Letter of 1873." *Literary World: A Monthly Review* (June 16, 1883): 191.
Higginson, Thomas Wentworth. *Contemporaries*. Boston and New York: Houghton, Mifflin, 1899.
———. "Helen Jackson, ('H. H.')." In *Short Studies of American Authors*, 1879. Reprint. New York: Longmans, Green and Company, 1906, 40–50.
———. "How Ramona Was Written." *Atlantic Monthly* 86 (November 1900): 712–14.
———. "Letter to a Young Contributor." *Atlantic Monthly* 9, no. 54 (April 1862): 401–11.
Hindus, Michael S., and Lynne E. Withey. "The Law of Husband and Wife in Nineteenth-Century America: Changing Views of Divorce." In *Women and the Law: A Social Historical Perspective*. Vol. 2, *Property, Family, and the Legal Profession*, edited by D. Kelly Weisberg, 133–53. Cambridge, Mass.: Schenkman, 1982.
Hofstadter, Beatrice K. "Southworth, Emma Dorothy Eliza Nevitte." In *Notable American Women, 1607–1950: A Biographical Dictionary*, edited by Edward T. James, Janet Wilson James, and Paul S. Boyer, 3:327–28. Cambridge: Harvard University Press, 1974.
Holland, Josiah G. "Sex and Wages." *Scribner's Monthly* 1, no. 1 (November 1870): 107–8.
Holland, Patricia G. "Lydia Maria Child as a Nineteenth-Century Professional Author." In *Studies in the American Renaissance, 1981*, edited by Joel Myerson, 157–67. Boston: Twayne, 1981.
Hollands, Hulda T. "Helen Hunt Jackson." *Bay View Magazine* (April 1, 1908): 481–83.
"The Holmes Breakfast." *Atlantic Monthly* 45, no. 268 Supplement (February 1880): 1–24.

Holt, Henry. *Garrulities of an Octogenarian Editor; with Other Essays Somewhat Biographical and Autobiographical*. Boston: Houghton Mifflin, 1923.
Howe, Daniel Walker. "American Victorianism as a Culture." *American Quarterly* 27, no. 5 (December 1975): 507–32.
Howells, M., ed. *The Life in Letters of William Dean Howells*. Garden City, N.Y.: Doubleday, 1928.
Howells, William Dean. *Literary Friends and Acquaintances: A Personal Retrospect of American Authorship* [1901], edited by David Hiatt and Edwin Cody. Bloomington: Indiana University Press, 1968.
Huddleson, Sarah M. "Mrs. E.D.E.N. Southworth and Her Cottage." In *Records of the Columbia Historical Society* 23 (1920): 52–81.
Huf, Linda. *A Portrait of the Artist as a Young Woman*. New York: Frederick Ungar Publishing Company, 1983.
Ives, Ella Gilbert. "Elizabeth Stuart P. Ward: A More Intimate Sketch of Her Personality." *Boston Evening Transcript*, February 4, 1911, pt. 3, p. 5.
Jackson, Helen Hunt (H. H.). *Bits of Talk about Home Matters*. 1873. Reprint. Boston: Roberts Brothers, 1891.
[_____]. *Mercy Philbrick's Choice*. Boston: Roberts Brothers, 1876.
[_____]. *Saxe Holm's Stories*, 1st and 2d ser. 1873, 1878. Reprint. New York: Charles Scribner's Sons, 1891.
James, Edward T., Janet Wilson James, and Paul S. Boyer, eds. *Notable American Women, 1607–1950: A Biographical Dictionary*. 3 vols. Cambridge: Harvard University Press, 1974.
Jeffrey, Kirk. "The Family as Utopian Retreat from the City: The Nineteenth-Century Contribution." *Soundings* (1972): 21–41.
Johnson, Arthur Franklin. "The Poetry of Louise Chandler Moulton." *Poet-Lore* (Winter 1908): 473–77.
Johnson, Thomas H. *Emily Dickinson: An Interpretive Biography*. 1955. Reprint. Cambridge, Mass.: Belknap Press, 1966.
Johnston, Johanna. *Runaway to Heaven: The Story of Harriet Beecher Stowe*. Garden City, N.Y.: Doubleday, 1963.
Jones, Howard Mumford. *The Age of Energy: Varieties of American Experience, 1865–1915*. New York: Viking Press, 1970.
Jones, W. A. "Female Novelists." *United States Magazine and Democratic Review* (May 1844): 484–89.
Kelley, Mary. *Private Woman, Public Stage: Literary Domesticity in Nineteenth-Century America*. New York: Oxford University Press, 1984.
_____. "At War with Herself: Harriet Beecher Stowe as Woman in Conflict within the Home." *American Studies* 19, no. 2 (1978): 23–40.
Kelly, Lori Duin. "'Oh the Poor Women'—A Study of the Works of Elizabeth Stuart Phelps." Ph.D. dissertation, University of North Carolina, Chapel Hill, 1979.
Kessler, Carol Farley. *Elizabeth Stuart Phelps*. Boston: Twayne, 1982.
_____. "A Literary Legacy: Elizabeth Stuart Phelps, Mother and Daughter." *Frontiers: A Journal of Women's Studies* 5, no. 3 (Fall 1980): 28–33.
_____. "'The Woman's Hour': Life and Novels of Elizabeth Stuart Phelps,

1844–1911." Ph.D. dissertation, University of Pennsylvania, Philadelphia, 1977.
———, ed. *Daring to Dream: Utopian Stories by United States Women, 1848–1919.* New York: Pandora Press, 1984.
———, ed. *The Story of Avis* [1877] by Elizabeth Stuart Phelps. New Brunswick, N.J.: Rutgers University Press, 1985.
Kessler-Harris, Alice. *Out to Work: A History of Wage-Earning Women in the United States.* New York: Oxford University Press, 1982.
Kilgour, Raymond L. *Lee and Shepard: Publishers for the People.* Hamden, Conn.: Shoestring Press, 1965.
———. *Messrs. Roberts Brothers, Publishers.* Ann Arbor: University of Michigan Press, 1952.
Kirk, Ellen Olney. "Women Fiction Writers of America." In *What America Owes Women,* edited by Lydia Hoyt Farmer, 194–204. Buffalo, N.Y.: C. W. Moulton, 1893.
Knopf, Alfred A. "Random Recollections of a Publisher." *Massachusetts Historical Society Boston Proceedings* 73 (1961): 92–103.
Kraditor, Aileen S. *The Ideas of the Woman Suffrage Movement, 1890–1920.* New York: Anchor, 1971.
Lentricchia, Frank. "Harriet Beecher Stowe and the Byron Whirlwind." *Bulletin of the New York Public Library* 70, no. 4 (April 1966): 218–28.
Leyda, Jay. *The Years and Hours of Emily Dickinson.* 2 vols. New Haven, Conn.: Yale University Press, 1960.
Lichtenstein, Nelson. "Authorial Professionalism and the Literary Marketplace, 1885–1900." *American Studies* 19, no. 1 (Spring 1978): 35–53.
Liedel, Donald E. "The Puffing of *Ida May*: Publishers Exploit the Antislavery Novel." *Journal of Popular Culture* 3 (Fall 1969): 287–306.
"Literary News—Saxe Holm." *Literary World* 4 (May 1874): 191.
"Literary Women." *The Living Age* (June 25, 1864): 609–10.
The Lounger. "E.D.E.N. Southworth." *Critic: An Illustrated Monthly Review of Literature, Art, and Life* 11, no. 31 (July 1887): 31.
Lyman, Joseph B. "Grace Greenwood—Mrs. Lippincott." In *Eminent Women of the Age; Being Narratives of the Lives and Deeds of the Most Prominent Women of the Present Generation,* edited by James Parton, 147–63. Hartford, Conn.: S. M. Betts and Company, 1869.
Mabie, Hamilton W. "Helen Jackson." *Christian Union* 32, no. 8 (August 20, 1885).
McCray, Florine Thayer. *Life-Work of the Author of Uncle Tom's Cabin.* New York: Funk and Wagnalls, 1889.
Madison, Charles A. *Book Publishing in America.* New York: McGraw-Hill, 1966.
"Many Grieve over Mrs. E. S. P. Ward." Clipping. Source unknown. AHS.
Marsden, Michael T. "Helen Hunt Jackson: Docudramatist of the American Indian." *Markham Review* 10 (Fall–Winter 1980–81): 15–19.
Martin, Minerva L. "Helen Hunt Jackson in Relation to Her Times." Ph.D. dissertation, University of Louisiana, Baton Rouge, 1940.
Mathes, Valerie Sherer. "Helen Hunt Jackson: Official Agent to the California Mission Indians." *Southern California Quarterly* 63, no. 1 (1981): 63–82.

"Mercy Philbrick's Choice." *Literary World* 7 (November 1876): 79–80.
Mott, Frank Luther. *Golden Multitudes: The Story of Best Sellers in the United States*. New York: Macmillan, 1947.
———. *A History of American Magazines*. 4 vols. Cambridge: Harvard University Press, 1957.
"Mrs. E.D.E.N. Southworth." *Book News* 11 (November 1890): 66–67.
Nevins, Allan. "Helen Hunt Jackson, Sentimentalist vs. Realist." *American Scholar* 10, no. 3 (Summer 1941): 269–85.
"News and Notes—Helen Hunt Jackson." *Literary World* 18 (February 5, 1887): 44.
"The New York Herald on Women's Work and Wages." *Woman's Journal* 4 (November 29, 1873): 381.
Noel, Mary. *Villains Galore: The Heyday of the Popular Story Weekly*. New York: Macmillan, 1954.
O'Brien, Sharon. "Tomboyism and Adolescent Conflict: Three Nineteenth-Century Case Studies." In *Woman's Being, Woman's Place: Female Identity and Vocation in American History*, edited by Mary Kelley, 351–72. Boston: G. K. Hall and Company, 1979.
Odell, Ruth. *Helen Hunt Jackson (H. H.)*. New York: D. Appleton-Century Company, 1939.
Our Famous Women: An Authorized Record of the Lives and Deeds of Distinguished American Women of Our Times by Twenty Eminent Authors. Hartford, Conn.: A. D. Worthington and Company, 1884.
"Our 'Forty Immortals.'" *The Critic and Good Literature* 4 (April 12, 1884): 169–70.
Page, Walter Hines. *A Publisher's Confession*. 1905. Reprint. Garden City, N.Y.: Doubleday, Page, and Company, 1923.
Papashvily, Helen Waite. *All the Happy Endings*. New York: Harper and Brothers, 1956.
Parker, Edwin Pond. "Harriet Beecher Stowe." In *Eminent Women of the Age; Being Narratives of the Lives and Deeds of the Most Prominent Women of the Present Generation*, edited by James Parton, 296–331. Hartford, Conn.: S. M. Betts and Company, 1869.
Parton, James, ed. *Eminent Women of the Age; Being Narratives of the Lives and Deeds of the Most Prominent Women of the Present Generation*. Hartford, Conn.: S. M. Betts and Company, 1869.
Pattee, Fred Lewis. *The Development of the American Short Story: An Historical Survey*. New York: Harper and Brothers, 1923.
———. *The Feminine Fifties*. New York: D. Appleton-Century Company, 1940.
Phelps, Austin. "Reform in the Political Status of Women." In *My Portfolio: A Collection of Essays*, 105–16. New York: Charles Scribner's Sons, 1882.
———. "Woman Suffrage as Judged by the Working of Negro-Suffrage." In *My Portfolio: A Collection of Essays*, 94–104. New York: Charles Scribner's Sons, 1882.
"Phelps, Elizabeth S." Unidentified clipping. UV.

Phelps, Elizabeth Stuart. *Austin Phelps: A Memoir*. New York: Charles Scribner's Sons, 1891.
———. *Chapters from a Life*. Boston: Houghton, Mifflin, 1896.
———. "A Dream within a Dream." *Independent* 26 (February 19, 1874): 1.
———. "George Eliot." *Harper's Weekly* 29, no. 1469 (February 14, 1885): 103.
———. "In Memoriam." *Independent* 33 (June 2, 1881): 1–2.
———. "A Plea for the Helpless." *Boston Herald*, March 27, 1901.
———. "Spirits in Prison." *Independent* 52, no. 2677 (March 22, 1900): 695–97.
———. *The Story of Avis*. Boston: James R. Osgood and Company, 1877. Reprint edited by Carol Farley Kessler. New Brunswick, N.J.: Rutgers University Press, 1985.
———. *The Struggle for Immortality*. Boston: Houghton, Mifflin, 1889.
———. "Too Much Conscience." *Independent* 23 (August 3, 1871): 3.
———. "The True Woman." *Independent* 23, no. 1193 (October 12, 1871): 1.
———. "What Shall They Do?" *Harper's New Monthly Magazine* 35 (September 1867): 519–23.
———. "Whittier." *Century* 45, no. 3 (January 1893): 363–68.
Poovey, Mary. *The Proper Lady and the Woman Writer*. Chicago: University of Chicago Press, 1984.
Pringle, Patrick. *When They Were Girls: Girlhood Stories of Fourteen Famous Women*. New York: Roy Publishers, n.d.
"Pseudonyms—Old and New." *Literary World* 8 (November 1, 1877): 102–3.
Pulsifer, Janice Goldsmith. "Gail Hamilton, 1833–1896." *Essex Institute Historical Collections* 104, no. 3 (1968): 165–216.
Putnam, George Palmer. "'Freestone'—Authors—Publishers." *Literary World* (May 29, 1852): 395–96.
[Putnam, George Haven] G. H. P. and J. B. P. *Authors and Publishers: A Manual of Suggestions for Beginners in Literature*. 1888. Rewritten with additional material. New York: G. P. Putnam's Sons, 1897.
"Ramona." *Overland Monthly* 2, no. 5 (March 1885): 330–31.
"Recent Fiction—Saxe Holm's Second Series." *Literary World* 9 (September 1878): 57.
"Recent Literature—*Mercy Philbrick's Choice*." *Atlantic Monthly* 39 (February 1877): 243.
"Recent Literature—*Verses* by H. H." *Atlantic Monthly* 28 (March 1871): 400.
"Recent Novels." *Nation* 26 (March 21, 1878): 202.
Reynolds, Quentin. *The Fiction Factory, or From Pulp Row to Quality Street*. New York: Random House, 1955.
Rice, Wallace. "Leaves from a Busy Life." *Dial* (September 16, 1901): 178–81.
Rich, Adrienne. "Vesuvius at Home: The Power of Emily Dickinson." In *On Lies, Secrets, and Silence: Selected Prose, 1966–1978*, 157–83. New York: W. W. Norton and Company, 1979.
Riley, Glenda. *Inventing the American Woman: A Perspective on Women's History*. Vol. 1, 1607–1877. Arlington Heights, Ill.: Harlan Davidson, Inc. 1986.
Robbins, J. Albert. "Fees Paid to Authors by Certain American Periodicals, 1840–1850." *Studies in Bibliography* 2 (1949–50): 95–104.

"Robbins, Sarah Stuart." Obituary. Source unknown. AHS.
Rollins, Alice Wellington. "Authors at Home: Mrs. Jackson ('H. H.') at Colorado Springs." *Critic: An Illustrated Monthly Review of Literature, Art, and Life* 3 (April 25, 1885): 193–94.
Rosenberg, Charles E. "Sexuality, Class, and Role in Nineteenth-Century America." *American Quarterly* 25, no. 2 (May 1973): 131–53.
Ross, Isabel. *Ladies of the Press*. New York: Harper and Brothers, 1936.
Ryan, Mary P. "The Empire of the Mother: American Writing about Domesticity, 1830–1860." *Women and History* 2, 3 (1982).
Savoyard. "Mrs. Southworth, Mr. Bonner, and the Ledger." *Washington Post*, September 4, 1904.
"Saxe Holm's Stories." *Woman's Journal* 5 (January 17, 1874): 21.
Scott, Donald M. "The Profession that Vanished: Public Lecturing in Mid-Nineteenth-Century America." In *Professions and Professional Ideologies in America*, edited by Gerald Geison, 12–28. Chapel Hill: University of North Carolina Press, 1983.
Scudder, Horace E. *Henry Oscar Houghton: A Biographical Outline*. Cambridge, Mass.: Riverside Press, 1897.
———. "Recent American Fiction—*Ramona*." *Atlantic Monthly* 55, no. 327 (January 1885): 127–30.
Sewall, Richard B. *The Life of Emily Dickinson*. 2 vols. New York: Farrar, Straus and Giroux, 1974.
Sheehan, Donald. *This Was Publishing: A Chronicle of the Book Trade in the Gilded Age*. Bloomington: Indiana University Press, 1952.
Shinn, M. W. "The Verse and Prose of 'H. H.'" *Overland Monthly* 2, no. 6 (September 1885): 315–23.
Showalter, Elaine. "Women Writers and the Double Standard." In *Woman in Sexist Society*, edited by Vivian Gornick and Barbara H. Moran, 452–79. New York: Basic Books, 1971.
Sklar, Kathryn Kish. *Catharine Beecher: A Study in American Domesticity*. New Haven: Yale University Press, 1973.
———. "Victorian Women and Domestic Life: Mary Todd Lincoln, Elizabeth Cady Stanton, and Harriet Beecher Stowe." In *The Public and Private Lincoln: Contemporary Perspectives*, edited by Cullom Davis, 20–37. Carbondale: Southern Illinois University Press, 1979.
"Some 'Lady Novelists' and Their Works: As Seen from a Public Library." *Literary World* 13 (June 3, 1882): 184–86.
"Southworth, Emma." In *National Cyclopedia of American Biography*, 1:432. New York: James T. White and Company, 1898.
Southworth, Emma D. E. N. *The Deserted Wife*. Philadelphia: T. B. Peterson and Brothers, 1855.
———. *The Hidden Hand*. 1888. Reprint edited by Joanne A. Dobson. New Brunswick, N.J., and London: Rutgers University Press, 1988.
Spofford, Harriet Prescott. Introduction to *The Poems of Louise Chandler Moulton*, by Louise Chandler Moulton, v–xix. Boston: Little, Brown, and Company, 1909.

———. *A Little Book of Friends*. Boston: Little, Brown, and Company, 1916.

Spring, Elizabeth T. "Elizabeth Stuart Phelps." In *Our Famous Women: An Authorized Record of the Lives and Deeds of Distinguished American Women of Our Time by Twenty Eminent Authors*, 560–80. Washington, D.C.: A. D. Worthington and Company, 1883.

Starr, Harris Elwood. "Austin Phelps." In *Dictionary of American Biography*, edited by Dumas Malone, 7:526–27. New York: Charles Scribner's Sons, 1964.

Stephens, Ann S. "Women of Genius." *Hesperian* (August 1839): 242–44.

Stewart, Randall. "'Pestiferous Gail Hamilton,' James T. Fields, and the Hawthornes." *New England Quarterly* 17 (September 1944): 418–23.

Stoddard, Charles Warren. "Mrs. Emma D. E. N. Southworth at Prospect Cottage." *National Magazine: An Illustrated Monthly* (May 1905): 179–91.

Stowe, Charles Edward. *The Life of Harriet Beecher Stowe: Compiled from Her Letters and Journals*. Cambridge, Mass.: Riverside Press, 1891.

Stowe, Harriet Beecher. "Can I Write?" *Hearth and Home* (January 9, 1869): 40–41.

———. "Faults of Inexperienced Writers." *Hearth and Home* (January 23, 1869): 72.

———. "How May I Know that I Can Make a Writer?" *Hearth and Home* (January 30, 1869): 88.

———. "How Shall I Learn to Write?" *Hearth and Home* (January 16, 1869): 56.

———. *Lady Byron Vindicated: A History of the Byron Controversy, from Its Beginning in 1816 to the Present Time*. 1870. Reprint. New York: Haskell House Publishers, Ltd., 1970.

———. "Writing Commercially." *Hearth and Home* (March 13, 1869): 184.

Stowe, Lyman Beecher. *Saints, Sinners, and Beechers*. Indianapolis, Ind.: Bobbs-Merrill Company, 1934.

Stronks, James B. "Author Rejects Publisher: Caroline Kirkland and *The Gift*." *Bulletin of the New York Public Library* 64 (1960): 548–50.

Sutherland, John A. *Victorian Novelists and Publishers*. London: University of London, Athlone Press, 1976.

Swinburne, Louis. "Reminiscences of Helen Jackson." *New Princeton Review* 2 (July 1886): 73–83.

Tassin, Algernon. "American Authors and Their Publishers." *Bookman* 39 (1914): 178–88, 268–81, 378–88, 526–38, 638–52.

Tebbel, John. *A History of Book Publishing in the United States*. 4 vols. New York: R. R. Bowker, 1975.

"Theophilus B. Peterson." *Publishers' Weekly* 39, no. 989 (January 10, 1891): 27–28.

Thorpe, Margaret Farrand. *Female Persuasion: Six Strong-Minded Women*. New Haven, Conn.: Yale University Press, 1949.

Thrasher, Max Bennett. "The Last Year of Gail Hamilton's Life, with Extracts from Letters Written by Her during that Time." *Arena* (December 1896): 112–19.

T. H. Y. "Biographical Sketch of the Author." In *The Haunted Homestead*, by E.D.E.N. Southworth, 29–42. Philadelphia, 1876.

Tompkins, Jane. "Masterpiece Theatre: The Politics of Hawthorne's Literary

Reputation." *American Quarterly* 36, no. 5 (Winter 1984): 617–42.
──────. *Sensational Designs: The Cultural Work of American Fiction, 1790–1860*. New York: Oxford University Press, 1985.
──────. "Sentimental Power: *Uncle Tom's Cabin* and the Politics of Literary History." *Glyph: Textual Studies* (1981): 79–102. Reprinted in *Sensational Designs: The Cultural Work of American Fiction, 1790–1860*, 122–46. New York: Oxford University Press, 1985.
Tomsich, John. *A Genteel Endeavor: American Culture and Politics in the Gilded Age*. Stanford, Calif.: Stanford University Press, 1971.
Tourgée, Albion W. "Study in Civilization." *North American Review* 143 (September 1886): 246–61.
Tryon, Warren S. *Parnassus Corner: A Life of James T. Fields, Publisher to the Victorians*. Boston: Houghton Mifflin, 1963.
──────, and William Charvat, eds. *The Cost Books of Ticknor and Fields and Their Predecessors, 1832–1858*. New York: Bibliographical Society of America, 1949.
Tuchman, Gaye, with Nina E. Fortin. *Edging Women Out: Victorian Novelists, Publishers, and Social Change*. New Haven, Conn.: Yale University Press, 1989.
T. W. M. "Publishers: Their Past, Present, and Future in the U.S.—The Present." *American Publishers' Circular and Literary Gazette* 1, no. 12 (November 17, 1855): 165–66.
Vedder, Henry C. *American Writers of Today*. New York: Silver, Burdett and Company, 1894.
Wagenknecht, Edward. *Harriet Beecher Stowe: The Known and the Unknown*. New York: Oxford University Press, 1965.
"Ward, Elizabeth Stuart Phelps." *Independent* 70 (February 2, 1911): 269.
Warner, Charles Dudley. "The Story of *Uncle Tom's Cabin*." *Atlantic Monthly* 78 (Spring 1896): 311–21.
Washburn, Mrs. E. H. "The Mother of 'H. H.'" *Independent* (September 17, 1885): 5.
Wayne, June. "The Male Artist as Stereotypically Female." *Art Journal* 32, no. 4 (Summer 1973): 414–16.
Welter, Barbara. "The Cult of True Womanhood, 1820–1860." *American Quarterly* 18 (Summer 1966): 151–75.
Whitaker, Rosemary. "Helen Hunt Jackson, 1830–1885." *Legacy: A Journal of Nineteenth-Century American Women Writers* 3, no. 1 (Spring 1986): 56–60.
"Who Saxe Holm Is." *New York Tribune*, May 12, 1877.
Wilkins, Thurman. "Helen Maria Fiske Hunt Jackson." In *Notable American Women: A Biographical Dictionary*, edited by Edward T. James, Janet Wilson James, and Paul S. Boyer, 2:259–61. Cambridge: Harvard University Press, 1974.
Wilson, Christopher P. *The Labor of Words: Literary Professionalism in the Progressive Era*. Athens: University of Georgia Press, 1985.
Wilson, Edmund. *Patriotic Gore: Studies in the Literature of the American Civil War*. New York: Oxford University Press, 1962.
Wilson, Forrest. *Crusader in Crinoline: The Life of Harriet Beecher Stowe*. New York: J. B. Lippincott Company, 1941.

Woloch, Nancy. *Women and the American Experience*. New York: Alfred A. Knopf, 1984.
"Woman in the Domain of Letters." *Knickerbocker Monthly: A National Magazine* (July 1864): 83–86.
Wood, Ann D. "The 'Scribbling Women' and Fanny Fern: Why Women Wrote." *American Quarterly* 23 (Spring 1971): 3–24.
W. P. H. "The Centennial Exhibition: How Shall Prizes Be Awarded?" *Publishers' Weekly*, no. 211 (January 29, 1876): 117.
Wylkom, Wat. "Our Native Authors: The Portraits of Inky Men and Women of Letters: William D. Howells, George William Curtis, Helen Hunt, and Henry James—The Real Persons Compared with Their Writings." *New York World*, May 3, 1885, p. 23.

Index

Abbot Academy, 170, 175
Abbott, John, 139, 141
Abbott family, 141
Abbott Institute, 139
Adams, Mary. *See* Phelps (Ward), Elizabeth Stuart—*Confessions of a Wife*
Alcott, Louisa May, 3, 69; in "Mr. Houghton's Mistake," 5
Alden, Henry Mills, 33, 37, 43, 47–48, 185
Aldrich, Thomas Bailey, 33, 155
Alliance, 132
American Literary Gazette, 41, 153
American Publishers' Circular and Literary Gazette, 31
Amherst Academy, 139
Amherst Record, 145
Andover Theological Seminary, 168, 169, 177
Androgyny, 12, 18. *See also* Dodge, Mary Abigail: androgyny/androgynous
Anonymity and pseudonymity, 13, 159. *See also* Dodge, Mary Abigail: anonymity and pseudonimity; Jackson, Helen Hunt: anonymity and pseudonymity; Phelps (Ward), Elizabeth Stuart: anonymity and pseudonymity
Appleton, Daniel, 33, 35, 37; regarding Southworth, 57, 65
Appleton, D., and Company, 57
Appleton, William, 46

Appletons. *See* Appleton, Daniel
Arabian Nights, The, 81
Arthur, T. S., 77
Atlantic dinner (1877), 2–3, 13, 28, 39, 203 (n. 1)
Atlantic Monthly, 2, 3, 20, 45, 89–90, 95; in "Mr. Houghton's Mistake," 5; office, 35; regarding Stowe, 89–90, 92, 97, 98, 99, 101, 102, 103–4; regarding Dodge, 120, 131; regarding Jackson, 142, 143, 145, 154, 155, 157, 160; regarding Phelps (Ward), 173, 185, 187, 190
Audience, 45–46
Aurora Leigh. *See* Browning, Elizabeth Barrett
Authorship. *See* Writer

Bailey, Gamaliel: and Southworth, 55, 56; and Stowe, 55, 89; and Dodge, 55, 108, 109, 110. *See also National Era*
Baltimore Saturday Visitor, 55, 60
Barnum, P. T., 69
Barr, Amelia, 165
Beecher, Catharine, 82, 83, 86, 87, 107, 108; views of women, 12, 82, 90, 91
Beecher, Edward, 88
Beecher, Henry Ward, 69, 104
Beecher, Lyman, 80, 81, 82, 90, 107
Beecher, Roxanna Foote, 81, 90
Bentley, Richard, 88
Best-sellers, 2, 42, 43, 51, 86, 169, 173
Blackwell, Elizabeth, 82
Blackwell, Emily, 82

Blaine, Harriet Stanwood, 112
Blaine, James G., 6, 112, 215 (n. 18); in "Mr. Houghton's Mistake," 5
Bloomer, Amelia, 33
Bok, Edward, 48; regarding Phelps (Ward), 187, 188, 191
Boker, George, 41
Bonheur, Rosa, 110
Bonner, Robert, 60, 97, 129–30; as Gentleman Publisher, 37, 46, 50, 69, 70, 74; as entrepreneur, 69; morality of, 70, 73, 74. *See also* Southworth, E.D.E.N.: relationship with Bonner
Bonner and Sons, 75
Book Publishers' Association, 31
Booth, Miss (editor, *Harper's Bazar*), 133
Booth, John Wilkes, 52
Boston Evening Transcript, 184
Boston Indian Citizenship Association, 146
Boston Miscellany, 84
Botta, Ann, 140, 141
Bowdoin College, 85
Bowles, Samuel, 144
Bremer, Fredrika, 66
Brontë, Charlotte, 56
Brown, Charles Brockden, 13, 56
Browning, Elizabeth Barrett, 15, 17, 147, 166, 172
Bulwer, Henry, 66
Burney, Fanny, 23
Businessman Publisher, 32, 47–48, 150; and masculinity, 48; and women, 48, 208 (n. 48)
Byron, Lady, 100–101, 102. *See also* Stowe, Harriet Beecher: Byron controversy
Byron, Lord (George Gordon), 81, 100, 102, 103. *See also* Stowe, Harriet Beecher: Byron controversy

Capitola. *See* Southworth, E.D.E.N.— *The Hidden Hand*
Carey, Matthew, 29–30, 40

Carey and Hart, 40
Cary, Alice, 124
Cather, Willa, 48
Century Magazine: office, 35; regarding Jackson, 158; regarding Phelps (Ward), 179, 185, 188, 191
Character. *See* Victorianism
Charlotte Temple, 29, 32. *See also* Rowson, Susanna
Child, Lydia Maria, 23, 217 (n. 58)
Christian Gentleman, 38
Christian Register, 55
Christian Union, 104, 154
Chubbuck, Emily, 16, 124
Church, William, 158, 162. *See also* *Galaxy*
Circular. *See American Publishers' Circular and Literary Gazette*
Clemens, Samuel (Mark Twain), 2, 203 (n. 1)
Clemmer, Mary, 177
Cobb, Sylvanus, 69, 70, 73, 211 (n. 48, 58)
Compensation, 39–41, 124, 207 (n. 29). *See also* Dodge, Mary Abigail: compensation; Jackson, Helen Hunt: compensation; Phelps (Ward), Elizabeth Stuart: compensation; Southworth, E.D.E.N.: compensation; Stowe, Harriet Beecher: compensation
Congregationalist, 110, 121, 132
Contracts, 41, 197; regarding Southworth, 71, 72, 211 (n. 48), 212 (n. 14); regarding Stowe, 86, 87, 97, 212 (n. 15)
Conway, Moncure, 140, 147, 151, 158, 161
Cooke, Rose Terry, 3, 20, 23–24; in "Mr. Houghton's Mistake," 5; compensation, 40
Coolidge, Susan. *See* Woolsey, Sarah
Cooper, James Fenimore, 66
Courtesy principle. *See* Trade courtesy
Cranch, E. P., 82
Critic, 62, 146, 147

Cummins, Maria, 3, 36
Cunctare. See Dodge, Mary Abigail: anonymity and pseudonymity

Dana, Richard, 15
Darwin, Charles, 46
Davis, Rebecca Harding, 3, 23–24, 26; in "Mr. Houghton's Mistake," 5; on Dodge, 106
Deacon, Edmund, 64, 67, 68
De Quincey, Thomas, 171
Derby, James, 45, 87, 110
Dial, 32
Dickens, Charles, 62, 66, 77, 89, 131
Dickinson, Austin, 164
Dickinson, Emily, 138, 141, 142, 145, 151, 153, 160, 161, 164, 221 (n. 52). *See also* Jackson, Helen Hunt: relationship with Emily Dickinson
Dime novels, 46
Dodd, Moses, 35
Dodge, H. Augusta, 25, 112–13, 117
Dodge, Hannah Stanwood, 106–7, 110
Dodge, James Brown, 106, 107
Dodge, Mary Abigail, 2, 7, 8, 106–35, 146, 197, 199; in "Mr. Houghton's Mistake," 4, 5, 6, 203 (n. 3); personality and description, 6, 108, 133, 134, 215 (n. 6); humor, 6, 109, 133; character, 8, 113, 115; views of women, 12, 104, 110–11, 112, 113–18, 119, 120, 124, 126, 128–29, 134–35, 148, 174; androgyny/androgynous, 12, 114, 115, 117, 119, 120, 134, 182; criticism of, 17, 113, 116, 119, 129, 130; attitudes toward authorship, 19, 26, 110–11, 153, 196; childhood, 22, 106–7; single and childless, 24, 111–12, 215 (n. 16); rejection of Gentleman Publisher's ideals, 38, 39, 104, 131, 132, 133, 134–35, 197; compensation, 40, 98, 109, 111, 120, 121–24, 132, 133, 134, 158; on Stowe, 101; controversy with James Fields, 103, 112, 120–28, 129–30, 131, 155, 186; reputation, 106, 110, 112, 113, 118, 120, 131, 196; family, 106–7, 112–13, 170; religious views, 107; education, 107, 139, 170; teacher and governess, 107–8, 109; attitudes toward working, 108, 110; anonymity and pseudonymity, 108, 110, 118–19; beginning of writing career, 108–10, 141, 147, 152, 172, 195; literary style and skills, 109, 116–17; Washington, D.C., and politics, 109–10, 112, 113, 215 (n. 18); writings, 111, 112, 120; attitudes toward money, 111, 126–27, 129, 132–33, 155, 156, 157, 184; work habits, 117–18; privacy, 118, 119, 160, 176, 215 (n. 12); editorial work, 120, 123, 132, 172; self-confidence, 130, 134, 172; vice-president of Society of American Authors, 134
—Works: *A Battle of the Books*, 39, 121, 122, 124, 125, 128, 130, 131, 133, 135, 155, 156; *Country Living and Country Thinking*, 120; *Divine Guidance*, 133; *Woman's Worth and Worthlessness*, 128; *Woman's Wrongs: A Counter Irritant*, 120

Dodge, Mary Mapes, 145

Edgeworth, Maria, 23, 66
Edwards, Mrs., 171
Edwards', Mrs., School for Young Ladies, 170
Eliot, George (Mary Ann Evans), 62, 174–75, 176, 177, 225 (n. 40)
Elliot, Charles W., 82
Emerson, Ralph Waldo, 2, 40, 115, 144, 171, 203 (n. 1), 226 (n. 61)
Ensign, H. L., 132
Era. See National Era
Estes and Lauriat, 131, 132
Evangelist, 84
Everett, Edward, 69, 97
Exclusive commitment: concerning Southworth, 51, 57, 64, 70, 97–98, 210 (n. 34); concerning Stowe, 96, 97–98, 100; concerning Dodge, 120,

126; concerning Jackson, 154; concerning Phelps (Ward), 185

Fanny Fern. *See* Parton, Sara Payson
Field, Kate, 160
Fields, Annie, 35, 94, 95, 96, 99, 100, 121, 131, 173, 185
Fields, James T.: as Gentleman Publisher, 33, 36–39, 41, 43, 46, 80; and Stowe, 92, 95, 96–97, 100, 196; and Jackson, 160; and Phelps (Ward), 168, 173, 175, 177, 185, 186. *See also* Dodge, Mary Abigail: controversy with James Fields; Stowe, Harriet Beecher: Byron controversy
Fields, Osgood and Company, 120, 129, 130, 142, 168
Fiske, Ann, 139
Fiske, Deborah Waterman Vinal, 138, 139
Fiske, Nathan Welby, 138, 139
Ford, J. B., 104
"Frost." *See* Thomas, Edith
Fruit and Floral Festival, Complimentary, 28, 31, 39, 45, 47

Galaxy, 40, 142, 162
Gaskell, Mrs. (Elizabeth Cleghorn Stevenson), 89
Genteel amateur. *See* Writer: genteel amateur/amateurism
Gentlemen Publishers, 28–48; and women, 28, 30, 32, 38, 44, 46–47, 48, 78; family-like, 33, 35–36, 206 (n. 19); male, 33–34; business, 35, 43–44, 208 (n. 39); loyalty and trust, 36–37; paternalism, 37–38; gender overtones, 38; inequality, 39. *See also* Compensation; Contracts; Moral goals/guardianship; Noncommercialism; Personal relationships; Publishing; Renaissance patrons of the arts; Trade courtesy; individual publishers; individual authors
Gilder, J. B., 146, 163

Gilder, Richard Watson, 36, 43, 48, 183, 185, 191, 222 (n. 63)
Gilman, Caroline, 33
Godey's Lady's Book, 23, 85
Godwin, Parke, 141
Goodale sisters, 165
Graham, George R., 37
Graham's Magazine, 56
Greeley, Horace, 69
Greeley, Philip, 86
Greenwood, Grace. *See* Lippincott, Sara Jane
Guiccioli, Countess. *See* Stowe, Harriet Beecher: Byron controversy
Gun Maker of Moscow, The. *See* Cobb, Sylvanus

Hale, Mr., Jr. See *Boston Miscellany*
Hale, Sarah Josepha, 23, 33, 85
Hall, James, 82
Hamilton, Gail. *See* Dodge, Mary Abigail
Harper, James, 34
Harper and Brothers', 43; and Southworth, 56, 57; and Stowe, 83; and Dodge, 131–32; and Phelps, 190–91
Harper brothers, 30, 39, 48
Harpers, 33, 34, 35, 206 (n. 12); and Stowe, 84; and Dodge, 133
Harper's. *See Harper's Monthly*
Harper's Bazar, 132, 133, 186, 187, 191
Harper's Monthly, 35, 185
Harper's New Monthly Magazine, 172
Harris, Mary Briggs, 177
Hart, Abraham, 57, 209 (n. 18)
Hartford Female Seminary, 82, 107, 108
Hartford High School, 108
Harvey, "Colonel," 48
Hawthorne, Julian, 131
Hawthorne, Nathaniel, 15, 37, 38, 39, 47, 97, 122, 124, 140, 151, 176, 183
Hawthorne, Mrs. (Sophia Peabody), 122, 125, 131
Hearth and Home, 131
Henshaw, Joshua L., 53

Henshaw, Susannah Nevitte, 53, 58
Hentz, Caroline Lee, 2, 82
Herschel, Caroline, 133
H. H. *See* Jackson, Helen Hunt: anonymity and pseudonymity
Higginson, Thomas Wentworth, 138, 142, 144, 145, 147, 155, 164, 166, 173, 195. *See also* Jackson, Helen Hunt: relationship with Thomas W. Higginson
Holland, Dr. (editor, *Scribner's*), 157
Holley, Marietta, 145
Holmes, Mary Jane, 2, 10
Holmes, Oliver Wendell, 2, 6, 7, 39, 90, 100, 102, 124, 145, 163, 176, 183, 203 (n. 1), 226 (n. 61)
Holt, Henry, 34, 36, 42, 43
Hooker, Isabella Beecher, 91
Hosmer, Harriet, 110
Houghton, Henry Oscar, 3–7, 37, 39, 198, 203 (n. 5); and Stowe, 104; and Jackson, 155, 158; and Phelps (Ward), 186, 187, 189–90
Houghton, H. O., and Company, 2
Houghton, Mifflin and Company, 176, 189, 191
Hours at Home, 172
Howe, Julia Ward, 38, 174
Howells, William Dean, 33, 35, 99; and Stowe, 101, 102, 103; and Jackson, 157; and Phelps (Ward), 183, 187
Hugo, Victor, 62
Hunt, Edward Bissel, 140, 141, 143–44, 164. *See also* Jackson, Helen Hunt: marriage (to E. Hunt) and motherhood
Hunt, Helen. *See* Jackson, Helen Hunt

"In a Cellar." *See* Spofford, Harriet Prescott
Independent: and Stowe, 89; and Dodge, 106, 109, 110, 113, 132, 133, 174; and Jackson, 142, 143, 147, 152, 153, 154, 156, 157, 158; and Phelps (Ward), 174, 177, 183–84, 185, 189

Ipswich Female Seminary, 107, 139
Irving, Washington, 15, 41, 66

Jackson, Helen Hunt (H. H. and Saxe Holm), 2, 138–66, 197; in "Mr. Houghton's Mistake," 5; childhood, 22, 138–39; marriage (to E. Hunt) and motherhood, 24, 140–41, 143–44, 145, 148, 155, 160; description and personality, 26, 140, 141–42, 143, 161, 162, 168, 199, 218 (n. 12); compensation, 40, 143, 156, 157–58, 162; relationship with Emily Dickinson, 138, 139, 140, 142, 143, 144, 145, 147, 152, 160, 162, 164–66; anonymity and pseudonymity, 138, 141, 143, 144, 145, 147, 152, 153, 154, 157, 158–62, 222 (n. 56); work habits, 138, 142, 152–53, 163; relationships with Gentlemen Publishers, 138, 143, 153–57; campaign for American Indian rights, 138, 144, 145–46, 148, 161, 162–64; reputation, 138, 144, 147, 159, 220 (n. 37); as mentor, 138, 165, 195, 222 (n. 63); education, 139; early writing, 139–40; literary friendships, 140; relationship with Thomas W. Higginson, 140, 142, 146, 147, 151, 152, 159, 160, 163, 164, 165; avoids social crusades, 140, 145–46; beginning of writing career, 141–43, 147–48, 195; illness, 143; marriage (to W. Jackson), 143–44; contribution to *A Masque of Poets*, 144, 160, 161, 165, 166; comparison with Stowe, 146, 163, 222 (n. 59); name, 147, 158, 160, 162, 163; death, 147, 177; views of women, 148–51, 154, 159, 160, 161, 163, 165, 166, 181; concept of individuality, 149–51, 152, 153, 159, 161, 166; attitudes toward money/market value, 150, 151, 154, 155–57, 159, 161–62, 163, 185; attitudes toward authorship, 151, 153, 156, 162, 196; literary style, 151–53, 165–66; negotiations, 154–55,

156–57, 159; lack of self-confidence, 158–59; privacy, 160, 176
—Works: *Bits of Talk about Home Matters*, 141; *A Century of Dishonor*, 146, 147, 151, 160, 163; "A Four-Leaved Clover," 149, 150; *Hetty's Strange History*, 144, 162; "A History of the Claimants," 162; "The Key to the Casket," 141; "Lifted Over," 141; *Mercy Philbrick's Choice*, 144, 148, 149, 150, 152, 158, 161, 162; "My Tourmaline," 149, 151; *Nelly's Silver Mine*, 144, 150; *Ramona*, 146–47, 158, 162, 163, 164, 219 (n. 21); *Verses*, 143; "Whose Wife Was She?," 143
Jackson, William Sharpless, 143–44, 146
James, Henry, Sr., 111, 134
James, Henry, Jr., 62, 119, 187
Jewett, John P., 86–88, 89, 90
Johnson, Mr. See *Evangelist*
Johnson, Robert Underwood, 188
Jordan, Elizabeth, 187, 191
Judson, Adoradim, 16
Judson, Emily. See Chubbuck, Emily

Kinney, Abbot, 146
Kirkland, Caroline, 40
Knopf, Alfred, 47, 48

Ladies Home Journal, 186, 187, 188, 191
Lane Theological Seminary, 82, 83, 85
Larcom, Lucy, 120
Ledger. See *New York Ledger*
Lee and Shepard, 41
Letters from a Cat. See Fiske, Deborah Waterman Vinal
Lippincott, Joshua B., 33, 35
Lippincott, Sara Jane (Grace Greenwood), 3, 10, 15, 16, 18, 109, 124, 195
Literary critics, 11–12, 15–16, 19
Literary professionalism, 104, 194–99, 227 (n. 4); history, 194; characteristics at end of century, 194, 198; demographics of women, 194–95; seriousness about work, 195; knowledge of business, 195–96; commitment, 196; autonomy, 196–97; acceptance of moral or cultural aims, 197; understanding of Gentleman Publisher's ethos, 197; discrimination, 198. See also Women writers
London Quarterly, 103
Longfellow, Henry Wadsworth, 2, 37, 89, 90, 177, 181, 183, 203 (n. 1), 226 (n. 61)
Lowell, James Russell, 33, 39, 90, 97, 102, 131; *The Cathedral*, 36
Lyon, Mary, 110

McClure, S. S., 48
McClure's Magazine, 186
Magnalia Christi Americana. See Mather, Cotton
Manual of Classical Literature. See Fiske, Nathan Welby
Marah. See Jackson, Helen Hunt: anonymity and pseudonymity
Martineau, Harriet, 66
Marvel, Ik, 37
Mather, Cotton, 81
Melville, Herman, 47
Methodist-Protestant, 55
Mifflin, George, 168, 179, 189, 190
"Mr. Houghton's Mistake," 3–5, 6, 20, 25, 26, 203 (n. 3)
Moral goals/guardianship, 14, 19, 34, 45–47, 48, 208 (n. 43); Southworth-Peterson, 64–66, 67; Southworth-Bonner, 73–74; Stowe-Fields, 80, 103; Jackson and publishers, 153. See also individual authors
Moulton, Louise Chandler, 3, 10, 15, 16, 160
Mt. Holyoke, 139
Mowatt, Anna Cora, 124
Munsey, Frank, 48

Nation, 141, 142, 154
National Era: and Southworth, 55, 56, 210 (n. 34); and Stowe, 85, 86; and Dodge, 108, 110

Nevitte, Charles LeCompte, 53
New Womanhood: Vision of, 10, 12, 18; New Woman writer, 18; and Dodge, 114; and Jackson, 148; and Phelps (Ward), 181
New York Association of Book Publishers, 28, 31
New York Evening Post, 38, 141, 142, 147, 159
New York Herald, 69
New York Ledger, 46, 51, 52, 57, 60, 68, 69, 73, 74, 75, 76
New York Merchant's Ledger. See *New York Ledger*
New York Society for the Suppression of Vice, 45
New York Tribune, 112, 132
Niles, Thomas, 37, 144, 153–54, 157, 158, 165, 221 (n. 53)
No Name series. *See* Roberts Brothers
Noncommercialism, 13, 14, 19, 34, 41–45, 48; and women, 44–45; in Southworth-Bonner relationship, 74–75, 76, 77; in Stowe-Fields relationship, 80; Dodge's rejection, 125, 126–28; concerning Jackson, 151, 153, 156
Noncompetition. *See* Noncommercialism
North American Review, 132
Norwood. See Beecher, Henry Ward

Old Corner Bookstore. *See* Ticknor and Fields
Origin of the Species, 46
Osgood, James R., 33; and Stowe, 96, 102, 103, 104; and Dodge, 123; and Phelps (Ward), 186
Osgood and Company, 96
Our Young Folks, 97, 120, 123, 172
Outdoor Papers. See Higginson, Thomas Wentworth

Page, Walter Hines, 42
Park, Edwards A., 171
Parton, James, 98, 129

Parton, Sara Payson (Fanny Fern), 3, 16, 19, 25, 69, 75, 98, 118, 120, 129, 130, 131; and *Ruth Hall*, 16, 18; on Dodge, 106, 107
Peabody, Elizabeth, 122
Perry, Bliss, 36, 37
Personal relationships, 34–39, 41, 48, 207 (n. 32); gender overtones, 37–39; Southworth-Peterson, 64, 67; Southworth-Bonner, 70–73, 77; Stowe-Fields, 80, 94, 95, 96, 102; Stowe-Jewett, 88; Dodge's rejection, 125–26, 127–28; Jackson and publishers, 153, 154; Phelps (Ward) and publishers, 168, 175, 185–86, 188, 189–91
Peterson, Henry, 56, 57. *See also* Southworth, E.D.E.N.: relationship with Henry Peterson
Peterson, Theophilus B., 57, 65, 75
Peterson, T. B., and Brothers, 77
Pettingill, Mr. (editor, *Hearth and Home*), 131
Phelps, Austin, 168–69, 171, 172, 175–76, 178, 179, 180, 223 (n. 4)
Phelps, Eliakim, 168
Phelps, Elizabeth (Stuart), 11, 169–70, 204 (n. 17), 223 (n. 6)
Phelps (Ward), Elizabeth Stuart, 2, 168–92, 197; childhood, 22, 168–72; beginning of writing career, 23–24, 171–73; married and childless, 24, 177–78, 180; negotiating strategies, 44, 177, 186, 191, 192; struggles with newer literary marketplace, 48, 166, 168, 180, 186, 187–92, 194, 198–99; reputation and criticism, 168, 173, 176, 183–84, 188, 191, 226 (n. 61); attitudes toward Gentleman Publisher's marketplace, 168, 175, 185–86, 188, 189–90, 191, 192, 196; family, 168–70, 174, 223 (nn. 4, 6); dual nature of assertion and self-denial, 170, 171, 174, 178–80; health and illness, 170, 175, 177, 178, 179, 180, 182, 184, 196, 225 (n. 40); education, 170–71, 223 (n. 10); views of women and femi-

nine strength, 171, 172, 177, 178, 179, 180–82, 185, 186, 192; religious and moral views and themes, 171, 173, 177, 178, 179, 182–84, 185, 187–88, 192, 224 (n. 26), 225 (n. 42); compensation, 172, 173, 188, 189, 192; lecturing, 174–75; women's rights, 174–75, 179, 180, 181, 183, 185; correspondence with publishers, 175, 177, 180, 190, 196; reform crusades (temperance and antivivisection), 175, 179–80, 183; losing self-confidence and support, 176–77; name, 178; description and personality, 178, 199; anonymity and pseudonymity, 179, 221 (n. 53); attitudes toward authorship, 182–85, 196; work habits, 184; attitudes toward money, 184–85, 226 (n. 51); attitudes toward changing literary tastes, 186–88; pride, 197
—Works: *Beyond the Gates*, 177; *Chapters from a Life*, 178; "The Chief Operator," 191; *Confessions of a Wife*, 179, 225 (n. 35); *Dr. Zay*, 177; *Donald Marcy*, 187; *The Gates Ajar*, 35, 168, 173, 175, 177, 179, 183, 186, 223 (n. 15), 225 (n. 42); *The Gates Between*, 177; *Jack, the Fisherman*, 183; "Jane Gurley's Story," 172; *An Old Maid's Paradise*, 174; "A Sacrifice Consumed," 172; *The Silent Partner*, 174; *A Singular Life*, 179, 188; *The Story of Avis*, 174, 175; "The Tenth of January," 172–73; "Trotty" stories, 172; *Up Hill, or Life in a Factory*, 172; "Victurae Salutamus," 175; *What to Wear?*, 174; *Within the Gates*, 179, 191
Phelps, Mary Johnson, 170
Phelps, Stuart, 177
Philbrick, Mercy. *See* Jackson, Helen Hunt—*Mercy Philbrick's Choice*
Phillips Academy, 171, 177
Phillips, Sampson and Company, 43, 88, 89, 95
Pierce, Franklin, 69

Pierce's, Miss Sarah, Female Academy, 81
Porter[s], Miss, 66
Press and Post, 140
Preston, Harriet, 145
Princhard, George, 36
Pseudonymity. *See* Anonymity and pseudonymity
Publishers' Weekly, 42, 43
Publishing: history and growth, 28–32; economics, 31, 32, 42–43, 48, 207 (n. 35); size, 34; offices, 34–35. *See also* Gentlemen Publishers
Putnam, George Haven, 34, 36
Putnam, George P., 33, 35, 37, 41, 206 (n. 12)

Quixote, Don, 115

Radcliffe, Anne, 23
Redpath, James, 132
Renaissance patrons of the arts, 28, 33
Riverside Bulletin, 42
Robbins, Sarah (Stuart), 169
Roberts Brothers, 3, 34, 143, 144, 153, 157, 158, 162, 221 (n. 53)
Robertson, Mr. (Hartford Publisher), 84
Rowson, Susanna, 23, 29–30
Runkle, Lucia, 145

Sand, George, 17, 66, 89
Saturday Club, 39
Saturday Evening Post, 56, 57, 63, 64, 68, 70
Saturday Night, 51, 72
Saxe Holm. *See* Jackson, Helen Hunt: anonymity and pseudonymity
Scott, Sir Walter, 62, 66, 80, 81
Scribner, Charles, 33, 34, 162
Scribner, Armstrong and Company, 144
Scribner's, Charles, Sons, 42, 48, 144, 153, 154, 157

Scribner's Monthly, 143, 154, 156, 157, 161, 185, 220 (n. 37)
Scudder, Horace, 37, 42, 162, 188, 190, 226 (n. 61)
Sedgwick, Catharine Maria, 14, 23, 66
Semi-colon Club, 82, 195
Separate spheres. *See* Woman's sphere
Sex and Education. See Howe, Julia Ward
Shakespeare: Southworth compared to, 62; Browning compared to, 172
Shurz, Carl, 146
Sigourney, Lydia H., 15, 23, 69, 83
Sill, Edward R., 177
Society of American Authors, 134
Southworth, E.D.E.N. (Emma Dorothy Eliza Nevitte), 2, 50–78, 197; popularity, 2, 51–52, 56, 208 (n. 2); morality, 8, 47, 60, 74, 91–92, 197; family, 21, 52–54, 55, 58, 106; education, 22, 53, 54; childhood, 23, 52–54, 80, 107; marriage and motherhood, 24, 54–55, 57–58, 196; negotiating strategies, 44, 75–76, 97, 196; relationship with Bonner, 48, 50, 54, 57, 63, 68–78, 80, 96, 99, 100, 104, 154, 196, 209 (n. 19), 211 (n. 48); views of women, 50, 54, 58–60, 63, 68, 72, 76–78, 80, 91, 104, 113, 114, 117, 148, 181, 182; literary skills/style, 50, 60–62, 64, 66–67; criticism of, 51, 52, 74, 151; compensation, 51, 55–56, 57, 58, 71, 72, 74–77, 158, 208 (n. 2), 211 (n. 61); name, 53, 119; religious beliefs, 54, 60, 65, 209 (n. 10); illness, 55, 56, 57, 58, 196; attitudes toward money, 55, 59–60, 76; teaching, 55, 108; beginning of writing career, 55–57, 109, 111, 141, 147, 209 (n. 18); praise of, 56, 62, 63, 64, 68–69, 70; relationship with Henry Peterson, 56, 63–68, 70, 76; work habits, 57, 71, 93, 196; relationship with Theophilus B. Peterson, 57, 72, 75, 77, 209 (n. 19); description, 58, 199; attitudes toward authorship, 60, 61, 63, 99, 153, 196; plagiarism attempts, 62–63; pride in work, 62–63, 197; contracts, 71, 72, 74, 75, 211 (n. 48), 212 (n. 14)
—Works: *The Curse of Clifton*, 51; *The Deserted Wife*, 53, 64, 65; *The Fatal Marriage*, 51; *The Hidden Hand*, 51–52, 58, 62, 75, 211 (n. 58); "The Irish Refugee," 55; *The Island Princess*, 70; "Miriam, the Avenger, or The Missing Bride," 65; "The Mother-in-Law," 56; "Retribution," 55–56; *Retribution*, 56, 57; *Self-Raised* and *Ishmael* ("Self-Made" serial), 51, 52, 60, 63, 71, 77; "The Wife's Victory," 55
Southworth, Frederick Hamilton, 54, 212 (n. 14)
Spofford, Harriet Prescott, 3, 6, 10, 17, 40; in "Mr. Houghton's Mistake," 4; and Dodge, 112–13; as author of Saxe Holm stories, 145
Springfield Union, 145
Springler Institute. *See* Abbott Institute
Stanton, Elizabeth Cady, 12
Stedman, Laura, 160
Stephens, Ann S., 16–17, 33, 67, 77
Stoddard, Elizabeth, 155
Stowe, Calvin E., 25, 82–85, 87, 88, 97, 100, 102, 103
Stowe, Harriet Beecher, 2, 69, 80–104, 106, 140, 164, 171, 197, 199; in "Mr. Houghton's Mistake," 3–4; relationship with Henry O. Houghton, 7, 104, 176; Byron controversy, 8, 74, 100–103, 104; literary style, 17, 92–93, 99, 213 (n. 30); self-confidence, 19, 83, 89, 90, 98, 99, 100, 212 (nn. 4, 11); beginning of writing career, 23, 82–85, 111, 147, 195; marriage and motherhood, 24, 83, 84, 85, 93–94, 144; compensation, 40, 82, 84, 85–86, 88, 89, 96, 97, 98, 124, 158; negotiating strategies, 44, 95, 97–98, 130, 132, 196, 214 (n. 40); friendship with

Southworth, 51, 61, 74; writers compared with, 62, 146, 147, 176; domestic feminism and views of women, 80, 81, 82, 85, 90–92, 93, 94, 95, 99, 101, 104, 113, 114, 117, 181; reputation and popularity, 80, 86, 89–90, 94, 95, 98, 103, 108, 110, 163; relationship with John P. Jewett, 80, 86–89, 94, 100; relationship with James Fields, 80, 90, 94–104, 120, 131, 214 (n. 50); family, 80–81, 82, 83, 85; childhood, 80–82, 107, 141; religious and moral views, 81, 85, 90, 91–92, 94, 102, 183; education, 81–82, 87, 107; teaching, 82, 87, 108; attitudes toward money and business, 83, 87, 89, 93, 96–97, 98, 131; name, 84; attitudes toward authorship, 93–94, 99, 153, 196, 213 (n. 33); attitudes toward publishing, 99; lecture tours, 103; on Dodge, 106, 120; friendship with Phelps, 171, 174; mentoring, 195; illness, 196
—Works: *Agnes of Sorrento*, 98; *Autographs for Freedom*, 87; *Dred: A Tale of the Great Dismal Swamp*, 89, 98; *Earthly Care: A Heavenly Discipline*, 85; "House and Home Papers," 92, 99; *The Key to Uncle Tom's Cabin*, 87, 88; *Lady Byron Vindicated*, 101, 103, 104; *The Mayflower*, 83, 85; *Men of Our Times*, 98; *The Minister's Wooing*, 17, 90, 98; *My Wife and I*, 103; *Oldtown Fireside Stories*, 101, 103; *Oldtown Folks*, 92, 93, 96–97, 98, 100; *Palmetto Leaves*, 103; *Pink and White Tyranny*, 103; *Poganuc People*, 103; "The True Story of Lady Byron," 94, 101, 214 (n. 46); "Uncle Lot," 82; *Uncle Tom's Cabin*, 2, 35, 43, 80, 85–90, 92, 93, 99, 108–9, 163, 183, 212 (n. 14);
Stuart, Moses, 168
Sue, Eugene, 66
Sumner, Charles, 39
Sunny Side: Or, A Country Minister's Wife, The. See Phelps, Elizabeth (Stuart)

Tennyson, Alfred Lord, 69
Terry, Rose. *See* Cooke, Rose Terry
Thomas, Edith, 165
Thoreau, Henry David, 47, 124, 226 (n. 61)
Ticknor, Howard, 123
Ticknor, William, 33, 35, 37, 124
Ticknor and Fields, 35, 43, 46, 80, 95, 120, 122, 123, 124, 185
Tomboys. *See* Women writers: alienation
Trade courtesy, 30–31, 37, 39, 206 (n. 12)
Trowbridge, John T., 120
True Woman/Women, 11, 12, 16, 23, 38; writer, 17. *See also* True Womanhood
True Womanhood, 10–12, 18, 22, 23, 204 (n. 17); Cult of, 10; and Southworth, 54, 55, 59, 74, 77; and Stowe, 81, 90, 91; and Jackson, 148, 150, 154, 159, 160, 161, 163, 165, 166; and Phelps (Ward), 181. *See also* True Woman/ Women
Twenty Years in Congress. See Blaine, James G.

Van Winkle, Rip. *See* Jackson, Helen Hunt: anonymity and pseudonymity
Victoria (queen of England), 69
Victorianism, 5, 7–8, 12–13, 14, 20, 21, 25, 92, 197, 203 (n. 7)

Walden. See Thoreau, Henry David
Ward, Herbert D., 177, 178, 186, 190, 224–25 (n. 32), 225 (n. 35)
Ward, William Hayes, 154, 156, 177, 185, 189
Warner, Charles Dudley, 145, 146, 147
Warner, Susan, 2, 35, 37
Warren, Margaret. *See* Jackson, Helen Hunt—"A Four-Leaved Clover"
Washington, George, 52, 127

Watchman and Reflector, 96
Western Female Institute. *See* Beecher, Catharine
Western Monthly Magazine, 82–83
Wharton, Edith, 48
Whipple, Bishop, 160
Whipple, E. P., 113
Whitman, Walt, 47
Whittier, John Greenleaf, 2, 39, 89, 90, 124, 198, 226 (n. 61); in "Mr. Houghton's Mistake," 3, 4, 5; and Southworth, 51, 56; and Dodge, 131, 215 (n. 16); and Phelps (Ward), 173, 175, 183
Whittier dinner. See *Atlantic* dinner
Wide, Wide World, The. *See* Warner, Susan
Woman question. *See* Women's rights
Woman's Journal: on Dodge, 108, 112, 113; and Phelps (Ward), 174
Woman's rights. *See* Women's rights
Woman's sphere, 8–10, 11, 12, 13, 15, 23, 25. *See also* New Womanhood; True Womanhood
Women of the North Distinguished in Literature, 110
Women's rights, 23, 40; and Southworth, 72; and Stowe, 91; and Dodge, 112, 115, 118, 120. *See also* Phelps (Ward), Elizabeth Stuart: women's rights

Women writers: popularity, 2, 17–18, 47, 208 (n. 46); views of, 5, 6, 7, 11–12, 15–19, 20; networks, 6, 25, 39 (male); discrimination against, 6, 13, 20–21, 39–40, 115–16, 118, 198, 205 (n. 36); social circumstances, 7; style, 16, 17, 204 (n. 32); subject matter, 16, 17; tone, 16, 17; self-confidence, 19–21; education, 21–22; description of, 21–26; intelligence, 22; alienation, 22, 54; economic necessity, 23; role models, 23; economic reward, 23, 24; children, 24; marital status and responsibilities, 24, 25, 205 (n. 50); negotiating strategies, 44–45. *See also* Literary professionalism
Wood, George, 110, 117, 121
Wood, Mrs. Henry, 77
Wood's Household Magazine, 132
Woolsey, Sarah, 140, 143, 145, 147, 152
Woolson, Constance, 154
Wordsworth, William, 171
Writer, 25; images of, 13–15, 19; genteel amateur/amateurism, 14, 19, 194, 227 (n. 1); great, 15. *See also* Women writers
Wuthering Heights, 46

Yard, Robert Sterling, 42

www.ingramcontent.com/pod-product-compliance
Lightning Source LLC
Chambersburg PA
CBHW021358290426
44108CB00010B/290